Lives That Made a Difference

An RSME Book for Schools

P. J. CLARKE

Strategic Book Group

Copyright © 2011
All rights reserved – P. J. Clarke

No part of this book may be reproduced or transmitted in any form or by any means, graphic, electronic, or mechanical, including photocopying, recording, taping, or by any information storage retrieval system, without the permission, in writing, from the publisher.

Strategic Book Group
P. O. Box 333
Durham, CT 06422
www.StrategicBookClub.com

ISBN: 978-1-60976-870-6

Book Design: Judy Maenle

For My Family
Brigitte, Virginie and Colleen

Contents

Introduction   1

PART ONE: FIGURES FROM THE PAST

Historic Leaders, Founders, Martyrs
- Jesus Christ   5
- Paul of Tarsus   12
- Ignatius of Antioch   17
- Patrick of Ireland   19
- Benedict of Nursia   23
- Hugh of Lincoln   28
- Francis of Assisi   32
- Joan of Arc   37
- Thomas More   41
- Ignatius of Loyola   44
- George Fox   49

Historic Artists and Architects
- Early Illuminated Manuscripts   53
- The Cathedral Architects   55

Historic Christian Thinkers
- Augustine of North Africa   60
- Thomas Aquinas   65
- Martin Luther   69
- Blaise Pascal   73
- Immanuel Kant   80
- Soren Kierkegaard   84

PART TWO: FIGURES FROM MODERN TIMES

Modern Writers
- Jonathan Swift   91
- Leo Tolstoy   95
- Fyodor Dostoyevsky   101
- G. K. Chesterton   108

Francois Mauriac	114
C. S. Lewis	119
J. R. R. Tolkien	123
Hilaire Belloc	127
Graham Greene	132
Malcolm Muggeridge	135
Alexander Solzhenitsyn	140

Modern Leaders

John Wesley	147
Angelo Roncalli	152
Jose Escriva	155
Brother Roger of Taize	158

Modern Humanitarians

William Wilberforce	164
John Bosco	167
Henri Dunant	170
Albert Schweitzer	172
William Booth	176
Thomas Barnardo	179
Damian of Molokai	182
Abbe Pierre	186
Leonard Cheshire	191
Jean Vanier	195
Chad Varah	199
Mother Teresa	202

Modern Activists

Trevor Huddleston	207
Desmond Tutu	211
Chiara Lubich	215
Dorothy Day	219
Simone Weil	223
Mary MacKillop	229

Modern Martyrs   **233**

Grand Duchess Elizabeth of Russia	233
Dietrich Bonhoeffer	235
Edith Stein	241
Titus Bransma	246
Maximillian Kolbe	249
Oscar Romero	252
Martin Luther King	256

Introduction

Making a difference

This book deals with a series of lives, both historical and modern, which are deemed to have made a difference. Some make a difference in fields of human endeavour such as science, technology and industry. Important as these fields are for the betterment of humanity, their direct effect is impersonal. What distinguishes those who feature in this book is the personal impact they have made on the lives of others. They have been chosen because they made a difference at the spiritual, moral, literary, artistic, social or humanitarian levels to the people and times in which they lived. In most cases their impact has been felt beyond their own time. As we shall see, the people here have made a difference either through their personal endeavours, their ideas, their art, their writings, or their example. In more modern times many have made a major difference to peoples' lives through the organisations they founded for the relief of human suffering.

A common perspective

Underlying all the lives covered there is a common thread: a certain perspective on life and life's values. This perspective is the one offered by the Christian tradition. Some represent that tradition by offering an admirable level of religious dedication and moral leadership. Others represent it in other ways, either through art or literature, or by way of working out what the Christian tradition implies either in terms of beliefs or ethical behaviour. Others again have embodied it by acting on the Christian inspiration to show love of neighbour by working out ways for the alleviation of poverty, ignorance, sickness and other forms of human deprivation.

Writers

Among those selected in this book, some, by their opinions or their writings openly defend the Christian vision of life. But the majority tend to deal with human life in a less clear-cut way, the way that is typical of the novel. Novelists tend to deal with the human condition as it is rather than how it should be. As a result, they show life with its ups and downs, its fortunes and misfortunes, its good as well as its more decadent side. Where faith comes in is a matter for the novelist, the character portrayed, and the reader. Usually religious faith is portrayed as an understandable challenge or struggle. In the face of human weakness men and women often find the demands of faith almost too much to bear. In the universal search for the holy grail of happiness, what can be more easily enjoyed, or attained, usually takes precedence over what is more difficult. Indeed while faith can claim to have the secret of human happiness at least through its promotion of a virtuous life, the reality is that its value is often seen as ambiguous or uncertain, resulting in varying degrees either of acceptance or rejection. From an ideal point of view this may not be life as it should be, but is life as it is. It is this reality the novelist endeavours to deal with.

Artists

Artists have traditionally played an important role in the Christian tradition, especially in the centuries leading up to the Reformation. Through frescos, mosaics, sculptures, drawings and paintings they have helped to give visual expression to the people and events at the heart of the historic Christian story. Of those artists who are well known it would be impossible to include even a few in the space of this book. Instead, those who are chosen are not known at all. They represent on the one hand the manuscript tradition, mainly carried out in ancient abbeys and monasteries by nameless monks and scribes. On the other hand are the equally anonymous architects and planners who produced the great cathedrals that still stand as testimony to their awesome achievements.

Founders, humanitarians, leaders, activists

Those who have been driven by the humanitarian ideal of making the world better by the relief of suffering form an important group in this selection. For them the top priority in life is finding ways to help others, particularly the disadvantaged, whether through misfortune, ignorance, illness or poverty. With a vision inspired by humanitarian concern for others, often rooted in religious faith, they have made a significant contribution to making the world a better place. Thanks to the organisations they founded, the work of poverty relief and the fight against ignorance, illness and disease was put on an organised and enduring foundation.

It goes without saying, however, that the headings under which lives are listed are not meant to indicate strict divisions. Most humanitarians were activists and leaders; some were founders, and some were martyrs.

Martyrs

In the early Christian tradition martyrs were usually those who were victimised because of their faith in God or Christ. In more modern times martyrs are of two kinds. One is where a person is made to suffer unjustly from the cruelty of others, and endures those sufferings with patience and resignation. The other kind are those who, without endangering others, earnestly put their lives at risk (often by refusing to be silenced) when faced with what they see as injustice done to their fellowman. They believed that in the circumstances they found themselves some risk to their lives were worth taking for the sake of a greater cause. In the Christian tradition this this has always been seen as the greatest testimony to a person's love for his fellowman. In the end it is their love of truth, goodness, and the rights of others before their own safety, that explains why such people are called martyrs.

Religious education

The selection of people from the Christian tradition is not to discount the value of other faiths. The aim of this book is merely to illustrate the contribution of one religious tradition to the understanding and the betterment of life. It is hoped that a knowledge of the work, example, ideas, beliefs, concerns, or capabilities of those featured here will lead others to appreciate their achievements, and in some way not only learn from them but emulate them also. Because the lives in question bring into focus universal issues about the meaning of life, and how far religious belief contributes to that meaning, they stand, I believe, as an important resource for religious education. However, it must be said that because of the relatively brief treatment of each life due to limitations of space and time, students are encouraged to gain further knowledge of each life and related issues through, say, the internet or other sources.

Moral education

It is arguable that all education is a form of moral education, an experience that leaves the recipient not only better informed but better disposed towards others, regardless of colour, class or creed. In other words education is not only about good knowledge but also about good will. Knowledge, to be complete, calls for a critical faculty: it is not just about what is, but what ought to be. Scientific knowledge of how nuclear bombs are made is generally regarded as partial without a knowledge of their dangers, and when, if ever, it is justified to use them.

Many would argue, therefore, that moral education is less about knowledge, than about the will to use that knowledge for the good. How that will is activated is a major question for the human condition and the inquiring mind. At a basic level the human will is undoubtably restrained by the fear of undesirable consequences. There is usually little moral credit for acting out of fear. At the higher levels it is obvious that something else is required. Many who feature in this book will raise a key question for the reader: if benevolence is not a natural condition, what is it that makes some individuals rise to often heroic levels of action in pursuit of the moral ideals of goodness, truth and justice in the interests of others?

RSME

In its comprehensive range, this book embraces religious, social and moral educational (RSME) themes. These may be seen as intertwining aspects of human life. Religion, for many, is a significant social aspect of life, and both religion and social life have an important moral aspect. To show how these aspects intertwine is one of the aims of this book.

Quotations

At the end of each life covered there is, in most cases, a selection of quotations that reflect the beliefs, wisdom and sometimes wit of the individual in question. Sometimes these quotations are directly from the individual, sometimes indirectly from their writings. In either case they can form a rich and rewarding basis for further discussion as to their meaning, value and application.

FIGURES FROM THE PAST

Historic Leaders, Founders, Martyrs

Jesus Christ

We begin with the person who is the founder and centre of the Christian faith, Jesus Christ. From a purely human or historical consideration how someone who was relatively undistinguished and unknown could become a major figure in western civilisation is itself an extraordinary question. The answer, of course, must lie in the faith that he evoked, and the cosmic significance which he held for his followers. But this, too, raises further questions, such as why one human being of apparent insignificance, could make such a difference to the outlook of peoples, and in so doing make such a mark on world history.

From obscurity to world significance

From a human perspective there was little to indicate that this man would be any more than a passing figure belonging to his time. For someone who did not, as far as we know, have the benefits of any formal education, social status, special skills or notable wealth, his subsequent fame would appear to be a mystery. But his followers were to see this mystery bound up with the explanation he gave for his presence in the world. He had come on a mission, he explained, a mission that included being the definitive spokesman for the God they knew from the Old Testament. When, after his crucifixion, he was believed to have risen from the dead, he gained a growing congregation of followers. This led to the extraordinary rise of what came to be known as the Christian faith, a faith that rapidly spread across the Roman empire and eventually became the key formative influence in what we know as western civilisation. The following description of him by one anonymous writer aptly sums up the contrast between his obscure beginnings and his later impact on the world:

> **ONE SOLITARY LIFE**
>
> He was born in an obscure village, the child of a peasant woman. He grew up in another village, where he worked in a carpenter's shop until he was thirty. Then for three years he was an itinerant preacher. He never wrote a book. He never held office. He never had a family or owned a house. He didn't go to college . . . He never visited a big city. He never travelled two hundred miles from the place where he was born. He did none of the things one usually associates with greatness. He had no credentials but himself. He was only thirty three when the tide of public opinion turned against him. His friends ran away. He was turned over to his enemies and went through the mockery of a trial. He was nailed to a cross between two thieves. While he was dying his executioners gambled for his clothing, the only property he had on earth. When he was dead he was laid in a borrowed tomb through the pity of a friend. Nineteen centuries have come and gone, and today he is the central figure of the human race and leader of mankind's progress. All the armies that ever marched, all the navies that ever sailed, all the parliaments that ever sat, all the kings that ever reigned put together, have not affected the life of man on this earth as much as that one solitary life.

1. Early Historic References to Jesus

One of the mysteries of the influence of Jesus Christ was the scarcity of any written records about his life and activities. Apart from the Gospels, which were written by his followers, only a few sources exist which throw any light on his existence.

Josephus, Roman historian (AD 37–AD 100)

"Now there arose at this time a source of further trouble one Jesus, a wise man who performed surprising works, a teacher of men who gladly welcome strange things. He led away many Jews, and also many Gentiles. He was the so-called Christ. When Pilate, acting on information supplied by the chief men around us, condemned him to the cross, those who attached themselves to him at first did not cease to cause trouble, and the tribe of Christians which has taken this name from him, is not extinct even today."

Tacitus, Roman historian (AD 55–AD 117)

"Consequently to get rid of the report, Nero fastened the guilt and inflicted the most exquisite tortures on a class hated for their abominations, called Christians by the populace. Christus, from whom the name had its origin, suffered the supreme penalty during the reign of Tiberius at the hands of one of our procurators, Pontius Pilate, and a most mischievous superstition, thus checked for the moment, again broke out not only in Judaea, the first source of the evil, but even in Rome, where all things hideous and shameful from every part of the world find their centre and become popular."

Suetonius, Roman historian (AD 69–AD 140)

"Punishment was inflicted on the Christians, a class of men given to a new and mischievous superstition."

2. What Religious Thinkers Have Said

> "If Christ is not risen our faith is in vain."
>
> St. Paul

> "When the fullness of time was come, God sent his son, made of a woman to redeem those who were under the Law, and give them the adoption of sons."
>
> St. Paul

> "He died, but he vanquished death; in himself he put an end to what we feared; he took it upon himself and he vanquished it; as a mighty hunter he captured and slew the lion."
>
> St. Augustine

> "Jesus, by your dying we are born to new life: by your anguish and labour we come forth in joy: despair turns to hope by your sweet goodness: through your gentleness we find comfort in fear."
>
> St. Anselm

> "It would be simpler to say that Christ is present in the Sacrament, and leave the manner to God"
>
> Erasmus

> "What Jesus has to bring us are not ideas but a way of life. One can have Christian ideas about God and the world and about human redemption, and still with all that be a complete heathen. And as an atheist, a materialist, and a Darwinist, one can be a genuine follower and disciple of

Jesus. Jesus is not the Christian world view, and the Christian world view is not Jesus."

KARL BARTH

"Christianity is a monotheistic faith . . . and is distinguished from other such faiths by the fact that everything in it is related to the redemption accomplished by Jesus of Nazareth."

FRIEDRICH SCHLEIERMACHER

"The resurrection is the foundation of our belief that Jesus Christ is the sovereign of this beautiful, endangered planet."

WOLFHART PANNENBERG

"Wolfhart Pannenberg, perhaps the greatest living systematic theologian in the world, has rocked modern, sceptical German theology by building his entire theology precisely on the historical evidence for the resurrection of Jesus as supplied in Paul's list of appearances."

GARY HABERMAS

"It would have been simply a contradiction of terms for an early Jew to say that someone was raised from the dead but his body still remained in the tomb . . . The empty tomb forms a veritable rock on which all rationalistic theories of the resurrection dash themselves in vain."

WILLIAM L CRAIG

"Easter is not the celebration of a past event. The alleluia is not for what was. Easter proclaims a beginning which has already decided the remotest future. The Resurrection means that the beginning of glory has already started."

KARL RAHNER

"Without a doubt, at the centre of the New Testament there stands the Cross, which receives its interpretation from the Resurrection."

HANS URS VON BALTHASAR

"To deny oneself is to be aware only of Christ and no more of self, to see only Him who goes before and no more the road which is too hard for us."

JOHN WESLEY

3. What the Church Fathers Said

"Await Him that is above every season, the Eternal, the Invisible, who became visible for our sake, the Impalpable, the Impassible, who suffered for our sake, who endured in all ways for our sake."

ST. IGNATIUS OF ANTIOCH (AD 50–110)

"The Eucharist is the flesh of our Saviour Jesus Christ, flesh which suffered for our sins and which that Father, in his goodness, raised up again."

ST. IGNATIUS OF ANTIOCH

"Many indeed are the wondrous happenings of that time: God hanging from a cross . . . yet no one of them can be compared to the miracle of my salvation."

ST. GREGORY NAZIANZEN (AD 329–389)

"When mankind was estranged from him by disobedience, God our saviour made a plan for raising us from our fall, and restoring us to friendship with himself. According to this plan Christ came in the flesh, he showed us the gospel of life, he suffered, died on the cross, was buried and rose from the dead. He did so that we might be saved by imitation of him and recover our original status as sons of God by adoption."

ST. BASIL THE GREAT (AD 330–379)

"The death of the Lord our God should not be a cause of shame for us; rather it should be our greatest hope, our greatest glory. By taking upon himself the death that he found in us, he has most faithfully promised to give us life in him, such as we cannot have of ourselves."

ST. AUGUSTINE (AD 354–430)

"The sin of our first parents destroyed, hell plundered, resurrection bestowed, the power given to us to despise the things of this world, even death itself."

ST. JOHN DAMASCENE (AD 675–749)

4. What Other People Have Said

"We always find that those who walked closest to Christ were those who had to bear the greatest trials."

ST. TERESA OF AVILA

"I believe that there is nothing lovelier, deeper, more sympathetic, more rational, more manly, more sympathetic than the Saviour . . . If anyone could prove to me that Christ is outside the truth, and if the truth did really exclude Christ, I should prefer to stay with Christ and not the truth."

FYODOR DOSTOYESKY

"Even those who have renounced Christianity and attack it, in their inmost being still follow the Christian ideal, for hitherto neither their *subtlety not the ardour of their hearts has been able to create a higher ideal of man and of virtue than the ideal given by Christ of old."*

FYODOR DOSTOYESKY

"Alexander, Caesar, Charlemagne, and I have founded empires. But on what did we rest the creation of our genius? On force. Jesus Christ founded his empire upon love."

NAPOLEON

"In his own lifetime Jesus made no impact on history. This is something that I cannot but regard as a special dispensation on God's part and, I like to think, an example of the ironical humour which informs so many of his purposes. To me, it seems highly appropriate that the most important figure in all history should thus escape the notice of memoirists, diarists, commentators, all the tribe of chroniclers who even then existed."

MALCOLM MUGGERIDGE

"A man who was merely a man and said the sort of things Jesus said would not be a great moral teacher. He would either be a lunatic or else the Devil of Hell. You must make your choice. Either this man was, and is, the Son of God; or else a madman or something worse. You can shut Him up for a fool, you can spit at Him and kill Him as a demon; or you can fall at His feet and call Him Lord and God. But let us not come with any patronising nonsense about His being a great moral teacher. He has not left that open to us. He did not intend to."

C. S. LEWIS

"As a child I received instruction both in the Bible and the Talmud. I am a Jew, but I am enthralled in the luminous figure of the Nazarene... No one can read the Gospels without feeling the actual presence of Jesus. His personality pulsates in every word. No myth is filled with such life."

ALBERT EINSTEIN

"A man who was completely innocent, offered himself as a sacrifice for the good of others, including his enemies, and became the ransom of the world. It was a perfect act."

MAHATMA GANDHI

"I am an historian, I am not a believer, but I must confess as a historian that this penniless preacher from Nazareth is irrevocably the very centre of history. Jesus Christ is easily the most dominant figure in all history."

H. G. WELLS

"John Newton, Clerk, once an infidel and libertine, a servant of slaves in Africa, was, by the rich mercy of our Lord and Saviour Jesus Christ, preserved, restored, pardoned, and appointed to preach the faith that he had long laboured to destroy."

JOHN NEWTON'S TOMBSTONE (AUTHOR OF *AMAZING GRACE*)

"Jesus is the God whom we can approach without pride and before whom we can humble ourselves without despair."

BLAISE PASCAL

"Despite our efforts to keep him out, God intrudes. The life of Jesus is bracketed by two impossibilities: 'a virgin's womb and an empty tomb.' Jesus entered our world through a door marked 'No Entrance' and left through a door marked 'No Exit'."

PETER LARSON

"How else but through a broken heart may Lord Christ enter in."

OSCAR WILDE

"Jesus was the first socialist, the first to seek a better life for mankind."

MIKAEL GORBACHEV, FORMER SOVIET PRESIDENT

"It is as wholly wrong to blame Marx for what has been done in his name, as it is to blame Jesus for what has been done in his."

TONY BENN, FORMER ENGLISH MP

"Jesus Christ was an extremist for love, truth and goodness."

MARTIN LUTHER KING

"Jesus Christ, without money or arms . . . without science or learning shed more light on things human and divine than all philosophers and scholars combined . . . Without writing a single line he set more pens in motion, and furnished themes for more sermons, orations, discussions, learned volumes, works of art, and songs of praise than the whole army of great men of ancient and modern times."

PHILIP SCHAFF

"Measured by his effect on history, Jesus is the most influential life ever lived on this planet."

KENNETH S. LATOURETTE

"Christ's technique . . . was to seek out obscure people, a few fishermen and farm people, a few ailing and hard-pressed men and women."

DOROTHY DAY

> **ALLEGORY: THE SPIRITUAL RAILWAY**
> The Line to heaven by Christ was made
> With heavenly truth the Rails are laid.
> From earth to heaven the Line extends
> To Life eternal where it ends.
> Repentance is the Station then
> Where Passengers are taken in.
> No Fee for them is there to pay
> For Jesus is himself the way.
> God's Word is the first Engineer
> It points the way to heaven so dear.
> Through tunnels dark and dreary here
> It does the way to glory steer.
> God's love the fire, his Truth the Steam,
> Which drives the Engine and the Train,
> All you who would to Glory ride
> Must come to Christ, in him abide.
> In First and Second, and Third Class,
> Repentance, faith and holiness.
> You must the way to Glory gain
> Or you with Christ will not remain.
> Come then poor sinners, now's the time
> At any Station on the Line.
> If you'll repent and turn from sin
> The Train will stop and take you in.
>
> Tombstone, South Porch Ely Cathedral

Paul of Tarsus (ca. 5–67 AD)

Originally known as Saul, Paul was born in Tarsus in Asia Minor, a place he famously boasted of it being *"no mean city"*. It appears that he was well educated, and became very learned in the Jewish Law which formed the ethical foundation of the Old Testament. Saul, as he then was, was present at the stoning of the first Christian martyr Stephen, described in Acts 7. This suggests that he may also have been present at the crucifixion of Jesus. In any case there is evidence that he took a close interest in the rise of Christianity and would be unlikely to have missed being present at the death of its Founder. He would have been well aware that the roots of the new faith were in Judaism, his own faith.

But he was determined to stamp it out by whatever means he could. As a result he was a well-known and an active figure in the persecution of the first followers of the man called the Christ.

> I, too, was convinced that I should do all that was possible to oppose the name of Jesus of Nazareth . . . On the authority of the chief priests I put many of the saints in prison, and when they were put to death I cast my vote against them . . . I even went to foreign cities to persecute them.
>
> Paul (Acts 20)

Dramatic conversion

As a devout Jew determined to put down the upstart new faith, Saul's historic conversion is all the more extraordinary. At the very moment when he was *"still breathing out murderous threats against the Lord's disciples"* and, more specifically, looking for names of new disciples *"that he might take as prisoners to Jerusalem"*, his life was turned upside down:

> As he neared Damascus on his journey, suddenly a light from heaven flashed around him. He fell to the ground and heard a voice say to him, "Saul, Saul why do you persecute me?" "Who are you Lord?" Saul asked. "I am Jesus whom you are persecuting," he replied. "Now get up and go into the city and you will be told what you must do."
>
> Account from Acts 9

The rest, of course, is history. Saul's Jewish name changed to the Roman Paul, and he went on to become the leading champion of the faith he once opposed and persecuted.

Missionary journeys

Paul now decided that he should travel as far and wide as possible to publicise the new faith in Jesus Christ. He made several journeys around the Mediterranean, taking in most of Asia Minor (modern Turkey), targeting several key population and trading centres such as Antioch, Ephesus and Corinth. His method of operations was to establish believing communities, or churches, which he would later communicate with through letters (or epistles). The records show that he was well liked by his followers, as testified in this moving passage:

> When he had finished speaking he knelt down with them all and prayed. By now they were all in tears; they put their arms round Paul's neck and kissed him; what saddened them most was his saying they would never see his face again. Then they escorted him to the ship.
>
> Farewell to Paul at Ephesus Acts 20.36ff

Paul in Athens

Probably his least successful visit was to Athens, the the intellectual capital of the ancient world. He chose to speak in two key locations, the synagogue and the market place, before making a major address at the busy meeting place called the Areopagus, a site directly overlooked by the Parthenon. Among the people he addressed were philosophers and teachers who found his message about the resurrection too much to believe. But the disappointing reception he got in Athens was not to be typical. His missionary journeys were an overall success, and by the end of them many of the areas around the Mediterranean had begun to embrace the new faith. It was mostly to Paul's credit that in a relatively short time the Christian faith was becoming an international phenomenon.

Writings

While on his missionary journeys, Paul reinforced his teachings by writing epistles to various communities, or churches, that he had founded. These epistles would become a permanent record of how he saw the significance of Jesus, especially the meaning of his death and resurrection. He would also lay down the social and moral obligations expected of a follower of Christ within the community of the Church. Paul's writings were to be hightly influential in shaping early Christian beliefs for centuries, but serious disagreements would arise about the correct meaning of some of his teachings.

A new way of life

Brought up in the studies of the Old Testament Law, Paul was aware of its dour and impersonal nature. He now saw its replacement in the more humane and charity-centred teaching of Jesus. Where the Law appeared tyrannical and oppressive, the teachings of Jesus were encouraging and liberating. One was a cold and overbearing system that made stern demands. The other was more of an invitation to a kinder way of life. But it needed the support of a close-knit community, the Church, to make its application possible. For Paul, being a follower of a person was different to being subject to some pre-set and impersonal code of Law.

Paul's arrest and martyrdom

Following the impact of his missionary journeys Paul had become a hated figure in Jewish circles. After one of his visits to Jerusalem he was the object of a Jewish assassination attempt. He was captured and taken prisoner to the coastal town of Caesarea where he was held for two years. Insisting that he had done nothing wrong, and fearing that his case would not go well if heard in Jerusalem he famously appealed to have his case heard in Rome before the Emperor. Since he was a Roman citizen Paul's request was granted. When he arrived in Rome around AD 62 he was held under house arrest, but was free to see visitors and allowed to continue his writings.

> **PAUL'S JOURNEY TO ROME**
> We boarded a ship ... and put out to sea ... We made slow headway for many days ... When the wind did not allow us to keep our course we sailed off the lee of Crete ... When neither sun nor stars appeared for many days and the storm continued raging we finally gave up all hope of being saved ... On the fourteenth night we were still being driven across the Adriatic Sea, when about midnight the sailors sense they were approaching land ... When daylight came they saw a bay with a sandy beach, where they decided to run the ship aground if they could ... Once safely ashore they found out that the island was called Malta ... After three months we put out to sea in a ship that had wintered in the island ... we put in at Syracuse ... And so we came to Rome ... The brothers had heard that we were coming ... and travelled ... to meet us ... Paul was allowed to live by himself with a soldier to guard him.
> Acts 27-28

Paul's death and legacy

Paul is believed to have been beheaded under Nero in AD 64 or 65. After that he disappears from history. But his memory was to endure, his letters becoming the earliest writings to form the inspired texts of the New Testament. They continue to be read and listened to in most of the world's languages to the present day.

> **PETER AND PAUL**
> St. Peter was in Rome at the same time as Paul. Legend has it that Peter decided he had enough of Rome, but was met by Paul on the great Roman road that leads south known as the Appian Way. Paul asked him "Quo vadis", meaning "where are you going"? Peter recognised the question as a reproach, and changed his mind. He returned to eventually face his own martyrdom. Today an ancient church marks the spot.

St. Paul quotes

Love

Though I speak with the tongues of men and angels . . . if I have not love I am nothing . . . Now these three remain: faith, hope, and love. But the greatest of these is love.

The Holy Spirit

Do you not know that your body is a temple of the Holy Spirit? . . . therefore honour God with your body . . . So I say, live by the Spirit and you will not gratify the desires of the sinful nature. The fruit of the Spirit is love, joy, peace . . .

Baptism

All of us who were baptised into Christ Jesus were buried with him . . . in order that just as Christ was raised from the dead, we too may live a new life.

Death

Where, O death, is your victory? Where, O death, is your sting? But thanks be to God! He gives us the victory through Our Lord Jesus Christ.

Resurrection

By his power God raised the Lord from the dead, and he will raise us also.

Eternal Life

The wages of sin is death, but the gift of God is eternal life in Christ Jesus our Lord.

Ignatius of Antioch (ca. 35–110 AD)

Ignatius is representative of the many bishop-leaders of the early Church who (like the Apostles) were called upon to give their lives for the emerging faith. Ignatius is specially important for three reasons. One, because he was among the first to be martyred for the new faith. Secondly, because he lived early enough to be virtually a contemporary of Christ, and may have met some of the Apostles. And thirdly, because he, like St. Paul, wrote letters to church communities of the time which still survive.

Antioch

The ancient city of Antioch, in modern Syria, was an important commercial centre with a large population. This made it a target city for the early Christian missionaries who knew it as a metropolis that attracted traders and travellers from all over the Roman empire. Antioch became part of the Roman empire in 47 BC. Not merely a commercial centre, it became one of the main Greco-Roman cultural centres on a par with Athens and Rome. Known as "Queen of the East", Antioch was the first place that the followers of the new faith were called "Christians". Today it is mainly a ruin. St. Paul made Antioch one of his first bases. From here he launched his famous missionary journeys. Tradition also has it that St. Peter the Apostle was the first bishop of Antioch. In early Christian times it was one of the four cities with the status of *patriarchates*. The others were Alexandria, Rome and Jerusalem.

Bishop of Antioch

Into this lively city Ignatius was born. Initially brought up as a pagan, he was converted to the new faith that was now gaining ground. According to the 4th century historian Eusebius, the apostles Peter and Paul planted the new faith in Antioch and left directions that Ignatius should be their successor as bishop, a post he probably took up shortly after the deaths of the two apostles. Some years later a persecution had broken out against the Christians under the emperor Domitian (AD 81–96). Ignatius was said to have "kept up the courage of his flock by daily preaching, prayer and fasting." Another wave of persecution began under the emperor Trajan (AD 97–108) who was deeply attached to his roman gods, whom he credited with winning him important victories in battle. After a dispute with the emperor, Ignatius was arrested for refusing to recognise Trajan's gods. He was sentenced to be taken to Rome where his fate would be decided.

Journey to Rome

His journey by boat involved many stops along the Asia-Minor coastline. During these stops he was often greeted by Christian leaders who had known of his courageous and saintly reputation in Antioch. During the long journey Ignatius managed to write several letters to various Christian communities, warning them to be prepared for insults, ridicule and even physical violence. In response, they should remain calm before their enemies, showing heroic patience and forbearance in the spirit of Jesus Christ:

> "And for the rest of mankind pray unceasingly—for there is in them hope of repentance... In the face of their outbursts of wrath be patient; in the face of their arrogant words be humble... Let our forbearance prove us their brethren... In all purity and sobriety abide in Christ Jesus in flesh and spirit."

According to his own report the sea journey to Rome was bad enough, but especially so for a passenger who was regarded as a criminal. He records being bullied and abused by his jailors, whom he compared to wild animals that nothing could pacify:

> "From Syria even to Rome I fight with wild beasts, by land and sea, by day and night, being bound amid ten leopards, even a company of soldiers, who only grow worse when they are kindly treated."

Desire for martyrdom

Knowing that many of his followers were prepared to do all in their power to save him from a violent death, Ignatius pleaded with them not deny him his wish. He wanted to endure it for the sake of Christ. In a powerful passage, he sees himself like the wheat that was ground to becomes the bread of the Eucharist, thus providing one of the earliest symbolic images of Christian martyrdom:

> "I am writing to all the Churches and I enjoin all that I am dying willingly for God's sake, if only you do not prevent it. I beg you, do not do me an untimely kindness. Allow me to be eaten by the beasts, which are my way of reaching God. I am God's wheat, and I am to be ground by the teeth of wild beast, so that I may become the pure bread of Christ."

Death in Rome

Ignatius was met outside Rome by some faithful followers who, though glad to see their beloved bishop, were greatly saddened by the near-certainty of his impending death. Arriving on December 20, during the emperor's games, he was quickly brought before the prefect who signed his death warrant. He was then taken to the Coliseum where he was thrown as fodder to the wild beasts. And so his wish for a martyr's death was fulfilled. As to his final resting place there is some doubt. Jerome, writing from Antioch some three hundred years later, said his remains "were placed in a cemetery outside the Daphne gate." But tradition has it that they were later removed to Rome in 637 in recognition of his martyrdom there.

Ignatius quotes

"It is the part of a great athlete to receive blows and be victorious."

"Stand firm as an anvil when it is smitten."

"All wounds are not healed by the same salve."

"Have a care for union, for which there is nothing better."

"I am a condemned man, who have my lot with those who are exposed to danger and condemnation."

"I do not command you as if I were someone great, for even though I be bound in the Name, I am not yet perfect in Jesus Christ."

"Remember in your prayers the church which is in Syria."

Patrick of Ireland (397–493 AD)

Patrick was one of the most influential of the early missionaries who took Christianity to the remoter parts of northern Europe. Despite the scarcity of written records either about his background or his later achievements, enough is known about him to make his name legendary. It is above all his success in converting the Irish from paganism to Christianity that has ensured his place in the history of western religion. Today he is ranked among the greatest of early missionaries and is venerated as a saint by the Catholic, Anglican, Lutheran and Orthodox churches.

Early years

How Patrick came into contact with the remote island of Ireland is a tale almost stranger than fiction. Very little is known about where Patrick came from, but it is probable that he was a native of Britain or Gaul, and may have been the son of a Roman official. His own account of his early life in what is called his *Confessio,* contains, strangely, no reference to his place of origin and no information about his family, upbringing or background.

A slave in Ireland

It seems likely that he lived near the sea, leaving him vulnerable to capture by the pirate gangs that roamed the western coasts picking up young men for the slave markets. Patrick tells us that he was indeed brought to Ireland by slave-traders where he was made to tend sheep on the Antrim mountains. He was held captive there for six years, during which time he had to endure the testing severity of Irish weather. But according to his own account he survived the harsh conditions, buoyed up by a remarkable piety:

> "(God's) fear increased in me more and more, and the faith grew in me, and the spirit was roused so that in a single day I said as many as a hundred prayers, and in the night nearly the same, so that whether in the woods or in the mountain, even before dawn, I was roused to prayer and felt no hurt from it, whether there was snow, or ice or rain."

Escape from Ireland

Eventually, almost by a miracle, he received news that a passing ship would help him to escape from Ireland and slavery. But in an extraordinary turn of events he would later decide to return to Ireland. It seems that somehow he had got to know people during his time of slavery, people with whom he formed a close enough attachment to later make him want to return.

He wrote, wistfully, as if describing a dream:

> I saw a man coming, at it were from Ireland. His name was Victorius, and he carried many letters, one of which he gave me. I read the heading: "The Voice of the Irish." As I began the letter, I imagined in that moment that I heard the voice of those very people who were near the wood of Foclut (probably in Mayo) which is beside the western sea—and they cried out, as with one voice: "We appeal to you, holy servant boy, to come and walk among us once more."
>
> Patrick, *Confessio*

Missionary and Bishop

When Patrick returned to the land that earlier had caused him such hardship, he came as a man of considerable rank and importance: an official (bishop) of the Christian Church. It is thought that after leaving Ireland Patrick lived on the Continent and eventually found his way to a monastic centre of learning, traditionally thought to be in Lerins, an island off the coast of Cannes in southern France, known for its ancient monastery. It is believed that he was educated there and ordained priest before embarking on his historic journey to Ireland. He is believed to have settled in Armagh, the recognised seat of the leader of Irish Christians ever since. From his base in Armagh he travelled throughout the island (either on foot or on horseback) taking the gospel message to the people. But these were a people who had very different beliefs.

The Druids

Under the influence of the Druids, the beliefs of the native Irish centred on nature festivals. They had *Beltaine (gaelic for May),* the festival of spring, *Lusanagh (gaelic for July)* a harvest festival, *Samhain (gaelic for November)* marking the beginning of winter; and probably *Yuletide,* a winter festival of life and light that had ancient Scandanavian origins. Taking on the druids would be a major challenge, but Patrick's fame owed much to his success in overcoming their power and influence.

King converted

Various legends describe his encounters with the druids. One describes how, at Easter, Patrick saw in the distance the fires of a druid festival at Tara. Despite the command of the High King that all other fires be put out, he daringly lit another fire on a nearby hill. The king allegedly said: "If that fire is not put out tonight it will burn forever." The prophetic remark would come true. By some means Patrick managed to convert the king and his court, paving the way for the later conversion of the whole of Ireland.

Hard-won success

But his success as a missionary spreading the new faith was not as easily achieved as history might suggest. The human challenges involved in interacting with a strange native people of different outlook are not difficult to imagine. A romantic belief that all was plain sailing would be quite misleading, something Patrick seems to confirm in this brief, but moving account of his encounters with the Irish:

> I came to the heathen of Ireland to preach the gospel and to bear insults from unbelievers, to hear the reproach of my going abroad and to endure many persecutions even unto bonds, the while that I was surrendering my liberty as a man of free condition for the benefit of others. And if I should be found worthy, I am ready to give my life for His name's sake ... and there (in Ireland) I desire to spend it until I die, if our Lord should grant it to me.
>
> Patrick, *Confessio*

Legends

Colourful legends associated with the saint include the belief that Patrick banished all the snakes from Ireland, although geologists claim that no snakes existed in Ireland after the Ice Age. Another, more likely legend, tells of how Patrick used the shamrock to illustrate the belief in the Holy Trinity. He is said to have held up the ubiquitous trefoil, showing that if three leaves on one stem make a single plant, God can be three persons (Father, Son and Spirit) sharing one divine nature, making a single God.

Legacy

Patrick's legacy is obviously his part in the Christianisation of Ireland and his subsequent influence on the history of the island. The later development of Irish monasticism strongly suggest his influence but few records survive to throw any light on this. Several landmarks are considered part of his legacy such as the mountain Croagh Patrick in Mayo, and the island of Lough Derg in Fermanagh, both long established penal places of pilgrimage. His remains are believed to rest in the cathedral in Downpatrick, Northern Ireland but strangely, unlike the case of many other saints, it never became a shrine or place of pilgrimage. This may be partly because Patrick himself was not normally associated with miracles, and there was never any cult of relics connected with him. As Philip Freeman, in his book *St. Patrick of Ireland* aptly puts it:

> Patrick's wish for an unmarked grave was prophetic. In an age obsessed with saints, relics, and pilgrimage sites, no one knows where Patrick died or was buried ... We know so little about the details of Patrick's life that it seem fitting that his death should be a mystery as well.

Benedict of Nursia (480–547)

Generally regarded as "the father of western monasticism", Benedict was born in Nursia, near Rome, of noble and wealthy parents. After an early decision to enter the religious life he gave up his inheritance and went on to lay the foundations for a way of life that would call for complete spiritual dedication, and would be a prominent feature of western Christianity for centuries. He is famous for establishing a monastic Rule that would be followed by virtually all western monasteries and nunneries. His importance as a religious leader made him a celebrated figure, and he became the subject of paintings by both Fra Angelico and Fra Phillipo Lippi. In 1964 Pope Paul VI named him the patron saint of Europe.

Early years

In the midst of his early studies in Rome Benedict began to question how he should spend his life. The prospect of an easy life cushioned by wealth and privilege was his for the taking, but he became strongly influenced by reading the life of Christ. It made him realise that self-denial for the sake of higher values such as love, truth and goodness was a challenge worth taking on. These, he saw, were the values that shone forth in the gospel story. But how could such noble, spiritual, values be pursued in the midst of a world of material interests? For him the answer lay in the monastic life.

Centres of spirituality

In Benedict's vision monasteries should be powerhouses of the spirit, places of religious and moral dedication which could make up, in his view, for the moral failings of the less fortunate in the world of sin and temptation. By living in a monastic environment the monk would be free to aspire to the higher things of life, the pursuit of goodness and holiness through work, prayer, worship and charity towards others.

The Rule of St. Benedict

Monasteries had existed by then in various parts of Europe and the Middle East. But many in Benedict's time had lost their sense of purpose and fallen into decline. Benedict proposed to tighten up the monastic system, laying down strict rules to cover the whole 24 hours of the monks' day. He saw the need to combine the spiritual work of study, piety and worship with the the more physical and worldly work of labour in the fields and the daily running of a monastic complex. By bringing all aspects of monastic activity under a single heading, everything could acquire a spiritual significance. The way of life he established became known as the "Benedictine Rule", a path to spirituality that would be followed by virtually all monasteries and nunneries in western Europe for centuries.

Worldly wisdom

As well as warnings about the ever present dangers of temptation and how to deal with it, the Rule contained much worldly wisdom on the intricacies of man-management, an important requirement in an environment that embraced many different types of individual. It also recognised the problems of dealing with ill or uncooperative members and showed foresight in anticipating the problems of fraud and corruption. Typically the Rule began with the responsibilities of the Abbot or Prior, the "father" of the monastery:

> It behoveth the abbot to be ever doing some good for his brethren rather than to be presiding over them. He must, therefore, be learned in the law of God... he must be chaste, sober and merciful, ever preferring mercy to justice, that he himself may obtain mercy.
>
> St Benedict, Rule

To work is to pray

But while monks would, in a sense, leave the world of material things, they would still belong to that world and need to survive in it. This meant that manual work and the production of those things necessary for everyday life were to be an essential part of the monastic life. Benedict recognised that the monastery must combine the work of spiritual development with the material labour involved in supporting its members. Monasteries were always considered places of *labore et ore* (work and prayer), but Benedict changed this to form a different motto. Henceforth the guiding principle of the monk's day was a merging of the two, so that one became the other. Labore et orare became:

> "Laborare est orare: to work *is* to pray."

While prayer was the direct worship of God the business of work, whether in the fields, or in the monastery or study, would now be seen as a form of prayer, a daily sacrifice to God through the grind of toil, sweat and intellectual endeavour.

> (The Rule of St. Benedict) was an epitome of Christianity, a learned and mysterious abridgement of all the doctrines of the Gospel, all the institutions of the Fathers, and all the counsels of perfection.
>
> Boussuet (1700)

Ways of the world

But monasticism as a way of life was not destined to last forever. History was to show both its remarkable success and its dramatic decline. Ironically, many monasteries became victims of their success as human organisations. Although theoretically "removed" from the world, in practice many of the great monastic abbeys became expert in the ways of the world. Intelligent, highly educated and skillful, many of the monks became experts in worldly affairs, such as agriculture and land reclamation, stock breeding and food production, as well as the development of basic farm machinery and tools. They were also expert in man management and human relations. Inevitably monks had also to become skilled in buying, selling, trading, storing and managing. But while they became major benefactors to the poor, their overall wealth was to lead to problems, as we shall see below.

Decline of monasticism

As time went on the wheel turned full circle. As before Benedict's time, abuses began to return, with some monasteries becoming more famous for their worldly achievements than for fulfilling their founder's aim to be beacons of spiritual dedication and moral leadership. Many monks gained reputations not for their virtue and asceticism but for good living, making them objects of scorn and ridicule. We get a glimpse of this in the Canterbury Tales (1380) where Chaucer takes a humorous swipe at the well-fed monk (or friar):

> "Now certainly he was a fine prelate:
> He was not pale as some poor wasted ghost.
> A fat swan loved he best of any roast."

Dissolution of the Monasteries

Eventually monasticism began to collapse under the weight of its material success and enormous wealth, all acquired in the centuries of their fame as religious institutions of great social, artistic and cultural importance. But in a changed social and religious climate such as that brought about by the Reformation, all that was to change. In Protestant countries the monastic way of life was rejected for being, among other things, out of date. The idea of a life of dedication was no longer seen as necessary. In this climate English monasticism was brought to an end by Henry VIII with his controversial Dissolution of the Monasteries. What was especially controversial was what many saw as the ruthless confiscation of their lands and wealth for the enrichment of the unworthy and the undeserving.

Benedict remembered

Had Benedict been able to see the final fate of the way of life he so valued, he would have rued not only the destructive winds of history, but man's own abiding tendency to failure and decline. But his own achievements and the original vision he embodied continued to be recognised and valued. In 1880, on the fourteenth centenary of his birth, a commemorative medal was struck showing a cross and other symbols of his life. On its vertical beam are the words *"Let the cross be my guide",* and on the horizontal beam the words *"Let not the dragon be my guide."* Around the margin are the words *"Begone satan, do not suggest to me your vanities"—evil are the things you proffer, drink your own poison."* The images of a raven and a cup also appear, recalling two legendary attempts to poison him. It is said that once when he blessed a poisoned drink the cup shattered. On another occasion when he blessed poisoned bread a raven flew past, a symbol of death.

Monte Cassino

The most famous Benedictine Abbey was Benedict's own monastery at Monte Cassino, near Naples. Monte Cassino had many ups and downs. It was destroyed by the Lombards in AD 577, and was needlessly (at it turned out) wrecked by Allied bombing in 1944 in a misguided attempt to remove German soldiers who had taken advantage of its high ground position to halt the allied advances from the south. Some noted the irony of its destruction:

> When the abbey of Monte Cassino was bombed last week, it was not only the destruction of the 1,400 year old religious and cultural monument that stirred the world. It was the thought that the Abbey of Monte Cassino, a unique beacon of the spirit lit at the very onset of the Dark Ages, was being demolished by the military necessities of a civilisation closer to the brink than any other has been since that earlier human crisis.
>
> Time magazine July 1944

After the war the monastery was famously rebuilt.

St. Benedict quotes

"Listen and attend to the ear of your heart."

"Let us ask God that He be pleased to give us the help of His grace."

"By the light of this life, we must hasten to do now what will profit us for eternity."

"(Those who) indulge their own wills, and succumb to the allurements of gluttony . . . of the miserable conduct of all such it is better to be silent than to speak."

"An Abbess who is worthy to be over a monastery . . . should show them all that is good and holy by her deeds even more than by her words, should show equal love to all (because she) holds the place of Christ."

"Let the Abbot be most solicitous in his concern for delinquent brethren, for it is 'not the healthy but the sick who need a physician'."

"The reason that we said that all should be called for counsel is that the Lord often reveals to the younger what is best."

"Just as it is proper for the disciples to obey their master, so also it is his function to dispose all things with prudence and justice."

"Do not: give way to anger, nurse a grudge, return evil for evil, be addicted to wine, be a great eater, lazy, a grumbler, a detractor. Attribute to God, and not to self, whatever good one sees in oneself."

"Now the workshop in which we shall diligently perform all these tasks is the enclosure of the monastery and the stability in the community."

"We descend by self-exaltation, and ascend by humility."

"We must be on our guard against evil desires, for death lies close by the gate of pleasure."

"Self-will has its punishment, but constraint wins a crown."

"Before all things and above all things care must be taken of the sick so that they will be served as if they were Christ in person."

"If any of the work of the craftsmen is to be sold, those responsible for the sale must not dare to practice any fraud."

"Let all guests who arrive be received tamquam Christi (like Christ)."

"In His loving kindness the Lord shows us the way of life."

> With his life and work St. Benedict exercised a fundamental influence on the development of European civilisation and culture, and helped Europe to emerge from the dark night of history that followed the fall of the Roman empire.
>
> Pope Benedict XVI (2006)

Hugh of Lincoln (1135–1200)

Also known as Hugh of Avalon, and Hugh of Burgundy, he was one of the outstanding religious leaders and social reformers of his day. A man of "cool and excellent judgement" as well as "singular and exquisite tact" he had a legendary sense of justice which made him a valued adviser to three popes. He was invited to England by the King, but his firm leadership in facing down the monarch and his sychophantic court to defend the interests of the ordinary people made him the people's bishop. His associations with Lincoln made him a revered figure, and he is remembered as much for his saintly life as his social and administrative achievements.

Early years

Hugh was born in a chateau of Avalon in Burgundy into a noble family, but his mother, Anna, died when he was eight. About 1159 he entered *Grand Chartreuse*, a Carthusian monastery in the mountains near Grenoble, widely reputed for the austerity of its rules and the piety of its monks.

> The monks of Grand Chartreuse were also famous for more secular reasons. Using a secret formula made up from 60 different herbs they produced two of Europe's most famous liqueurs, Green and Yellow Chartreuse, still popular (and expensive) today.

Sent to England

Not only Hugh's saintly reputation, but also his great leadership qualities, became widely known and in 1179 he was sent as prior to the Carthusian (Charterhouse) monastery of Witham in Somerset. This was founded by Henry II in supposed recompense, it was said, for the murder of Thomas Beckett. Henry had heard of Hugh, and begged for his services in England, a request that was first refused, then reluctantly granted by his Order.

Temporary site

But when Hugh arrived in Somerset the monastery there was in a poor state. No permanent buildings had yet been erected, and the monks, many of whom had come over from France, were living in log huts and other makeshift buildings that offered little protection against the severe West country weather. Many blamed the king for refusing to expend the necessary money to build a proper monastery. Henry, it appears, was reluctant to upset many of his subjects who were already tenants on the monastery estate, and were providing valuable revenue to the royal chest. But with the arrival of Hugh, plans were soon submitted for the building of a new monastery complex.

Trouble over lands

When Hugh arrived he discovered that the monastic lands belonged, not to the king but to the church. He therefore insisted, quite properly, that since the land belonged to the church the tenants ought to be expelled. He eventually got his way but, typically, he insisted that proper compensation be paid by the king to those who had to move. Hugh soon began to make his mark as a forceful, but fair, church leader. Not surprisingly, his stay in the relatively quiet surroundings of the West country was to be brief: as events turned out, his services were urgently needed for a more challenging post. This was the vacant see of Lincoln.

Bishop of Lincoln

But Hugh was reluctant to move. Lincoln was a hotbed of social, political and religious controversy. Not only were the state and the church at loggerheads, but the local church was riven by internal disputes. Hugh was seen as the ideal man to sort out these problems. When he arrived in Lincoln he found that, like in Somerset, certain royal arrangements were in place that made little sense. He told the king that some well-established appointments that had royal approval were little more than a waste of money, and had to be removed. Other reforms soon followed, including law-changes forced on local foresters who had a monopoly on timber supplies. This made him unpopular among certain interest groups, including the nobility and elite, but he considered this a small price to pay to defend the interests of his people, especially the poor. He saw that his diocese was riddled by class and privilege with little regard being shown for such basic services as poverty relief, social care and other provisions, including, especially, education. He was also aware that certain minorities were being victimised in the city.

Conflict with the king

Hugh was soon recognised as a man of forceful authority when it came to standing for justice and right. In 1198 he again came into conflict with the the new king, Richard I, over a long-standing custom of providing knights and materials to the monarch for fighting foreign wars. This did not please the king, but Hugh argued that it was an unjust burden on the people who were really the one's shouldering the cost. His decision was applauded and copied by other bishops. In a reluctant compliment, Richard told his courtiers: "If all the prelates of the Church were like him, there is not a king in Christendom who would dare raise his head in the presence of a bishop." The following year Hugh denounced a persecution of Jews in Lincoln. To do this he had to face hatred and hostility from anti-Semite elements in the city. But nothing would thwart his aim to restore a proper respect for people of all classes and beliefs, regardless of rank or privilege. In doing so he brought a new level of order, peace and prosperity to the formerly troubled diocese.

Death of Hugh

As an exemplary Christan leader, Hugh saw his primary mission as one of helping the poor and deprived. He began by raising the standards of education for the young by making available much needed schools and teachers. He also started the rebuilding of one of England's most famous cathedrals which had recently suffered heavy damage from an earthquake in 1185. As it turned out, Hugh only lived to see the completion of the cathedral's magnificent quire. As a result of a fever contracted on his way back from France, Hugh died in London at the residence of the Lincoln bishops. His remains were removed to Lincoln, and interred in the north transept of the cathedral in the presence of the new King John. Following his canonisation as a saint by Pope Honorius III in 1220, they were removed to a special site in the cathedral's south transept, the trace of which can still be seen.

Hugh's Shrine

Afterwards Hugh's tomb became a holy shrine that attracted thousands of pilgrims for years to come. But at the Reformation, some four hundred years after the time of Hugh, it suffered the fate of others. His body was removed and the shrine robbed of its gold and jewellery, because at the time they were considered items:

> "with which all the simple people be moch deceaved and brought into greate supersticion and idolatrye."

Critics noted, dryly, that while there might be some doubt about the idolatry, there was no doubt about the monetary value of the gold and jewels that adorned the tomb! But this was not all. With the current king, Henry VIII, deciding to confiscate all monastic property throughout England, Hugh's monastic foundation was to be no exception. All its buildings, plant, lands, life-stock and other property were taken and added to the royal chest, and the monastery disbanded.

Hugh's memory

But Hugh's memory was not forgotten. St. Hugh's College Oxford is named after him, and outside the library is a statue of the saint holding on one hand an effigy of Lincoln cathedral, and on the other the figure of a swan, Hugh's traditional emblem. Legend tells of how a swan became famously attached to the saintly bishop, even guarding him while he slept! Hugh is the patron of sick children, sick people—and swans. In the 19th century a memorial tower was built by the Carthusians at his birthplace of Avalon in his native France.

Francis of Assisi (1181–1226)

One of the most romantic figures of the high middle ages, Francis of Assisi helped to highlight the deficiencies of the Church as a time when it was losing contact with the ordinary people. He brought to attention the need for a mission to the poor, and set a personal example in fulfilling that mission. His legacy was continued by the Franciscan Order which he established, a religious community dedicated to fighting poverty and ignorance, with foundations throughout the world.

Early years

Giovanni di Bernardone was a noble young man born into a rich family. As the son of a wealthy cloth merchant he was expected to follow in his father's footsteps and enjoy, in his turn, the life of wealth and fame that was marked out for him. But his father had not reckoned on his rebellious and independent-minded son.

Disowned

Things came to a head when he had the audacity to give away some of his rich clothing to a beggar. His father reacted with anger, virtually disowning him. Soon afterwards his wayward son got caught up in one of the local wars that were common in the Italy of the time. Never one to shirk a challenge, he took part in a local rebellion against the neighbouring town of Perugia. For his pains the future saint found himself locked up for a year in prison!

Eligible young man

When the eligible young Francis was asked by his friends if he was ever going to get married and settle down he answered:

> "yes, but to an unlikely lady, a fairer bride than any of you have ever seen, the lady poverty."

He then disappeared, taking time off to reflect on his life, and look for guidance and enlightenment. When he eventually returned to Assisi it appears that in his absence he had acquired some building skills, for it is known that he set about restoring a faded local church. This was the church of San Damiano, and it was here that his life took a decidedly new turn. During some restoration work that he had begun with some helpers, he had a strange vision in which heard a voice say: "Go and repair my house, which you can see is falling into ruin."

The call to leadership

Francis was not sure what this meant. Was the voice referring to the poor state of San Damiano, or to the decrepit state of the Church as a whole? Francis knew that the Church's reputation was being tarnished by wealth and corruption. This made him convinced that the voice was a call to take on a serious mission: to set about doing something for Christ and the Church. From his contemplation of the gospels he knew that Jesus had shunned wealth and status and spent most of his time with the poor. He wanted to do the same.

Mission to the poor

No airy fairy idealist, Francis's believed that he was being called to take the hard steps to bring the gospel directly to the cities and towns. This had become a neglected mission. The dominant spirituality, based on a view of the world as evil and sinful, had become too concentrated in the monasteries and convents with the result that the ordinary faithful were being overlooked. Outwardly the Church looked strong, healthy and influential, but in reality it had become remote and ineffective, identifying with the rich and comfortable, and neglecting the poor and disadvantaged.

Example of Christ

Francis and his friars (or *frartres,* brothers), in contrast to the more isolated monks, saw the world, not as evil and sinful, but as the place where the majority of people lived, and where human, social, and even religious problems needed to be faced. Drawing inspiration from the example of Christ, Francis saw the problems of the world in a spiritual light. Problems like poverty, deprivation, injustice and suffering were those that Christ had addressed, who often used them as the background against which he presented his own spiritual message about concern for others. In his identification with Christ, Francis was reviving the old way of seeing the Christian gospel as a call to fight material values with the weapons of faith and self-renunciation.

The Order of Franciscans

By 1205 his ideas began to take shape. He formed a small community of followers who would together devote themselves to the problems of social poverty, and the deprivations it caused. Out of humility, they all renounced joining the Church's elite as ordained priests. They preferred instead to see themselves as *"poor friars"* on a par with the poor and destitute they set out to serve. In 1209 Francis had obtained the approval of the Pope, and the way was clear to form a new Order, to be known henceforth as Franciscans. The numbers of his followers gradually increased, and by 1217 they had spread to many European countries. Francis himself travelled widely, even forming a personal friendship with the Sultan of Egypt who, in an extraordinary gesture, gave him safe-passage (a form of diplomatic protection), to enable him to visit the Holy Land, dear to him as the historical source of his life's inspiration.

Practical impact

Francis, of course, could have been dismissed as some well-meaning do-gooder, another eccentric campaigner on behalf of the less privileged. But this was not to happen. A man gifted with intelligence, with a practical outlook and a steely resolve, he was taken seriously as a dedicated reformer who knew what he was doing. Soon his Order was one of the most effective social agencies of the time in the fight against poverty and ignorance.

Poet and romantic

But alongside his practical bent, Francis also had a romantic, even poetic, side to his character. It was he who first introduced the idea of the Christmas crib, the colourful tableau of the figures in the Nativity, something that would become a popular feature of Christmas for centuries to come. Known also for his imaginative writings, he is regarded by literary critics as among the first Italian poets (see below).

Champion of the environment

Another facet of his personality that became legendary was his remarkable rapport with birds and animals. This was an integral part of his well-known love of the environment, or as he would have put it, the beauty of creation. For this reason his name has a special resonance today with those resolved to save the earth and its ozone layer from a growing deterioration. In 1986 Assisi was chosen as the venue for the international congress of the World Wildlife Fund. The occasion saw 235 world representatives join together with representatives of five major world religions to discuss the growing problems of the world's environment, under his patronage. In the following canticle Francis celebrates the glories of creation through the lens of his own profound religious vision.

> **CANTICLE OF THE CREATURES**
> We praise you Lord for all your creatures,
> especially for Brother Sun
> who is the day through whom you give us Light.
> And he is beautiful and radiant with great splendour,
> of you Most High he bears your likeness.
> We praise you Lord for Sister Moon and the stars,
> in the heavens you have made them bright, precious and fair.
> We praise you Lord for Brothers Wind and Air,
> fair and stormy, all weather's moods,
> by which You cherish all that You have made.
> We praise you Lord for Sister Water,
> so useful, humble, precious, pure . . .
> We praise you, Lord, for Sister Earth,
> who sustains us with her fruits, coloured flowers and herbs . . .
> We praise and bless You, Lord, and give You thanks,
> and serve You in all humility.

Death of St. Francis

Francis of Assisi is revered today as a saint by Christians of all denominations. He was painted by the greatest artists of the day, including Giotto, Cimabue, Jose de Ribera and El Greco. He died in Assisi dictating his spiritual testament, surrounded by his beloved friars. His remains were placed in the Lower Basilica in Assisi, which was later decorated with frescos by the great Giotto. They depict the life of Christ in conjunction with Francis seen as the devoted follower of his Master.

Assisi today

Since his death Assisi has become a popular centre of pilgrimage for people of all backgrounds, all faiths, and none. In 1997 Assisi suffered severe damage by an earthquake which brought down the roof of its cathedral, the destruction of art works and the death of some worshippers. But tragic though it was, the quake was seen by many as an event that evoked one of Francis's fundamental beliefs: that this world is fragile and passing, and earthly life is fleeting. In contrast, the values of the life of the spirit and the life to come are, by comparison, permanent and enduring.

> Time magazine ranked Francis of Assisi first among the top ten most important figures of the second millenium, a tribute to one of the most influential figures of the medieval church.

St. Francis quotes

"Not to hurt our humble brethren (animals) is our first duty to them."

"If you have men who will exclude any of God's creatures from the shelter of compassion and pity, you will have men who will deal likewise with their fellowmen."

"Above all the grace and the gifts that Christ gives to his beloved is that of overcoming self."

"I have been all things unholy. If God can work through me he can work through anyone."

"If a superior give any order to one who is under him which is against that man's conscience, although he does not obey it yet he shall not be dismissed."

"It is not fitting when one is in God's service, to have a gloomy face and a chilling look."

"When you are proclaiming peace with your lips, be careful to have it even more fully in your heart."

The Prayer of St. Francis

"O Lord, make me an instrument of Thy peace!
Where there is hatred make me sow love;
Where there is injury, pardon;
Where there is discord, harmony;
Where there is doubt, faith;
Where there is despair, hope;
Where there is darkness, light, and
Where there is sorrow, joy.
O Divine Master, grant that I may not
seek to be consoled as to console;

to be understood, as to understand;
to be loved as to love; for it is in giving that we receive;
It is in pardoning that we are pardoned;
and it is in dying that we are born to Eternal Life."

Joan of Arc (1412–1431)

One of the most fascinating but tragic figures of the high middle ages, Joan of Arc became a national phenomenon in her native France. She defied comprehension by her achievements as a military leader while still under the age of 19, proving her critics as well as enemies wrong by her astute judgement, calm intelligence and victory in the field. But she descended into history as a true heroine and martyr after the injustice of a mock trial that labelled her a heretical witch, a condemnation that led to her savage burning at the stake in the old market at Rouen.

Patron saint

The absurd injustice was later reversed when her true character was assessed, but this was far too late to save the saintly Joan. Her name became synonymous with innocence, courage and victimisation, and an enduring embarrassment to the fanatical judges who mixed religion and politics to destroy an innocent 19 year old at the peak of her powers. Today she stands, along with St. Denis, St. Martin of Tours, St. Louis IX, and St. Teresa of Lisieux as one of the patron saints of France.

Early years

Joan was born of peasant stock in the town of Domremy in eastern France. Domremy was situated in Lorraine in territory surrounded by Burgundians who were in an alliance with the English. Frequently the town was attacked for its stubborn supporter of Charles VII, the prospective king of France. There was at first little to indicate the fame Joan would achieve before her youth was over, but by the age of 13 she began to experience what she felt was a divine call to save France from its enemies. At first she was dismissed as a fool, but after much persistence convinced Charles to allow her to join his army.

Military leader

France at the time was being carved up between the English and the Burgundians. The French army was weak and Orleans, the one strategic city holding back the English advance, came under critical siege. Joan, driven by a religious conviction, pleaded with the generals to allow her to lead the French forces. Dressed as a soldier-knight she directed the army on how the siege could be lifted. To the astonishment of her critics the city held out and Orleans was saved. As the historian Stephen Richey put it:

> "Only a regime in the final straits of desperation would take any heed of an illiterate farm girl who claimed that the voice of God was instructing her to take charge of her country's army and lead it to victory . . . She proceeded to lead the army in an astounding series of victories that reversed the tide of war."

Peacemaker

Other notable victories against the English and the Burgundians followed, and Charles VII was duly crowned king of France in Reims cathedral in Joan's presence. But Joan, now the Maid of Orleans, was more concerned with peace than war. She wrote to the Duke of Burgundy:

> "I pray you that you make no more war with the kingdom of France . . . and on behalf of the gently king of France I say he is ready to make peace with you, by his honour."

But the plea failed. In the end she became the victim of intrigues and political deceptions all designed to effect her capture. It was a measure of her power and importance that her enemies, the Burgundians and the English, wanted her eliminated. No other commander in the king's army was more feared or sought after.

Capture

Joan was eventually betrayed and captured near the town of Compeigne. The Burgundians, it was said, were more overjoyed at her capture than if they had defeated half her army. Soon afterwards she was sold to the English and held under high security. The conditions under which she was held were later exposed for being unjust, cruel and inhuman. She was denied female guards and was left at the mercy of male soldiers and jailors. Attempts in the meantime to buy her back by the king, both by ransom and an exchange of prisoners all failed. The next stage was her public humiliation and trial.

Trial

Her trial took place in Rouen, the seat of the English occupation government. She was denied legal counsel and, in her own words, was surrounded only by partisans who were, to a man, her enemies. Although the trial was clearly political, aimed at revenge for her military successes, it resorted to religious charges to bring her down. Based on her claims of hearing divine voices, Joan was tried for heresy, that is, false religious beliefs. A fair trial was impossible. The first question put to her was loaded. Was she in God's grace? If she said yes she was clearly a heretic, since nobody is alleged to know how they stand before God. If she said no she would automatically be confessing her own guilt. To the astonishment of the judges who thought her simple, her astute reply was a masterstroke of evasion:

> "If I am not may God put me there. If I am may God keep me there."

But notwithstanding her cool defence against these and other charges, which included the absurd charge of dressing as a man (Her defence: "if you fight as a soldier you dress as a soldier"), she was convicted of heresy by the leading judge Cauchon. The bishop, an English sympathiser, sentenced her to a savage death: to be burned at the stake. To prevent her having a martyr's grave her ashes were cast into the Seine. Today, in the centre of Rouen, a cross marks the spot where she was burned at the stake.

Hearing voices

One of the great controversies surrounding Joan's life was her claim to have heard voices from God telling her to recover her homeland from English domination. Fearing that she might be in league with the devil, the king's advisers carried out an early examination of her character. A commission of inquiry was held at Poitiers in April 1429 which cleared her name and declared her to be:

> "of irreproachable life, a good Christian, and possessed of the virtues of humility, honesty and simplicity."

But her enemies insisted that the final proof that she was not a witch would be victory at Orleans! Church leaders too questioned whether she was a saint, a devil, a witch or a sorceress. At her trial she was ridiculed as such by the religious judge Pierre Cauchon. Some, however, like the agnostic George Bernard Shaw so admired her character that he wrote a play (St. Joan) defending her integrity regardless of her visions. These, he explained, were the insights of a highly gifted individual who had an exceptionally clear view of her vocation. They were simply evidence of a vivid imagination which naturally drew on her religious background. As he astutely put it: *"Because she was not malicious, selfish, cowardly or stupid, her sanity was never in doubt."*

Retrial and innocence

A retrial was held in July 1456, which included clergy and lawyers from all over Europe. The original court was declared unlawful and biased, and Joan was found innocent of all charges. Pierre Cauchon was declared a heretic for convicting an innocent woman on pseudo religious grounds in pursuit of a political vendetta. The retrial named her a martyr.

Cultural impact

Joan of Arc has remained an important figure in western culture, both for her achievements and her cruel sufferings. As a victim of gross injustice and cruelty at the hands of men, she stands out as a woman of exceptional virtue, courage and ability who defied the odds against her. In exemplifying universal virtues such as faith, bravery, and patriotism in pursuit of justice, she remains a figure of continuing interest. Her serenity in the face of false accusations which led to her death has made her a figure of romance. She has figured frequently in religious art, and was painted by Ingres, Delaroche, Millais, Lapage and Sherrer, among others. In literature she has been honoured by Schiller *(die Jungfrau von Orleans)*, Berthold Brecht *(die heilige Johanna der shlackthofe)*, Mark Twain *(Personal Recollections of Joan of Arc)*, G B Shaw *(St. Joan)* and Maxwell Anderson *(Joan of Lorraine)*. In music, by Verdi *(Giovanna d'Arco)* and Tchaikovsky *(Opneakar deca)*. Her life has also been the subject of numerous films and plays. Joan of Arc remains one of the most romantic and tragic figures of European history. Her military and political achievements were immense, but she is largely remembered as a wronged individual whose piety, courage and integrity outlived the efforts of those who tried to discredit her.

Joan of Arc quotes

"I am not afraid. I was born to do this."

"Act and God will act."

> "Children sometimes say that people are hanged for speaking the truth."
>
> "One life is all we have and we live it as we believe in living it. But to sacrifice what you are and to live without belief, that is a fate more terrible than dying."

Thomas More (1478–1535)

Author, lawyer, religious thinker and statesman, Thomas More occupied the post of Lord Chancellor under Henry VIII, but fell into disfavour when he took a principled position against the king's attempt to obtain a divorce so that he could marry Ann Boleyn. Later, by refusing to take the Oath of Supremacy because he rejected Henry's claim to be the supreme head of the Church of England, he was convicted of high treason, and beheaded in the Tower of London. His historical reputation is such that he was voted number 37 on a poll of the 100 most famous Britons ever. He was canonised a saint in 1935.

Early years

Thomas More was born near the ancient City of London, and attended St. Anthony's school in Threadneedle street. After his studies in Oxford he returned to London to train as a lawyer. An indication of his strong spiritual orientation was his choice to lodge with the Carthusian monks in Charterhouse, near Smithfield Market, while he trained at Lincoln's Inn. By this time he was also gaining a reputation as a well-read religious scholar. He formed a close friendship with Erasmus, the famous Dutch humanist who, although sympathetic to many of the ideas of the Reformers, remained loyal to the Catholic Church. More and Erasmus were regarded as the leading humanist thinkers of their time.

Member of parliament

After struggling with the idea of leading a religious life, perhaps as a monk, More decided that life in the world was where he could make his greatest contribution. But he retained a strong leaning towards the monastic life. He led a personal life of strict mortification, even secretly wearing a highly uncomfortable hair shirt next to his skin as a form of penance. Needing more room for his growing family, More moved to Chelsea. After his election to parliament in 1504 he became a regular traveller down the Thames from his home there. As his reputation for leadership, intelligence and sound judgement gained ground, he was eventually honoured with the post of Lord Chancellor to the king in 1529.

Lord Chancellor

The lofty post was to become a poisoned chalice. More found himself at odds with the king when Henry demanded a divorce from his wife Catherine of Aragon. This was something that More, as a loyal Catholic, could not agree with. When Henry went further and claimed to be legally head of the Church after imposing the Act of Supremacy, More was left in an impossible position. As a result, he was imprisoned in the Tower to await the fate of a traitor, newly defined to include anyone disloyal to the king.

Refusal to compromise

But More, despite attempts to change his mind, refused to compromise his moral or religious beliefs. When his beloved daughter tried to persuade him to agree with the king and preserve his social status and its many privileges, he reminded her of the unthinkable foolishness of selling one's soul for the short-term benefits of material gain. Supposing, he told her, that by some unlikely event he managed to secretly survive his death, his death certificate would already ensure that his material possessions had passed to his inheritors. Thus at a stroke he would be a stranger in his own house!

Death of Thomas More

More is especially remembered for the cool way he conducted himself as he approached his untimely end. A man of his intelligence would have been keenly aware of the personal tragedy of losing his life at so early an age. But he remained fully in charge to the end, showing a masterly courage and a gentle wit as he faced the most daunting event to confront mortal man. The historian William Roper gives an account of how he approached the moment of his beheading:

> So remained Sir Thomas More in the Tower more than a seven-night after his judgement . . . from thence he was led to the place of execution. There, going up the scaffold, which was so weak it was ready to fall, he said merrily to the Lieutenant: "I pray you, Master Lieutenant, see me safe up, and for my coming down let me shift for myself." Then desired he all the people thereabout to pray for him . . . This done, he kneeled down, and after his prayers said, turned to the executioner with a cheerful countenance, and said unto him: "Pluck up thy spirits, man, and be not afraid to do thine office; my neck is very short, take heed therefore thou strike not awry, for saving of thine honesty."

> A man of angel's wit and singular learning. I know not his fellow. For where is the man of that gentleness, lowliness, and affability? And, as time requireth, a man of marvellous mirth and pastimes, and sometimes as of sad gravity. A man for all seasons.
>
> Robert Whittington (1520)

More the Londoner

More was a Londoner who loved its streets and alleyways and the special buzz it created then and still does by its busy crowds, colourful streets and bustling markets. As a lawyer he would have known well its seedier side, from which he probably gained some employment as a lawyer. But he was more likely to rejoice in the good things it offered: theatres, taverns, busy markets, unending opportunities for companionship, and the meeting of strangers from all corners of the earth. He knew it was a city of rogues and villains as well as aristocrats and gentlemen. He would have known many of the former. The following is a poignant imagining of how More might have lamented the leaving of his beloved city:

> **THOMAS MORE'S LONDON**
> Across from the Tower, over a modern river of rushing cars, is a plaque on the green where More was beheaded. It states that Thomas Cromwell and one of the commissioners inquiring into More's treason did not long survive Henry's whim; he was sent to the block in 1540. A brisk breeze blows from the river, as it might have the day More died. We can see a square of Roman wall, just as More did before he saw no more. The material world around him was the single most important network of More's life. The very presence of London churches was an emblem of the divine community on earth; the nature of his society was heralded in ritualistic and symbolic forms down the streets in which he walked. His Catholicism was imbued with the spirituality of the material world—each was a token of the other. For him the streets of London could become, on one level, the City of God.
>
> Peter Ackroyd (More's biographer)

Thomas More quotes

"*I die the king's good servant, and God's first.*"

"*The clearness of my conscience has made my heart hop for joy.*"

"My case was such in this matter through the clearness of my own conscience, that though I could have pain I could not have harm, for a man in such a case could lose his head and not be harmed."

"Were it my father on one side and the devil on the other, his cause being good, the devil should have his right."

"I never intend, God being my good Lord, to pin my soul to another man's back, not even the best man that I know this day living: for I know not where he may hap to carry it."

"I would have people in time of silence take heed that their minds are occupied with good thoughts, for unoccupied they will never be."

"Earth has no sorrow that Heaven cannot heal."

"An enchanted world is one that speaks to the soul, to the mysterious depths of the heart and the imagination where we find value, love and union with the world around us."

"Every tribulation which ever comes our way either is sent to be medicinal, if we will take it as such, or it may become medicinal if we make it such, or is better than medicinal, unless we forsake it."

"For Boethius says: for one man to be proud that he has rule over other men is much like one mouse being proud to have rule over other mice in a barn."

"I never saw a fool yet who ever thought himself other than wise ... if a fool perceives himself a fool, that point is not folly, but a little spark of wit."

"If honour were profitable, everyone would be honourable."

> There were also Protestant martyrs at the time of the English Reformation, mostly in the reign of Queen Mary. Notable among them were John Lambert, who was burned to death at Smithfield, London; Hugh Latimer, Nicholas Ridley and later Thomas Cranmer, all of whom were burned at the stake outside Balliol college in Oxford.

Ignatius of Loyola (1491–1556)

Famous as an outstanding spiritual authority, counsellor, mystic, and religious leader, Inigo Onas Lopez became one of the most renowned figures in the Catholic Church in the wake of the Reformation. The

Jesuits whom he founded were known as "foot soldiers" of the Pope. Their first mission was to purify and defend the Church, and restore its battered image after it was vilified and condemned by the Reformers as corrupt in its teachings, failing in its leadership, and untrustworthy in its fidelity to the truths of the gospel. For his work and organisation in responding to the Reformers; for his commitment to truth and justice; and for the sanctity of his life, Ignatius Loyola was canonised a saint on March 13, 1662.

Early years

Inigo's early life saw him involved in warring conflict on behalf of the Viceroy of Navarre. But it was also an opportunity to display his powers of diplomacy and calm leadership, both of which would later come to the fore in his work for the Church. Although a survivor of many earlier battles, in 1521 he was wounded in the legs by a cannon ball, an injury which left him lame. During his convalescence he set about reading spiritual texts on Christ, and the lives of the saints. This led to a spiritual awakening in which he resolved to imitate other great spiritual leaders such as St. Augustine and St. Francis of Assisi, and give his life to the cause of the gospel.

Inspiring vision

During a visit to the monastery at Monserrat near Barcelona he hung up his military uniform before a statue of the Virgin. He then retired to a cave near the town of Manresa where he experienced a spiritual vision. This inspired him to follow a self-imposed programme of prayer, fasting and repentance. Afterwards he made a pilgrimage to the Holy Land before moving to Paris to study at the Sorbonne. There he became a distinguished scholar and gained the nickname "Master Ignatius". Between 1522 and 1524 he wrote his *Spiritual Exercises*, a rigorous spiritual programme consisting of prayers, meditations and other devotions spread over 30 days. They were to become a classic of spiritual direction, and subsequently the guiding handbook of the Jesuit Order which he founded (also known as the *Society of Jesus)*.

Society of Jesus

By 1534 he had attracted a small group companions, most of whom he had got to know during his student days in Paris. Together they formed the first members of the Jesuit Order. Their original mission was to "enter upon hospital and missionary work in Jerusalem, and to go without questioning wherever the Pope might direct." Ignatius was appointed the first Superior General of the Order, and under his leadership his followers grew in numbers, and became engaged in various forms of Christian service. But it was their involvement in education that became their hallmark. This was to be expected, since the original inspiration of their founder was to engage in the battle for ideas, combating especially the dangers he saw in the teachings of the reformers.

Feared reputation

As a result of their dedication and drive, the early Jesuits gained a feared reputation outside Catholic circles. They were accused of allegedly using the worldly methods of subversion and deceit in support of their supposedly fanatical loyalty to the Catholic cause. This made them objects of suspicion in countries that had rejected the papacy, where they were often held responsible for involvement in anti-government activities. Henry Garnet, a leading English Jesuit was hanged for his alleged involvement in the *Gunpowder Plot,* and another, Oswald Tesimond, managed to escape arrest.

Treason

As a result, in England especially, the Jesuits gained a notorious reputation as potential traitors. After another Jesuit, John Ballard, was executed for his alleged part in a plot to assassinate Queen Elisabeth they became public enemies to be hunted down. Since the loyalty to the papacy and the English monarchy were seen to be incompatible, for a Jesuit to enter England was to risk capture and death. This was the fate of one of the most famous Jesuit martyrs, Edmund Campion, who, after many years on the run, was put to death for treason by being hanged, drawn and quartered in Tyburn, London.

Political involvements

In Europe, the Jesuits were not always popular within their own church. They sometimes became involved in heated religious disputes, as exemplified in the writings of Pascal. In 1773 the Order was suppressed in many European countries because of tactless political involvements, but restored in 1814. But they had another side. In a humanitarian connection, the Holocaust memorial in Jerusalem honours 12 Jesuit priests for risking their lives to save Jews; and a plaque commemorating 152 Jesuit priests who gave their lives during the Third Reich stands in the Jesuit university of Kansas City, Missouri.

Liberation theology

In more modern times they have caused controversy for their involvement in political struggles for human rights and social justice. In Latin America they became public enemies of repressive governments. Leading Jesuits gave their lives for speaking out against regimes that ignored the poor. They argued that since Christ in the gospel defended the poor, it was their mission to do likewise. Their understanding that the gospel provided a warrant to justify policical involvement where injustice is rife, became known as *Liberation Theology*.

Assassinations

Acting on this vision brought them into conflict not only with violent regimes that favoured the rich, but also with leaders of their own church. They were criticised for causing embarrassment to the Church by getting involved in troublesome politics rather than staying within the bounds of their religious mission. But the people they helped did not see it this way, and their fame increased after the assassination of 6 Jesuit priests in the university campus of El Salvador on November 16, 1989 by government troops on the trumped up charge of "subversion".

Jesuits today

Despite their chequered history, Jesuits today enjoy a special reputation for their contribution to human development across the world. In one area, going back to their foundation, they continue to provide impressive leadership, namely education. Today Jesuit schools and universities embrace students of all faiths and backgrounds worldwide. Operating in a multi-cultural secular society, Jesuit schools and universities continue to be highly subscribed by students from all backgrounds, valued for their commitment to free enquiry, high scholarship, scientific research and the pursuit of culture.

Christian principles

But in doing so they hold an unswerving regard for the Christian principles of human development through personal morality and social justice. The Jesuit motto *ad majorem Dei gloriam* (for the greater glory of God) is no longer seen in a narrowly "religious" sense. Today it stands for a widely accepted principle: that any activity, or any profession, as long as it conforms to what is right and good, can be meritorious, rewarding and worth pursuing. Such a principle recognises the new multi-faith and multi-cultural reality of today's world, and stands for a Christian vision that continues to gain respect for its part in building bridges across all boundaries of the modern secular age.

Jesuit education

An amusing insight into the tough Jesuit education in his day is given by James Joyce, in which the author recalls his time at the Jesuit school of Clongowes Wood, near Dublin:

> "Then he asked Fleming and Fleming said that the word had no plural. Father Arnall suddenly shut the book and shouted at him: Kneel there in the middle of the class. You are one of the idlest boys I ever met... A silence filled the classroom and Stephen, glancing timidly at Father Arnall's dark face, saw that it was a little red from the wax he was in... He had heard his father say that they were all clever men. They could all have become high-up people in the world if they had not become Jesuits... The door opened quietly and closed: the prefect of studies (Father Dolan)... Any idle loafers want flogging here, Father Arnall?... He came to the middle of the class and saw Fleming on his knees... Hoho, Fleming! An idler of course. I can see it in your eye... Fleming held out his hand. The pandybat came down on it with a loud smacking sound... 1, 2, 3..."
>
> James Joyce, *Portrait of the Artist*

St. Ignatius quotes

> *"In the light of the Divine Goodness, it seems to me ... that ingratitude is the most abominable of sins ... It is a forgetting of all the graces, benefits and blessings received, and as such it is the cause, beginning, and origin of all sins and misfortunes."*
>
> *"Let no one seek to be considered a wit, or to affect elegance, or prudence or eloquence, but look upon Christ, who made nothing at all of these things, but chose to be humbled and despised by men for our sake rather than to be honoured and respected."*
>
> *"We should not dispute stubbornly with anyone; rather we should patiently give our reasons with the purpose of declaring the truth lest our neighbour remain in error, and not that we should have the upper hand."*
>
> *"If the matters being discussed are of such nature that you cannot or ought not be silent, then give your opinion with the greatest sincerity*

and humility, and always end with the words *salvo meliori iudicio*—
with due respect for a better opinion."

"The negligent do not struggle against self, (and) they never achieve
peace of soul, and never possess any virtue in its fullness, while the
energetic and industrious make notable advances on both fronts."

Prayer of St. Ignatius

"Take, O Lord, and receive my entire liberty, my memory, my understanding, and my whole will. All that I am and that I possess You have given me: I surrender it to You to be disposed according to Your will. Give me only Your love and Your grace; with these I will be rich enough, and desire nothing more.
Lord, teach me to be generous.
teach me to serve you as you deserve;
to give and not to count the cost,
To fight and not to heed the wounds,
to toil and not to seek for rest,
to labour and not to ask for reward,
save that of knowing that I do your will.

George Fox (1624–1691)

As the son of a weaver who was apprenticed to a cobler there was little in the early upbringing of George Fox to suggest the impact he would have in the history of Christian thought and practice. A man of exceptional courage, Fox is remembered for his innovative proposals for how Christianity should be practiced, both at the level of worship and the level of daily living. He took the pacifist teaching of Jesus to new lengths, and he departed sharply from the established idea that worship should involve word and sacrament: what commonly goes on inside a traditional church. In Fox's view there was no need for priests, sacraments, sermons or church buildings. For these revolutionary views he was to pay dearly.

Early years

George Fox was born in the village of Drayton-in-the-clay, not far from the city of Leicester in England. His family upbringing was puritan, that is, a form of Christianity separate and distinct from the established Church of England. George Fox received little or no formal education, but he was a man of considerable intelligence with a capacity to speak and write with warmth and insight. His profound spiritual ideas about how faith, if it is to be genuine, must transform the inner man, have continuing relevance in an age bedevilled by external religious divisions and the secularism they have partly spawned.

Revolutionary thinker

Puritans were generally looked down upon as rebels and eccentrics. Fox, like Wesley after him, looked down on the established church for its pretentions and, in his view, its hypocrisy. Instead of being, as it pretended to be, the true way to God and Jesus Christ, he saw it as essentially an obstacle to people's search for God and true spiritual enlightenment.

Rebel and troublemaker

If the puritans thought that the Church of England was out of touch, Fox went even further, making the puritans themselves look rooted in the past. One of Fox's main targets was the idea that priests and ministers were necessary to mediate between human beings and God. In his view God could be approached much more effectively by people themselves. By turning to the Bible people could encounter the voice of Jesus directly, and more importantly, could receive personally the Holy Spirit's inspiration to guide and inspire them in their daily lives. As he put it:

> "As a Quaker I find I can most easily "turn to the light", and try to live my life as I should, in the silent community meeting for worship and the search for truth. I find I can worship God with people of many different traditions. But for me the Quaker silence, in a simple meeting house, without any symbols, is the most direct way I can find communion with God."

Fox was so taken with this idea that he often caused disturbances by going around interrupting church services. He mockingly called churches "steeple houses". In his travels round the countryside preaching he became a marked man. He was imprisoned six times between 1653 and 1673 for civil disobedience. He and his followers wore distinctive wide-brimmed hats and had a cheerful reputation for refusing to doff their hat to anyone. Fox once famously refused to doff his hat to a judge in court, insisting that no man was superior to any other: all were equally inferior to Jesus Christ.

The Quakers

One of Fox's key ideas was the so-called *inner light*, a direct perception of the Christian message that would transform a person from the inside. This could be obtained by meeting with others in simple surroundings and waiting for inspiration either by listening to the word of God in the Bible, or to others who might wish to share their thoughts. In this way a person learns from others, and gains the important insight that there is something divine (of God) in everyone. As he put it:

> "By cherishing *that of God* in everyone, I have come to see religion as a form of liberation, which abolishes social oppression and injustice, and allows those on the edge of society to be brought into the middle. It also allows me to see all warfare and violence as opposed to the will of God, and to understand the sacredness of creation."

The new movement later became known as "Friends" or the "Society of Friends". But its original name was Quakers. This came after Fox once had the temerity to tell a judge to *"tremble at the word of the Lord."* The name stuck.

Quaker worship

Quakers have no formal worship, but meet in silence before the Bible until one of their number feels moved to give a message. The ideals of the movement are widely respected but quakerism never had a wide following. It has little emotional or communal appeal and depends on small followings for its dynamics to work. Notably its stress on intelligent understanding means that it has little appeal for children. However, its essential message is a warning about the sometimes artificial nature of church-centred worship, and it remains a champion of the inner conscience.

Quaker influence

But for all their modest size Quakers have never been an insignificant movement. They have a widespread following worldwide, and historically have had some leading names among their number, including former US presidents. Both Herbert Hoover and Richard Nixon came from Quaker stock. Quakers have always been at the forefront of the pacifist movement, and were often made to suffer for appealing to conscience to avoid fighting in time of war. So-called "conscientious objectors" were always regarded with contempt, despite often being prepared to serve their country in other, no less demanding, ways.

George Fox quotes

> *"Be patterns, be examples in all countries . . . that your carriage and life may preach among all sorts of people, and to them; then you will come to walk cheerfully over the world, answering that of God in everyone; whereby in them you may be a blessing, and make the witness of God in them to bless you."*

> *"The Lord showed me that he did not dwell in temples that men built, but in peoples hearts. His people were his temple, and he dwelt in them."*

> *"I heard a voice which said, there is one, even Jesus Christ, who can speak to thy condition, and when I heard it my heart leapt for joy."*

> *"I also saw that there was an ocean of darkness and death, but an infinite ocean of light and love which flowed over the ocean of darkness."*

> *"Keep within for Christ is within you. They are seducers who draw your mind out from the teachings within you."*

Historic Artists and Architects

Early Illuminated Manuscripts

The term *illuminated manuscript* refers to works written on vellum (animal skin) or parchment (more durable than paper), usually on religious subjects such as bible or gospel texts, psalms, prayers and so on. Their artistic value comes from the exceptional quality of their writing (calligraphy) and the excellence of their colourful imagery (illumination). The majority of illuminated manuscripts were done in the medieval period in Europe, but the earliest ones were done in Ireland, Constantinople and Italy between roughly AD 600–800. Unlike later works of religious art whose creators are known, the early manuscripts are the work of anonymous artists, almost certainly monks. Here we look briefly at two of the most famous from the period known as the Dark Ages.

The Book of Kells.

Famous illuminated manuscript, and one of the earliest, it was created by highly skilled Celtic monks in Kells in Ireland around 800 AD. It is regarded as the most famous book to have survived from the pre-medieval period, and is considered the zenith of religious calligraphy and illumination. Its brilliant illustrations decorate the Latin text of the gospel. To its first readers its pages were said to have *"looked like jewels in the cold northern light."*

> Celtic, or Irish, monasteries that specialised in art and learning included Kells, Durrow and Clonard in Ireland, and Lindisfarne in Northumbria. The most famous manuscript, *The Book of Kells,* escaped damage from a Viking raid, although its jewelled cover was lost. The *Lindisfarne Gospels* (see below) were probably produced by the same artistic school.

Abstract and pictorial art

The Book of Kells is famous for its "carpet pages", colourful pages of mostly mesmeric abstract creations designed to enhance the initial letters of each chapter occurring throughout the gospel text. Pictorial imagery is limited, and includes symbols of the Four Evangelists, Christ, and scenes from the Passion. Alongside these are frequently recurring images of real or mythical animals and birds. One remarkable image, so small that it is hardly visible to the naked eye, shows two cats holding the Eucharistic host, while on their backs sit two mice. The image echoes the harmony of nature promised by Isaiah as a mark of the Messianic Age.

Significance today

But most of the book's imagery is abstract, consisting of intricate designs of great beauty that are baffling to the eye. The book has been held at Trinity College, Dublin since the 17th century, and has been on public display in the historic library since the 19th century. Today it is the main tourist attraction of the college, and is presented in a climatically controlled ultra modern display-centre which shows off the book's awesome achievement as a work of artistic, religious, cultural and historical significance. Each day one page is turned.

> **THE BOOK OF KELLS (TRINITY COLLEGE, DUBLIN)**
> "The book contains the harmony of the Four Evangelists according to Jerome (Latin text), where for almost every page there are different designs distinguished by varied colours. Here you may seen the face of majesty divinely drawn, here the mystic symbols of the Evangelists ... Fine craftsmanship is all about you, but you might not notice it. Look more keenly at it and you will penetrate to the very shrine of art. You will make out intricacies, so delicate and so subtle, so full of knots and links, with colours so fresh and vivid, that you might say that all of this were the work of an angel and not of a man."
>
> Gerald of Wales, 12th century

The Lindisfarne Gospels.

A highly prized document similar in many respects to the Book of Kells with equally brilliant workmanship, it was probably created on the island of Lindisfarne in Northumbria around 700 AD. It is one of the show-pieces of the British Library in London (see box).

> The Lindisfarne Gospels is one of the main treasures of the British Library in London. It is an "illuminated manuscript" of the gospel texts, the product of an unknown monk, or monks, of Lindisfarne Priory on Holy Island in Northumbria. The manuscript is a work of superb craftsmanship and visual artistry created sometime in the early 8th century. "(The artist's) remarkable skill and power of invention are strikingly evident in the opening pages of each gospel. A painting of the gospel's Evangelist is followed by a "carpet" page, so-called because the whole page is covered with intricate pattern. Next is the "incipit" page, that is, an opening page in which the first letters of the gospels are greatly elaborated with interlacing and spiral patterns."
>
> British Library Internet site

The Cathedral Architects

The building of the great cathedrals which are still dotted around Europe is usually dated to around 1000 AD, or the first millenium. Earlier cathedrals and basilicas had been built, but in a style that was called Norman, or Romanesque. This style was typified by the round arch, and relied on heavy, thick, walls to support the roof. But in the years following the millenium a new style of building came into vogue. It was in this period that most of the great European cathedrals which stand today were built, using the principles of the newly discovered gothic architecture.

Gothic architecture

The earliest of the great cathedrals are a mixture of Norman and gothic, such as Durham, Lincoln and Peterborough. The Norman parts of these buildings can be identified by the use of the heavy roman arch, and windows which tended to be small. With the arrival of gothic the pointed arch came into play. This made possible the creation of much higher buildings, with walls that were supported by so-called "flying" buttresses. These were great arches attached to the walls from the outside, and looked like oars attached to a boat. As a result of this technique lighter walls could be built which allowed the insertion of great windows, some as large as a tennis court. These windows were filled with stained glass (see below) and became the hallmark of high gothic.

Unknown artists

Most of the cathedral builders were artists who, like those who created the illuminated manuscripts, are unknown. The resulting buildings were produced by teams of architects, engineers, designers, carpenters, masons and workmen. How such buildings were erected before the existence of machines, earth movers, lifting gear, safety equipment, and the high technology that today makes such mega-structures comparatively easy to erect, is a wonder in itself.

Brilliance of engineering

While the building of the great cathedrals was no doubt inspired by religious faith and devotion, the standards of structural excellence that they reflect were based on more than "a wing and a prayer". Their survival over centuries to the present day testify to their unerring fidelity to the highest standards of structural engineering. Proof of this can be seen in their awesome height and mass, the artistic perfection of their detail, and by their remarkable, and often difficult to believe, solidity. The fact that some were seriously damaged in the course of time was usually the work of man. War, revolution and other human conflicts caused some to be ruined, most notably Coventry in England, but happily the majority have survived, most ranked today as World Heritage Sites.

Art and education

Each Cathedral was built by a team of master masons who worked on designs based on precise geometric principles and proportions. For instance, most of the cathedral facades fit perfectly either inside a square or a circle. When the structural work was complete a team of religious artists worked on sculpture, statuary, painting and stained glass to form a unity of religious imagery designed to uplift the spirit, provoke wonderment and inspire devotion. They also functioned as an important source of religious education by bringing alive pictorially many of the events and personages that made up the "history of salvation" (Old Testament prophets, Christ, the Virgin, the Evangelists and the Apostles).

Religious experience

The sculptured figures and holy images which adorn each cathedral were in each case intelligently planned to form part of a grand theological scheme. A recurring idea was to show how the history of the faith shows a chronological progression from the pre-Christian Old

Testament to its fulfilment in the life of Christ. Windows in particular frequently contained schemes of imagery illustrating how incidents from the Old Testament prefigured, and were fulfilled by, events in the New. As a result each cathedral became an architectural, artistic and religious experience in one.

> Some cathedrals, like Chartres, paid tribute to figures from the ancient world for their wisdom and enlightenment, thus recognising their contribution to man's onward march in knowledge, of which faith, with its spiritual insights, was seen as a crowning moment. These included figures like Socrates, Aristotle, Euclid, and Pythagoras.

Stained Glass

Windows are always the most fragile and vulnerable parts of any building. The move from Norman to Gothic meant that walls could support much larger windows (the west window of Canterbury is larger than a tennis court). This meant that glass would become an important medium for illustrating the figures who played a prominent part in the historic drama of the Christian faith. All the great cathedrals had windows that showed this drama and were considered of great beauty and splendour. But time and history would not be kind.

> It has often been pointed out that since a stained glass window can only be seen from inside the church, it symbolises the way faith itself (as a special form of insight, or seeing things in a "different light") can only be understood by those who are "on the inside" as believers within the Church.

Destruction of medieval stained-glass

The medieval stained glass of many of the great cathedrals has been lost, often due less to the ravages of nature than to the destructive forces of war and vandalism. On the continent only Chartres retains its complete set of stained glass windows. Many cathedrals were attacked, particularly during the French Revolution, and elsewhere; and much destruction was caused in Europe during both world wars. In England, the stained glass heritage suffered early on from Puritan iconoclasts in the years following the Reformation . In some cases windows survived by good fortune (see box below), while others (as at Canterbury), partially survived through the lucky intervention of local townspeople, fiercely proud of their local cathedral.

> In the bleak mid-winter of 1643, early in England's civil wars, an inspector sent by Parliament to find and destroy idolatrous images, toured the churches and colleges of Cambridge. On 26 December, late in the short and gloomy day, William Downing made a slapdash survey of Kings College chapel and vaguely noted the "one thousand superstitious pictures" in its stained glass windows. He had many more visits to make on his Puritan mission of sacred vandalism. Besides, some Parliamentary troops were already in the chapel and shielded from the bitter weather by that Popish glass. So through tiredness, prudence or oversight, one the greatest works of visual art ever created in England managed to survive. In Henry VII's chapel in Westminster Abbey, by contrast, the iconoclasts did their shattering worst.
>
> Boyd Tonkin on *The Kings Glass* by Carola Hicks,
> The Independent 11 January 2008

Some Famous Cathedrals

Chartres (France)

Famous for its twin spires and unique
collection of undamaged stained glass
The glass can be taken down and buried secretly in
case of war or civil disturbance. Look for the *belle*
verriere window of Madonna and Child. Search
For images of Aristotle, Pythagoras and other representatives of ancient wisdom.

Amiens (France)

Tallest gothic building in the world.
Glass largely destroyed from effects
of two world wars. Look for the famous weeping
angel behind the high altar, sent home as postcards by soldiers
as poignant reminder of millions killed in battlefields nearby.

Durham (England)

Famous for the beauty of its proportions
and brilliance of design. Note how the pillars
are decorated differently, and how the height
of each pillar is equal to its circumference
forming a circle in a square

Canterbury (England)

Famous as site of martyrdom of St. Thomas Beckett and immortalised in Chaucer's *Canterbury Tales*. Notice the cathedral's massive bulk and wonderful setting. Look out for the "miracle windows" around the Trinity Chapel.

Ely (England)

Rising like a massive ship from the flat landscape of the Fen, Ely is famous for its octagonal tower made of wood and suspended within the cathedral as a masterpiece of engineering and design. Look for the missing (vandalised) heads of saints in the Lady chapel.

Burgos (Spain)

Burial place of *El Cid*. Note the splendour of its spires, towers and pinnacles, and the darkness of the cool interior, a defense against the often intense heat of sunny Spain.

Cologne (Germany)

Famous for its soaring twin spires rising beside the banks of the Rhine. Was iconic war-time image of survival among the ruins caused by Allied bombing.

St. Peter's (Rome)

Built in Italian basilica style based on the Greek cross of equal length and sides surmounted by a dome, designed by Michelangelo. Admired for its massive scale and the marble splendour of its interior space.

> In the East there were buildings of comparable magnificence that reflected aspects of the faith typical of Orthodox Christianity, not covered in this book. Examples of great eastern religious buildings include Hagia Sophia in Istanbul (now a mosque), St. Basil's Cathedral in Red Square Moscow (now a museum). The influence of the East may also be seen in the splendid mosaic-covered churches for which Ravenna is famous.

Historic Christian Thinkers

Augustine of North Africa (354–430 AD)

Made Bishop of Hippo in modern day Algeria after achieving wide fame as a renowned scholar and academic, Augustine was regarded as one of the leading creative thinkers of the early Church. He is recognised by the Orthodox, Roman Catholic and Anglican Churches as a saint, and pre-eminent *Doctor of the Church*. His teachings on various Christian beliefs were highly influential not only in the early Church but later among the reformers, Luther and Calvin. But what gave Augustine an extra edge was his openly-admitted early life of sin and debauchery. His later conversion, and subsequent pronouncements on human behaviour, carried much more weight as a result.

Early Years

Augustinus Africanus was born in Tagaste, modern day Algeria, of a Christian mother, Monica, and a pagan father. In 373 AD he went to the University of Carthage where he stayed as a teacher for nine years. Fed up with the unruly atmosphere of Carthage and its mediocre standards, he looked for an opening in one of the mainstream centres of learning such as Rome or Milan. In Milan he was attracted by the prospect of meeting the highly intellectual and well-liked bishop Ambrose. Following a mystical experience there (see box) he decided to enrol for a course of instruction in Christianity, and was finally baptised by Ambrose in 387. Four years later he was ordained priest, and shortly afterwards appointed as Bishop of Hippo Regius, a coastal city, where he was to remain until his death.

Augustine's Confessions

In his *Confessions* Augustine describes his early life which he remembered as a time full of devilment of which he later became ashamed. One of the memories that troubled him was of stealing pears from an orchard, an episode which later made him realise how easily we drift towards pointless misbehaviour. Trivial though it was, he recalled it as stealing:

> "for the sake of stealing ... I lusted to thieve ... nor cared I to enjoy what I stole, but joyed in the theft and the sin itself."

Another phase of his early life involved sexual indulgence. He formed a lengthy relationship to a woman who eventually bore him a son. This, in the light of his later religious beliefs, he saw as wrong and foolish. He reflected that his wanton behaviour brought him more pain than happiness because it always seemed to land him in suspicion, jealousy and quarrels. As he put it in his *Confessions:*

> "Through an immoderate inclination towards these goods of the lowest order, the better and higher are forsaken—Thou, our Lord God, Thy truth, and Thy law ... To love, then, and be beloved was sweet to me; but more when I obtained to enjoy the person I loved. I defiled, therefore, the spring of friendship with the filth of concupiscence, and I beclouded its brightness with the hell of lustfulness ... (But I) was with joy fettered with sorrow-bringing bonds, that I might be scourged with the iron burning rods of jealousy, and suspicions, and fears, and angers, and quarrels."

Augustine's Conversion

Augustine's conversion to Christianity, no doubt, owed much to his meeting with Ambrose. But it also owed much to a personal crisis that he had been going through. In the end, it was an extraordinary experience in a garden in Milan in the summer of 386, that made him make up his mind:

> This controversy in my heart was self against self only ... So was I ... weeping in the most bitter contrition of my heart, when, lo! I heard from a neighbouring house a voice, as of a boy or girl, I know not, chanting and oft repeating, "Take up and read", Take up and read" ... So checking the torrent of my tears, I arose; interpreting it to be no other than a command from God, to open the book, and read the first chapter I should find ... I seized, opened, and in silence read that section on which my eyes first fell: *not in rioting and drunkenness, not in chambering and wantonness, not in*
>
> (continued)

> *strife and envying; but put ye on the Lord Jesus Christ, and make not provision for the flesh in concupiscence.* Instantly at the end of this sentence, by a light as it were of serenity infused into my heart, all the darkness of doubt vanished away.
>
> St Augustine, *Confessions*, Bk 8

Augustine the thinker

After the experience, Augustine decided to give up his teaching post in Milan and devote his life to celibacy and dedication to the Christian life. But Milan's loss was the Church's gain: he became the outstanding thinker of his time, throwing new light on Christian beliefs and values.

Augustine saw the Christian faith as an historical drama involving three key moments: Creation, Redemption and Salvation:

> The divine plan of creation was ruined by the *first man* (Adam). The damage was made good by the *second man* (Christ). The task of the believer is to become the *third man*, the man transformed by the grace of Christ.

Like the ark of Noah, a vehicle of salvation is needed to make the third man possible. This is the Christian community of the Church, what Augustine saw as a City, a spiritually oriented community harbouring the seekers of goodness and truth, what he famously called the *City of God*.

Good and evil

The prevailing view in Augustine's north Africa, (and once shared by Augustine himself), was that there were two opposing forces governing the world, the forces of light and the forces of darkness, one representing good and the other evil. Augustine broke away from this *Manichaean* view, and held that God was the only supreme power in the world, and he held the power of good. What appeared to be an evil power was simply the power of evil, something that for all its baleful effects, has no existence in itself.

Conquering evil

Instead of evil deriving from some evil power, it is only an illusion, an appearance of being something real and often good. In Augustine's view it was simply "an absence of good", about as real as the shadow cast by the sun—the sun of morality and goodness. Not only does evil not come from an evil power neither does it come from a good power. Its source is in the human heart, and its defeat is dependent on how far the human being is subjected to the inspiring influence of the power of good (God).

> I came to Carthage, where I found myself in the midst of a hissing cauldron of lusts. I had not yet fallen in love, but I was already in love with the idea of it, and this feeling that something was missing made me despise myself for not being more anxious to satisy the need. I began to look around for some object of my love, since I badly wanted to love something.
> St. Augustine, *Confession*

The Bible

Augustine saw the Bible as the key to understanding the history of salvation, the hidden theme behind its message. But despite his apparently literal understanding of events such as the sin of Adam, he also showed an early awareness of some of the problems that come from a too literal understanding of events such as creation. He said that:

> "When the scriptures are at variance with our rational faculties, we must remember that it was not the intention of the Spirit of God to teach men anything that would not be of use to them for their salvation."

In other words it is not necessary to take everything in the Bible at face value. In more modern times this became a key idea in the science—religion controversy which still, to this day, revolves around the interpretation of the Bible.

St. Augustine quotes

"Hope has two beautiful daughters. Their names are anger and courage: anger at the way things are, and courage to see that they do not remain so."

"A thing is not necessarily false because badly uttered, not true because spoken magnificently."

"Beauty is indeed a good gift of God; but that the good may not think it a great good, God dispenses it even to the wicked."

"Charity is no substitute for justice withheld."

"Do you wish to be great? Then begin by being. Do you wish to construct a vast and lofty fabric? Think first about the foundations of humility. The higher your structure is to be, the deeper must be its foundation."

"Don't you believe that there is in man a deep so profound as to be hidden even from him in whom it is?"

"Faith is to believe what you do not see: the reward of this faith is to see what you believe."

"Find out how much God has given you and take what you need; the remainder is needed by others."

"God had one son on earth without sin, but not without suffering."

"God judged it better to bring good out of evil than to suffer no evil to exist."

"He that is kind is free, though he is a slave; he that is evil is a slave, even though he be a king."

"He who created us without our help will not save us without our consent."

"If we did not have rational souls we would not be able to believe."

"If we live good lives the times are also good. As we are, such are the times."

"If you believe what you like in the gospels, and reject what you don't like, it's not the gospel you believe, but yourself."

"Seek not to understand that you may believe, but believe that you may understand."

"In the absence of justice, what is sovereignty but organised robbery."

"Indeed, man wishes to be happy even when he so lives as to make happiness impossible."

"It was pride that changed angels into devils; it is humility that changes devils into angels."

"Patience is the companion of wisdom."

"Pray as though everything depended on God. Work as though everything depended on you."

"Men go abroad to wonder at the heights of mountains, at the huge waves of the sea, at the long courses of the rivers, at the vast compass of the ocean, at the circular motion of the stars, and they pass by themselves without wondering."

"Since love grows within you, so beauty grows. Love is the beauty of the soul."

"What does love look like? It has the hands to help others. It has the feet to hasten to the poor and needy. It has eyes to see misery and want. It has the ears to hear the sighs and sorrows of men. That is what love looks like."

"There is something in humility that strangely exalts the heart."

"To seek the highest good is to live well."

"What then is time? If no one asks me I know what it is. If I wish to explain it to him who asks, I do not know."

"Who can map out the various forces at play in one's soul? Man is a great depth, O Lord. The hairs of his head are easier by far to count than his feeling, the movements of his heart."

"Grace is to will as the horse is to the rider."

"Thou hast made us for thyself, O Lord, and our hearts are restless until they find their rest in thee."

"If by fate anyone means the will or power of God, let him keep his meaning but mend his language: for fate commonly means a necessary process which will have its way apart from the will of God or men."

"My mind withdrew its thoughts from experience, extracting itself from the contradictory throng of sensuous images, that it might find out what that light was wherein it was bathed ... and thus, with the flash of one hurried glance, it attained to the vision of That Which Is."

"We are certainly in a common class with the beasts; every action of animal life is concerned with seeking bodily pleasure and avoiding pain."

Thomas Aquinas (1225–1274)

Philosopher and religious thinker

Renowned for the clarity of his thought and the depth of his intellect, Thomas Aquinas was one of the leading philosopher-theologians of the Middle Ages. His ideas on a wide range of issues from man's understanding of religion to the question of how to judge ethical behaviour, continue to be studied into modern times. His unique approach of writing from a non-believer's perspective makes him of continuing interest in a secular age. Although his life's work was dedicated to expressing and explaining the Church's religious and moral teachings, he dealt with more universal issues such as the existence of God, how knowledge is obtained, and how the human will should be guided in order to act morally.

Philosophy and theology

A theologian is someone concerned to show the significance of religious faith from a believer's perspective. As a theologian Thomas was a leading authority in analysing and explaining points of religious belief such as the significance of Christ, and other related teachings of the Church. But in the process of doing so he also had to be a philosopher, using the principles of human knowledge and reason. Philosophy is a human science which examines all aspects of how and what people think and believe. Thomas addressed many questions that unbelievers ask. His aim was to show how religious beliefs can be justified rationally, and how they help towards an understanding of life and the world. One of the issues he was particularly concerned with was the existence of God.

The existence of God

Briefly, his approach was to argue that our experience of the world led to some blind alleys when we begin to ask fundamental questions. For instance when we look at the world we see that everything has a cause. But you cannot go back infinitely looking for causes. There must have been a first cause. And this is what people call God. Equally we can see that everything in the world appears to be designed to achieve an objective. Man is guided by reason, animals by instinct, and inanimate things by the laws of physics. This suggests a hidden intelligence or designer guiding all things to their end. This is what people call God.

Limitations of philosophy

These arguments are of course helpful to believers who find in them a certain rational support for their belief in God. But while he believed that his arguments were strong, he knew that his reasoning may not be accepted by non-believers, since nobody can be compelled to accept an argument based on reason alone. From his wide experience as a teacher in some of Europe's leading universities he was aware of the paradox that the rational mind only accepts conclusions that it already believes to be true.

Problems with reason

Aquinas also came under fire from religious leaders. The idea of using reason to back up faith was challenged by the reformers on religious grounds. According to Luther, faith does not need reason and should never be supported by it. To do so is to insult the Almighty. Instead it should be accepted for itself, on its own terms. This is because it is a unique form of enlightenment given to mankind as a gift of a gracious God.

Reason and faith

Others have defended Aquinas, pointing out that he never claimed that reason could be a substitute for faith, and arguing that he himself did not rely on rational arguments for his own faith. From his writings it is clear that he saw faith as a freely accepted spiritual insight into religious truth. Others claim that the reformers had misunderstood Aquinas. He was not saying that faith needed additional backing. He was primarily trying to show non-believers that faith could be defended by reason, which is itself a God-given gift.

Morality and natural law

Aquinas also had an important influence with his ideas on morality and behaviour. Influenced by Aristotle, he taught that happiness was the key test of our behaviour. Happiness comes not from following our desires or wishes, but from doing those things that bring inner satisfaction. He concluded that happiness was a sense of fulfilment in doing what was right according to our conscience. He argued that man is equipped with reason to see that certain laws of behaviour (moral laws) follow from the way we are made, both as individuals and members of society. Murder, theft, stealing, fraud, exploitation, dishonesty and so on, are really different ways of going against our nature. When people act in these ways they always bring suffering to other human beings. This Aquinas called natural law, something that he saw as reflecting the will of the Creator.

Later years

But after many years of teaching and being involved in conferences and disputes Aquinas found himself down in spirits and in failing health. He even began to doubt if his teaching career had not been a failure. "Everything I have written seem like straw to me", he famously lamented. In the end he resigned his teaching post at the Sorbonne in Paris, and returned to Italy.

Death of Aquinas

He spent some time convalescing in Monte Cassino before his eventual death near Rome. His last prayer was a moving testimony both to his humanity and deep spirituality:

> "I receive Thee, ransom of my soul. For love of Thee I studied and kept vigil, toiled, preached and taught..."

He was honoured by later Popes as one of the Doctors of the Church, and in the *Divine Comedy* Dante sees him in heaven, calling him "the great Teacher". Today his ideas continue to be widely studied in schools and universities throughout the world.

> Thomas Aquinas was a pan-European. He studied and taught at three major European universities: Cologne, Naples and Paris. His relics are in the Dominican church in Toulouse in southern France.

Thomas Aquinas quotes

"Better to illuminate than merely to shine, to deliver to others contemplated truths than merely to contemplate."

"Reason in man is rather like God in the world."

"Faith has to do with things that are not seen and hope with things that are not at hand."

"By nature all men are equal in liberty, but not in other endowments."

"There is nothing on this earth more to be prized than true friendship."

"A scrap of knowledge about sublime things is worth any amount about trivialities."

"To live well is to be engaged in a good activity."

"Good and evil, which are objects of the will, are in things. Truth and error, which are objects of the intellect, are in minds." (quoting Aristotle).

"Most men seem to live according to the senses than according to reason."

"Man cannot live without joy. When he knows not spiritual joy he turns to carnal pleasures."

"It is requisite for the relaxation of the mind that we make use, from time to time, of playful games and jokes."

"Well-ordered self-love is right and natural."

"Poets and philosophers are alike in being big on wonder."

"Not everything that is more difficult is more meritorious."

"The highest manifestation of life is governing one's own actions."

"Happiness is secured through virtue."

Martin Luther (1483–1546)

Few people made a greater impact on the religious and social history of Europe and, by extension the world, than the former monk from Eisleben in Germany. With his radical understanding of Christianity, and above all the Church, Martin Luther began a movement that had far reaching religious, social and political consequences. Each of the countries that embraced the Reformation became radically changed in organisation, outlook and practice. Some, like England, underwent significant religious, social and cultural change, resulting in a radical reassessment of its religious and cultural heritage. Above all a new rift opened up in European society, dividing people for the first time into Catholic and Protestant, often with bitter consequences.

Early years

Martin Luther was born of hard-working and relatively well-off parents who were desirous of good schooling for their son. But the young Martin did not take easily to the disciplines of education and learning. His rebellious nature revealed itself early in his blunt opinion of his first school. *"It was,* he recalled, *"a time of purgatory and hell."* Later, when he joined the University of Erfurt his mood hadn't changed. He described it as *"a beerhouse and whorehouse"* whose lectures left him bored and depressed. Having to rise at 4 a.m. each morning to face *"a day of rote learning and often weary spiritual exercises"* was not to his taste. Yet he grimly soldiered on, gaining a masters degree at the age of 22.

Troubled spirit

Following his father's advice, he enrolled in law-school with a view to joining the legal profession, but soon dropped out. He felt that law represented uncertainty, something he detested. Deeply religious and devout, he appears to have been obsessed with the search for truth and certainty about life and the hereafter. Philosophy, with all its pretentions about truth and knowledge, he found full of arrogant claims. Its claims that reason was the one path to truth left him cold. Believing that human beings were weak, shifty, unreliable and perverse, he had no confidence in human nature or human reason. He believed instead that the Bible, the word of God not the word of man, held all the answers he was looking for.

Importance of the Bible

In line with the standard beliefs of his day Luther saw the Bible as the record of God's revelation to mankind. But while he saw it as a privileged book that provided a unique insight into the meaning of life, he felt that the Church had fallen down on its responsibility to proclaim its true message. First it had allowed its teaching to become confused and corrupted, putting itself forward instead as the true guide to the Christian faith. And second, it had deliberately kept the sacred book to itself by keeping it in Latin, a language the ordinary people could not understand.

The meaning of faith

For Luther, one of the Bible's most important teachings was the meaning of faith. Turning to the writings of St. Paul, Luther proclaimed that faith was something that owed nothing to human reasoning, his old bug-bear. As St. Paul said, the beliefs of faith are "foolishness" to the eyes of reason. Following reason was alright in relation to everyday human affairs, but not in relation to God. Reason can never be trusted because men were corrupt and sinful, and are always likely to use reason to justify their egotism and selfishness. Here Luther extended his criticism of reason to include the attitude of the Catholic Church which, in his eyes, had made faith a matter of "beliefs". In Luther's view faith was not meant to be about beliefs. It was much more about trust. If you trusted in God all would be well, regardless of your beliefs.

Terrifying experience

Luther' new conviction that faith was about trusting in God, and depending on him absolutely for salvation, was put to the test by an unexpected trauma that brought him face to face with all his inner fears about life and death. Returning to university one winter evening, he was caught in a thunderstorm, an event that terrified him so much that he vowed to become a monk if he survived.

Sale of indulgences

Soon after entering a monastery Luther was advised by his superiors to take time off to ease his despair and morbid introspection. He was advised to pursue an academic career as a university teacher. Luther took the advice, gained a Doctorate degree and took up a teaching post at the University of Wittenberg. About this time an Dominican friar called Johann Tetzel came from Rome to raise money for the rebuilding of St. Peter's Basilica. In doing so he claimed that the Church could issue "indulgences" (spiritual pardons for sin) to those who were good enough to make a contribution. It was as if he had set off a bomb.

Break with Rome

An enraged Luther saw it as an example of the church's corruption. This, he fumed, was fraudulent blackmail: selling spiritual benefits in return for a material investment. God, he warned, could not be bought in so crude a way. Nailing his objections to the church door of All Saints Church in Wittenberg, he accused the Catholic authorities of abandoning the Bible in favour of its own version of Christianity. As he saw it, it was personal faith not allegiance to the Church that was the key to salvation:

> Jesus Christ, our Lord and God, died for our sins and was raised again for our justification... All have sinned and are justified freely, without their own works or merits, by His grace through the redemption that is in Christ Jesus, in His blood (Romans 3. 23-25)... This is necessary to believe. This cannot otherwise be grasped or acquired by any work, law or merit. Therefore it is clear and certain that this faith alone justifies us.
>
> Martin Luther

The Reformation

Luther's objections, which received a welcome boost by the recent invention of printing, soon became well known across Europe. Before long his influence began to spread and the Reformation he started began to take root. Papal power in many European countries was overthrown, replaced by the new, "Protestant", or "Reformed" faith. While Luther began with some fundamental convictions regarding faith and the central importance of the Bible, he gradually began to reject well-established Catholic practices such as confession and the role of priests, praying for the dead and, above all, the central act of worship the Mass. All these he saw as obstacles, not helps, in man's search for God and salvation.

Bible translated

Luther went on to distinguish himself as a considerably able scholar, composing a catechism of his beliefs, writing hymns, and producing a reputable translation of the Bible into German which, with the benefit of the newly discovered printing press, became widely known and read. Making the Bible available in the vernacular (German), Luther encouraged people to stop relying on priests and bishops for religious and moral guidance. They could now have this guidance for themselves by reading the Bible. In this way the Bible became the badge of Protestantism, the new alternative to papal authority.

Impact of Luther

The impact of Luther and his ideas was to be far-reaching. Europe became newly divided into Catholic and Protestant, southern Europe generally remaining loyal to Catholicism, while the northern countries turned Protestant. The result was a period of deep-seated hostility between the two sides which has continued well into the modern era. Whether Luther deserves praise or blame depends on which side answers the question. But what cannot be disputed is that few men made a greater impact on the religious, social, and political history of western Europe in the last five centuries than Martin Luther.

Martin Luther quotes

> "Here I stand, I can do no other. God help me. Amen."
>
> "Faith is permitting ourselves to be seized by the things we do not see."
>
> "I more fear what is within me than what is without."
>
> "I have held many things in my hands and I have lost them all; but whatever I have placed in God's hands that I still possess."
>
> "Peace if possible, truth at all costs."
>
> "Every man must do two things alone; he must do his own believing and his own dying."

"Where God built a church there the devil would also build a chapel."

"Beautiful music is the art of the prophets that can calm the agitations of the soul; it is one of the most magnificent and delightful presents that God has given us."

"Whatever your heart clings to and confides in, that is truly your God."

"Our Lord has written the promise of resurrection, not in books alone, but in every leaf at springtime."

Blaise Pascal (1623–1662)

French mathematician, physicist and philosopher, Pascal was a child prodigy who became one of the most eminent figures of his time. But following an unexpected religious experience in 1654 in a Paris church, he later gained a reputation as an outstanding religious thinker. Keenly impressed by the wonders of nature and science, he found that human beings by comparison were a disappointing enigma. Given that they had extraordinary intellectual powers they tended, almost naturally, to use them badly. As a result, they found themselves (if they really thought about it), unable to cope either with the mystery of life, or the mystery of themselves. But the earlier Pascal did not always take life so seriously.

Early years

Earlier, as a man of the world, the young Pascal became well known in Paris for his far from pious life-style. Born in Clermont-Ferrand in central France, his mother died when he was three; but his father was highly educated with an interest in science and mathematics, an interest later taken up by his precocious son. After moving to Paris his father received an important post as tax inspector in nearby Rouen. Although he was initially of a quiet nature, Pascal became an independent minded young city gent. He was often seen in the company of freethinkers, theatre-goers, gamblers and *bon viveurs* during their frequent crawls through the hot spots of the capital.

Overall man of genius

There were many sides to Pascal's life. As a mathematician and physicist he had few equals. He was a recognised authority on scientific matters, and was regarded as a writer of style, substance and originality. As early as 16 he was so advanced as a student that he was writing academic papers and solving mathematical problems. When one of his works was shown to the great philosopher Descartes the latter refused to believe it was done by one so young. When Descartes visited him in 1647 they argued about the current scientific problem of the vacuum. Descartes went away saying that the biggest vacuum was in Pascal's head! Proving the great philosopher wrong Pascal achieved further renown by inventing an early form of calculator (or computer) which his father used in his tax business.

Outstanding Writer

Pascal's writing ability was seen at its best in his *Provincial Letters (1657)*. The letters were highly regarded at the time for their literary excellence, and they became an exhilarating read, partly because of Pascal's readiness to attack the unpopular Jesuits (see box below). But it was his use of wit, satire, humour, mockery, irony and sarcasm, as well as his polished prose, that made the *Letters* stand out as something new and refreshing, throwing further light on Pascal's originality and genius. The *Letters* became recognised as a key influence in the later development of French literature, particularly the works of Rousseau and Voltaire. The latter praised them, saying:

> "All kinds of eloquence are contained in these letters, they are the best written book that has yet appeared in France."
>
> Voltaire

Change of direction

But as he was about to contemplate marriage a disturbing event happened that led to a complete change in his attitude to life. Riding along one day on a four-horse carriage he lost control of the unruly animals and ended up suspended over a bridge near Neuilly, outside Paris. Badly shaken by the accident he took it as a sign to take stock of his life. The event was to mark the beginning of a spiritual journey that would turn him into one of the most penetrating religious thinkers of his day.

Disillusionment about life

Pascal's conversion gave him a sharp awareness of the difference between what really mattered and what didn't matter in life. Some say his increasing poor health made him despair of how little life had to offer. He was subject to frequent headaches, insomnia and acute dyspepsia. He could not have known that these problems would eventually lead to his early death of a brain haemorrhage at the age of 39. In the short time he had left Pascal became urgently, perhaps even neurotically, concerned with questions about life: his own life and life in general. He became particularly worried about the consequences of moral failure, sin and guilt; the need for forgiveness, and how his "poor soul" stood before God.

Religious thinker

Pascal began with philosophical questions about man and his place in the world. He concluded, like Kierkegaard, that the final solution to all human problems lay in religious faith. He began by concentrating on the enigma of life, posing the central question: what brings ultimate happiness? Or what makes life worthwhile? Pascal saw that the best answer to these questions was provided by the Christian faith. But he had this typically Pascalian warning: religious faith involves knowing yourself as well as knowing God:

> **KNOWING YOURSELF**
> It is equally dangerous for man to know God without knowing his own wretchedness, and to know his wickedness without knowing the Redeemer who can cure him of it. Knowledge of only one of these points leads either to the arrogance of the philosophers ... or to the despair of the atheists."
>
> Pascal, *Pensees*

Darkness and light

Pascal collected his deepest thoughts on life and faith over a four year period. They were published after his death as simply his *Thoughts* or, as they are better known, the *Pensées*. Man, he believed, prefers to live as if life went on forever. Rarely getting down to consider the big questions, such as the relative shortness of life or what things in life are really important, he becomes absorbed instead in trivial activities and pass-times simply because such questions are too disturbing to deal with. For the same reason man mistakenly looks to science to provide him with truth and happiness, not realising its impotence to provide a way out of man's real needs. Without the real truth about life provided by religious faith man remains a perpetual enigma to himself. Here is a typical extract from the *Pensees:*

> **THE BLINDNESS OF MAN**
> "What after all is man in nature? A nothing in relation to infinity, all in relation to nothing, a central point between all and nothing and infinitely far from understanding either. The ends of all things, and their beginnings, are impregnably concealed from him in an impenetrable secret. He is equally incapable of seeing the nothingness out of which he was drawn and the infinity in which he is engulfed ... The only good thing for men therefore is to be diverted from thinking of what they are, either by some occupation which takes their mind off it, or by some novel and agreeable passion which keeps them busy, like gambling, hunting, some absorbing show ... What people want is not the easy peaceful life that allows us to think of our unhappy condition ... that is why we prefer the hunt to the capture."
>
> Pascal, *Pensees*

The heart versus the intellect

Pascal rejected the idea that God's existence can be proved. Ahead of his time, he realised that arguments for God's existence are "not of such a nature that they can be said to be entirely convincing." There is always "both evidence and obscurity (enough) to enlighten some and confuse others." An atheist will never be convinced by one-sided intellectual arguments, since they can always be interpreted in another way. Instead, Pascal believed that faith came, not through the intellect but through the heart, the feelings, the intuitions, the emotions. Famously, he said:

> "The heart has reasons that the mind knows nothing of."

Focus on man

For Pascal the way to God was by understanding ourselves. He saw man as a great enigma. He is more noble than the universe because he had the power of thought and consciousness. But he is also a wretched creature that misuses his great gifts in the pursuit of short term gains. In this respect he gambles wrongly. Despite his great powers he is vulnerable to a sudden end: a respiratory illness is enough to kill him. As he put it:

> **FRAGILITY OF LIFE**
> Man is but a reed, the most feeble thing in nature, but a thinking reed. The entire universe need not arm itself to crush him. A vapour, a drop of water suffices to kill him. But if the universe were to crush him, man would be still more noble than that which killed him, because he knows that he dies... the universe knows nothing of this. Since all our dignity consists in thought... let us endeavour to think well; this is the principle of morality.
>
> Pascal, Pensees

Pascal's wager

Pascal was a contemporary of the philosopher Descartes whose rationalist views about human knowledge he regarded as naive and limited. He regarded Descartes as out of touch:

> "People are more concerned with card—playing, horse-racing, theatre-going and hunting than with obtuse questions of philosophy," he scoffed.

Far more important, Pascal believed, was making a bet on what really mattered in life. His line of argument is famously known as the Wager. The wager states that the meaning of life is a gamble. The gamble is between there being something or nothing after death. The odds might appear in favour of their being nothing, but in either case the issue is a serious one, which only a fool could ignore. The outlay is small but the stakes are big. If you bet on there being something you might win. If you bet on there being nothing you might lose, and the loss would be great. As he put it: "If there is nothing you lose nothing. If there is something (God) you win eternity."

> His argument may be summarised thus:
> 1. Man can not be satisfied by earthly things.
> 2. There is a big moral difference between a virtuous life, and a life of egotism and self-indulgence.
> 3. The satisfaction that comes from egoism cannot be compared to that which comes from virtue.
> 4. A God, if he exists, wants people to be virtuous.
> 5. To be virtuous is to lay the foundation for happiness.
> 6. To risk a non-virtuous life is to gamble with eternity.

Death of Pascal

Pascal short life ended after a long battle with ill-health. His last words were full of poignancy: "May God never abandon me." He was buried in the Paris cemetery of Saint Etienne du Mont. After his death a piece of parchment was found sewn inside his cloak. He had carried it all his life. It contained an account of his earlier religious experience together with his fundamental belief that "the God of the philosophers" (based on reason) bore no relation to the God of faith:

> "I thank you Lord God who has not revealed yourself to the philosophers, but to those who recognise you as the living Father of Abraham, Isaac and Jacob."
>
> Blaise Pascal

Pascal quotes

"Nature is an infinite sphere of which the centre is everywhere and the circumference nowhere."

"Man's greatness lies in the power of thought."

"Through space the universe encompasses me and swallows me up like an atom; through thought I comprehend the world."

"The heart has reasons the mind never thought of."

"The supreme function of reason is to show man that some things are beyond reason."

"To deny, to believe and to doubt are to a man as a race is to a horse."

"All err the more dangerously because they follow a truth. Their mistake lies not in following a falsehood but in not following another truth."

"Perfect clarity would profit the intellect, but damage the will."

"Our notion of symmetry is derived from the human face. Hence we demand symmetry horizontally and in breadth only, not vertically nor in depth."

"We never love a person, but only qualities."

"Our nature is movement, absolute rest is death."

"You always admire what you really don't understand."

"I should be much more afraid of being mistaken about finding out that Christianity is true than of being mistaken in believing it to be true."

"There are two kinds of people one can call reasonable: those who serve God with all their heart because they know him, and those who seek him with all their heart because they do not know him."

"There is a God-shaped vacuum in the heart of every man which cannot be filled by any created thing, but only by God, the Creator, made known through Jesus."

"It is right that so pure a God should disclose himself only to those whose hearts are purified."

"Knowing God without knowing our wretchedness makes for pride.
Knowing our own wretchedness without knowing God makes for despair.
Knowing Jesus Christ strikes the balance, because he shows us both God and our own wretchedness."

"All our reasoning ends in surrender to feeling."

"Between us and heaven or hell is only life, the frailest thing in the world."

"Do you wish people to think well of you? Don't speak well of yourself."

"Few friendships would survive if each one knew what his friend says of him behind his back."

"The more I see of men the more I like my dog."

"Human beings must be known to be loved; but Divine beings must be loved to be known."

"I have made this letter longer than usual only because I have had not time to make it shorter."

"If man made himself the first object of study, he would see how incapable he is of going further. How can a part know the whole?"

"In faith there is enough light for those who want to believe, and enough shadows to blind those who don't."

"It is natural for the mind to believe and for the will to love; so that, for the want of true objects, they must attach themselves to false."

"Jesus is the God whom we can approach without pride and before whom we can humble ourselves without despair."

"Men despise religion. They hate it and are afraid it may be true."

"Men never do evil more completely and cheerfully than when they do it from a religious conviction."

"Diversion is the only thing that consoles us in our wretchedness, yet diversion is itself the greatest of our miseries. For it is diversion above all that keeps us from taking stock of ourselves and so leads us imperceptibly to perdition."

"Nothing gives rest but the sincere search for truth."

"The knowledge of God is very far from the love of Him."

"The only shame is to have none."

Immanuel Kant (1724–1804)

One of the most outstanding philosophers in the history of western thought, Immanuel Kant remains high on the agenda of all students of modern philosophy to the present day. His studies on the inner mechanics of how we experience things, and how knowledge is acquired, have made him a landmark thinker: he showed that our knowledge is as much the product of our inner minds, as it is of the outward experiences we think it is based on. For instance, he held that space, time and causality have no reality in themselves, but are essential elements used by the mind to organise our perceptions and turn them into experience.

Early years

Immanuel Kant was born in the East German city of Konigsburg, and would spend the rest of his life there, from his student days to his years of professorship at the local university. Kant was one of the first professional philosophers, earning his living not only as a teacher of others' ideas but as an original creator of new ideas of his own. Brought up in a strict religious household, he was a devout Christian who lived by discipline and piety. But his later thinking was to subordinate the knowledge gained from religious faith to the greater authority of reason. If something did not stand to reason, there was no point in arguing that it came from God.

Morality and duty

Kant was also renowned for his ideas on morality. Morality was the product of our sense of duty. Knowing our duty is knowing what we should do. We should never act from feeling or inclination, for Kant the fatal enemies of duty. In Kant's view acting morally means never taking the easy way out. Kant was also against doing, or not doing, something because it might benefit others. This would be putting the cart before the horse: doing our duty must come first, benefit to others comes second, and usually does. What he was really against was egoism, acting out of self-interest. Doing our duty would see to that.

Morality and reason

Kant became the supreme champion of reason, arguing that reason is man's most distinguishing characteristic. To ignore reason was to be like an animal. The power to reason sets man apart from the beasts, thereby undermining one of the key ideas of evolution, namely, that man is no more than a biological descendent from the animals. For Kant, man is totally unlike the animals simply because he does not have to be a slave of instinct. He can, if he chooses, do what goes against his instincts and follow what his reason tells him.

Morality and religion

With his humanitarian theory of reason as the supreme guide to life and behaviour, Kant appeared to be on very firm ground. Yet he was accused of being unrealistic. It was allright for a philosopher with plenty of time on his hands to work out how we should behave. In the real world people rely on guidance and direction. This has historically been provided by moral codes such as the Ten Commandments. Kant would hardly dispute this, but his aim was to show that even divine laws had to stand to reason (which was also a God-given gift), if they were to command respect. He felt that religion had a more important function: to give an extra human impetus to why people should act morally. As a result, he believed that faith was an important personal and social benefit, being "more in keeping with mans ultimate welfare" than unbelief.

The dignity of human beings

In this respect he saw religion as providing a fundamental principle that offered a key to moral behaviour: the idea that man had inherent value in himself. Some things have value that comes from their use. Gold is not valuable in itself but only in relation to its demand—and its price: its value is dependent on how useful it might be in making me wealthy. Spiritual things like love, truth, goodness and beauty are different. Their value is intrinsic, not dependent on the use to which they are put. They are what Kant called "ends in themselves". Human beings are in the same category: they are ends in themselves. If this is ignored the alternative is to treat humans as means, that is, a means or stage to a further end. To appreciate human dignity is to realise that the inherent value or worth of a human being rules this out. Forgetting this (as has often happened) is the degrading of human beings, making them serve some further purpose. Historically this has led to slavery, exploitation, cruelty, injustice and other forms of inhumanity.

> **PRICE AND DIGNITY**
> Everything has either a price or a dignity. Whatever has a price can be replaced by something else as its equivalent; on the other hand whatever is above all price, and therefore admits of no equivalent, has a dignity. Such a thing is an end in itself and does not have mere relative worth, that is, a price. It has an intrinsic worth, and therefore a dignity.
>
> Immanuel Kant

Kant's moral argument

Although Kant was instrumental in dismissing many of the traditional arguments of God's existence, such as the arguments of Aquinas (see above), he is also renowned for putting forward his own special argument in support of faith. He argued that since morality and happiness do not necessarily go together, it would be a mistake to suppose that morality is not worth pursuing. This would lead to despair about life. You cannot feel compelled to be good, knowing that nothing will come of it. Instead, he argued, it is more reasonable to suppose that one day those who deserve the fruits of a moral life, happiness, will enjoy their deserts. Only the existence of a God could make this possible. Therefore it is reasonable to believe in God.

> Two things fill the mind with ever increasing wonder and awe: the starry heavens above me and the moral law within me . . . I see them before me and connect them immediately with my existence.
>
> Immanuel Kant

Immanuel Kant quotes

"It is not necessary that whilst I live I should live happily; but it is necessary that as long as I live I should live honourably."

"Science is organised knowledge. Wisdom is organised life."

"Have patience awhile; slanders are not long-lived. Truth is the child of time; erelong she shall appear to vindicate thee."

"So act that your principle of action might safely be made a law for the whole world."

"Happiness is not an ideal of reason, but of the imagination."

"He who is cruel to animals is hard also in his dealings with men. We can judge the heart of a man by his treatment of animals."

"Immaturity is the incapacity to use one's intelligence without the guidance of another."

"If a man makes himself a worm, he must not complain when he is trodden on."

"It is beyond doubt that all our knowledge begins with experience."

"Experience without theory is blind, theory without experience is mere intellectual play."

"Always recognise that human beings are ends. Therefore do not use them as a means to your end."

"Nothing is divine but what is agreeable to reason."

"In law a man is guilty when he violates the rights of others. In ethics he is guilty if he only thinks of doing so."

"The possession of power unavoidably spoils the free use of reason."

"Morality is not about happiness but how to deserve happiness."

"It is less important to live happily than to live honourably."

"Religion is about seeing all our duties as divine commands."

"Man must be disciplined, for he is by nature raw and wild."

"Ingratitude is the essence of vileness."

Soren Kierkegaard (1813–1855)

Born in what was then a relatively obscure Denmark, he became widely known and studied for his ideas about human life and, in particular, the understanding of life revealed by the Christian faith. His penetrating insights into the significance of life and faith have made him one of the most influential figures in modern thought. Kierkegaard straddles both philosophy and theology. As a philosopher he raises fundamental questions about human life. As a theologian he sees the Christian faith as the key to to its full understanding.

The problem of existence

His influence in philosophy is such that he is regarded as the father of the philosophical movement known as existentialism. Existentialism is a secular, individual-centred, philosophy that calls attention to the problems of making sense of one's life in the face of the certainty of one's own death. Other forms of philosophy were more intellectual and theoretical. Existentialism was more practical: it was about how one should order one's own life. Kierkegaard was the first in a line of many eminent thinkers to call attention to the enigma of human existence, something that was previously thought to be a purely religious question. But for Kierkegaard it was a question that was bound up with the object of all human enquiry, the search for truth. As he warned, it would not be an easy search:

> "The task (of finding truth) must be made difficult, for only the difficult inspires the noble-hearted."

Early years

Soren Aabye Kierkegaard was born in Copenhagen, the product of a morbid and complex family background. It was dominated by his wealthy, but pious, father who grew up with a guilt complex for once "cursing God" while herding sheep on a windswept heath. Although Kierkegaard inherited his father's depressive nature, he formed a close attachment to him. He described his death, enigmatically, as:

> "the last sacrifice which he made to his love for me ... he died for me, in order that , if possible, I might turn into something. Of all that I have inherited from him, the recollection of him ... is dearest to me, and I will be careful to preserve (his memory) safely hidden from the world."

Yet he would later make the poignant admission of having had a sad childhood:

> "I never had the joy of being a child. The terrible torments which I suffered from knowing the tranquillity there must be in being a child, having things in one's own hands, being occupied, etc., delighting one's father ... for my inner unrest meant that I was always, always, outside myself."

Broken relationship

But if the influence of his father had an important bearing on his later life and thought, a perhaps greater influence was a personal relationship with his girl friend Regina Olsen. His decision to break off his engagement with her was to cause him great and lasting anguish. If his father reminded him of Abraham, the Bible's towering figure of faith, Regina was Isaac, the innocent human victim who had to be sacrificed for a greater cause. For him the greater cause was to write about and publicise his beliefs on the truth about life.

The divine and the human

After breaking off his relationship with Regina he went on to pursue theological studies at the University of Copenhagen. Kierkegaard first began writing under a pseudonym, *Johannes Climacus,* who represented a confessed non-philosopher. The name was adopted from a Greek monk who lived at Mt. Sinai and held that life was like ascending a ladder to heaven under the influence of a divine inspiration. Kierkegaard saw this profound idea corrupted by the current eminent philosopher Hegel, who held that human thought could "reach heaven" without any help from God. Hegel believed that human beings were self-contained, and that all truth was accessible to them through reason. Man had only to realise that he was the product of unstoppable historical forces in order to understand himself and his place in the world.

Importance of the individual

Kierkegaard rejected outright Hegel's man-made philosophical scheme, deriding it as "the great system", the product of someone from within history attempting to speak as if he was outside history. He therefore rejected Hegel's claim that the collective force of history could outweigh, even overcome, the force of individual human choice. Where Hegel stressed the anonymity of the individual swept along by the great events of history, Kierkegaard adamantly stressed the uniqueness of the individual, both in the world and before God, insisting that the individual human person makes history, not the other way around:

> "A person can relate to God in the truest way only as an individual, for one only acquires the sense of his own unworthiness alone."

Believing in the absurd

Kierkegaard believed that a rational vision of life contained no solution to the problems of living. Human existence, doomed to be cut off by death, was an enigma that needed a solution if man was to find fulfilment and avoid angst and despair. The only solution was an act of faith, a belief in a miracle, a readiness to accept what is rationally absurd. For Kierkegaard this was the death and resurrection of Jesus Christ, what St. Paul called "foolishness in the eyes of the world."

Faith as privileged insight

Kierkegaard saw faith as both a personal decision and a miracle. Once the act of faith is made, eternal truth enters time, and what is absurd becomes a moment of enlightenment, a vision of the supreme reality. With this view Kierkegaard rejected the time-honoured Socratic belief that all knowledge was already in the human domain. Socrates had said that all truth, being recollection, was already contained in the human mind. For Socrates there was "nothing new under the sun" *(nec novum sub sole)*. Kierkegaard disagreed. There was, happily, another kind of truth, eternal truth, something entirely new, which comes from beyond mankind and not accessible to reason. Such truth is contained in the Christian story. This story is so strange that it is almost a contradiction, what he called an "offence" (to reason), something "absurd", a "paradox", involving the near incredible. In the divine becoming human in the person of Christ, the "absurd" makes sense, and what appears paradoxical and offensive becomes ultimate truth.

Object of ridicule

Kierkegaard was convinced that too many so-called believers lived at the superficial level of card-carrying church members. This,they assumed was enough to guarantee them a place in heaven. When he extended his scathing criticism to the officials of the Church for their bland complacency and indifference, he became an object of ridicule in the Danish press. But he forged on regardless, insisting that for the Christian faith to work it needed to be taken seriously. In own his words it required nothing less than *"intense passionate inwardness"*.

The prince and the maiden: faith as free

Kierkegaard believed that the enigma of faith itself was God's intention. Its value was hidden, not obvious. It was not something so obvious that people would be forced to see its importance and accept it. Instead, faith was to be a free response to divine love and goodness, not something we are compelled to accept. To make this point he used the parable of the prince and the maiden. The prince (God) can easily win the hand of the maiden (the human subject) if he reveals himself fully. But if he does so, the maiden will marry him not for who he is, but because he is a prince. It is therefore necessary for the prince to come in disguise (as for Kierkegaard he did, in the person of Christ). Only then will the maiden be free to marry him for the right reasons. But, in his usual way, he warned that having faith for the right reasons would never be easy:

> "The real conflict between Christianity and man lies in the fact that Christianity teaches... that there is something absolute, and demands of the Christian that his life express that something absolute exists... I have never seen anyone whose life expressed that."

Death and legacy

Kierkegaard died after being taken ill on a public street near his home in Copenhagan. He was buried in the local cemetery following his funeral in the Cathedral of Our Lady. Today his grave is specially marked for the benefit of tourists. His works were little read until well after his death, but were gradually translated into other languages. His writings and ideas, both philosophical and religious, have produced a massive body of literature, and he continues to be studied as a major thinker in most western universities.

Kierkegaard quotes

> *"People understand me so little that they fail even to understand my complaints that they do not understand me."*

"People demand freedom of speech in compensation for freedom of thought which they never use."

"Most men pursue pleasure with such breathless haste that they hurry past it."

"Prayer does not change God; it changes him who prays."

"Christianity is a power which is not to be jested with."

"Good and evil do not exist outside freedom, since this distinction exists precisely by virtue of freedom."

"In Danish letters these days the fee even for authors of repute is very small, whereas the tips dropped to the literary hacks are very considerable. Nowadays the more contemptible a writer the better his earnings."

"If the truth is put to the ballot, then there is untruth."

"In so far as there is, in a religious sense, a "congregation" this is a concept that does not conflict with "the individual" and which is by no means to be confounded with what may have political importance: the public, the crowd, etc."

"If there is, then, something eternal in man, it must be able to exist and to be grasped within every change . . . For repentance is precisely the relation between something past and someone that has his life in the present time."

"The person who will only one thing that is not the Good . . . is (under a) deception that he wills only one thing . . . let your hearts in truth will only one thing for therein is the heart's purity."

"To be able to despair is an infinite advantage (over the beasts), and yet to be in despair is not only the worst misfortune and misery, no, it is ruination . . . to despair over something is not despair proper . . . to despair over oneself, in despair to will to be rid of oneself—this is the formula for all despair."

"For what is despairing other than to have two wills? The inability to wrench oneself away from the bad, and the unwillingness to tear oneself away from the Good."

"There is only one proof that the Eternal exists: faith in it."

"I find it indescribably unfortunate to raise a child rigorously in Christianity, because you then confuse a man's life on a most horrific scale until he is somewhere in his thirties . . . and this Christianity never *intended ... how could someone who believes in the forgiveness of sins possibly become young enough to fall erotically in love!" ... you must have lived your life a bit to feel the need for Christianity."*

"From a distance Christianity appears to human eyes be an amiable thing."

"They have made Christianity too much of a consolation and forgotten that it is a demand."

"Christ truly willed the Eternal in the eternal sense, yet in the temporal order he became distinguished by being repudiated, and so accomplishing but little ... and so it has gone with so many witnesses of the Good and the true in whom this eternal will has burned fiercely."

"To be true to himself in this eternal vocation is the highest thing that a man can practice, and, as that most profound poet (Shakespeare) has said, "Self-love is not so vile a sin as self-neglecting." There is then but one fault, one offence: disloyalty to his own self or the denial of his own better self."

"Everyone shall render his account to God as an individual ... for, after all what is eternity's accounting other than that the voice of conscience is forever installed with its eternal light to be the exclusive voice?"

"If you genuinely will the Good, if you hold fast to God, then you are in unity with all men."

"In the material sense the way is an external reality ... In the spiritual sense, on the contrary, the way cannot be physically pointed out. It does indeed exist whether anyone travels it or not; and yet in another sense it only really becomes a way ... for each individual who travels it; the way is how it is travelled."

"If the purpose of suffering is to be the way, then there is a breath of air, then the sufferer breathes, then it must lead to something."

"There is so much talk about being offended by Christianity because it is so dark and gloomy, offended because it is so rigorous etc. but ... the real reason why men are offended by Christianity is that ... its goal is not man's goal, because it wants to make man into something so extraordinary that he cannot grasp the thought."

"A genius is born ... an Apostle is not born: an Apostle is a man called and appointed by God, receiving a mission from him ... If an Apostle becomes neither more nor less than a genius—then good night Christianity."

"(The Gospel) does not speak about us men, you and me, it speaks to us men, you and me, and it speaks about the requirement that love shall be known by its fruits."

"I know what Christianity is, my imperfection as a Christian I myself fully recognise, but I know what Christianity is . . . My tactics were, by God's aid, to employ every means to make it clear what the requirement of Christianity truly is . . . but never have I wished to develop a pietistic severity . . . to over-tax human existences."

"Christianity has misgivings about erotic love and friendship because preference in passion or passionate preference is really another form of self-love . . . Paganism held these to be genuine love. But Christianity which made manifest what love is, reckons otherwise."

"Christianity has never taught that one must admire his neighbour—one shall love him."

"Love to one's neighbour has the perfection of the eternal—this is perhaps why it seems to fit in so imperfectly with earthly relationships . . . and why in any case it is very thankless to love one's neighbour."

"The wife shall first and foremost be your neighbour; the fact that she is your wife is then a narrower definition of your special relationship to each other."

"I am not a holy man; in short, I am a spy who is spying. In learning to know all about questionable conduct and illusions and suspicious characters, all the while he is inspecting he is himself under the closest inspection."

"Let the heavens fall and the stars change their place in the overturning of all things, let the bird die and the lily fade—yet thy joy in worship outlives, and thy joy dost outlive, even now today, every destruction."

"The whole of existence makes me anxious, from the smallest fly to the mysteries of the Incarnation. Its all inexplicable, myself most of all. For me all existence is contaminated, myself most of all. Great is my distress, unlimited. No one knows it but God in heaven, and he will not comfort me."

"I shall work on coming into a far more intimate relation with Christianity; up to now I have been in a way standing altogether outside it, fighting for its truth. I have borne the cross of Christ in a quite external way, like Simon of Cyrene."

FIGURES FROM MODERN TIMES

Modern Writers

> Literature is an aspect of the fallen world and one of its tasks is to clarify the nature of the fall.
>
> Anthony Burgess

In this section we look at a selection of writers who can all be categorised as Christian. Some reveal themselves as Christian in a more specific sense than others, especially when they write of their own beliefs, whether critically or in defence of them. Others would consider themselves less as writers who write Christian novels than as Christians who happen to write novels. This is a way of saying that they attempt to deal, via the novel, with life as they see it, not how it should conform to some religious or moral ideal. But all in some way touch on Christian beliefs and values as they relate either to their own lives, or to the characters they write about. In doing so they bring into focus problems that are universal: life, death, love, hate, suspicion, jealousy, deceit, infidelity and so on.

Jonathan Swift (1667–1745)

Swift was an Irish satirist, political commentator, poet and cleric who became famous as the Dean of St. Patrick's Cathedral in Dublin. He used his sharp tongue and scathing but often brilliant wit to serious effect. At heart he was a champion of justice and a ruthless critic of hypocrisy and human arrogance. He is perhaps most famous for his novel *Gulliver's Travels* (1726), still widely read today but in an expurgated form to make it suitable for children. On the face of it, it is a story of Gulliver's encounters with various races and peoples in far away places. But a deeper reading shows it to be a story of human follies, with humans always hovering between the base and the noble, usually leaning towards the former. He said his purpose in writing it was "to mend the world".

Gulliver's Travels

The book, a work of highly involved satire, is in 4 parts. In the first part, pompous people whose arrogant self importance ties them up in petty intrigues, are cast as pygmies to show their insignificance. The second part is in a kingdom of giants who are obsessed with their own importance. The king laughs at Gulliver with incredulity when he hears stories of the glories of England and the kind of society that exists there. In his devastating assessment of England it is not clear whether it is the king or Swift who is speaking:

> "It doth not appear from all you have said, how any single virtue is required towards the procurement of any one station among you; much less that men are enobled because of their virtue, that priests are advanced for their piety or learning, soldiers for their conduct or valour, judges for their integrity, or counsellors for their wisdom ... From what I have gathered ... I cannot but conclude the bulk of you natives to be the most pernicious race of little odious vermin that nature ever suffered to crawl upon the face of the earth."

The third part is peopled by quack philosophers and pseudo scientists who are so obsessed with their own special studies that they forget their humanity and become heedless of the good of society. The fourth part is about a land governed by horses that behave with reason and judgement. But they are served by bestial creatures in debased human form (people, really). This illustrates the depths to which mankind can sink when it allows selfish passion to overcome reason. In the end Gulliver returns home, preferring the company of horses to that of his own family!

Satirist and champion of justice

Swift had originally spent time in England, and was initially unhappy with his Irish posting. But after he settled there he became a robust champion of social justice, often criticising England's treatment of the native Irish. He became famous for his use of bitter, scathing satire to express his views. Blaming the English landlords for the poverty of Ireland, he once made the mock proposal of ameliorating Irish poverty by butchering children and selling them as food to wealthy English aristocrats! In this way parents would be relieved of the burden of caring for their children, the rich would be happy, and everyone would benefit. His point of course was that there were other, more acceptable, ways of achieving the same result: landlords for instance could stop the oppression of the peasants, and show some practical decency to ease their lot.

Staunch Anglican

Swift was very much a man of his time, passionately attached to the Anglican church (also called the Church of Ireland) and holding other churches in open contempt. One of his satirical tales involved three people who were given three coats by the Almighty. One was not happy with his coat because it was too ornate. He represented the non-conformist churches (Baptists, Presbyterians etc) who frowned on ornamentation. Another was not happy because his coat was too shabby. He represented the Roman church which loved ornamentation. The third was happy because his coat was just right. He, of course, represented the Established, or Anglican, Church. But despite his time-bound sectarian allegiance, Swift had a high moral sense, and knew that religion was often more honoured in the breach than in the observance. He famously said:

> "People had enough religion to make them hate, but not enough to make them love."

Personal travails

In his personal life he was haunted by dilemmas and indecision. He failed to make up his mind about which of two lovers he should marry. This brought the criticism, probably unfair, that although he was capable of strong friendship and even tender feelings, he was incapable of love. Yet his writings and sermons were widely enjoyed, especially for their often hard-hitting but wildly humorous satire, as in this brilliant example:

> **THE PLACE OF THE DAMNED**
> All folks who pretend to religion and grace
> Allow there's a hell but dispute of the place:
> But if hell may by logical rules be defined
> *The place of the damned*—I'll tell you my mind.
> Wherever the damned do chiefly abound
> Most certainly there is hell to be found . . .
> Damned senators bribed, damned prostitutes slaves;
> Damned lawyers and judges . . . damned blockheads and knaves . . .
> And into the bargain . . . damned prelates . . . damned lords
>   and damned liars.
> For we all know that these mark the place of the damned:
> And hell to be sure is at Paris or Rome
> How happy for us that it is not at home!
>
> Satirical Poem by Jonathan Swift

Illness and death

Towards the end of his life Swift's health declined gradually. He was subject to depression, attacks of dizziness and other ailments. These made him keenly aware of his failing powers, leaving him with a growing sense of his fading influence. A stroke eventually left him paralysed, and his person and estate were entrusted to guardians. His remains were buried in St. Patrick's Cathedral where a plaque and epitaph are the "must see" for countless visitors. Unfortunately for most, the original is Latin. Literally translated it reads:

> Here is laid the body of Jonathan Swift, Doctor of Sacred Theology, Dean of this Cathedral Church, where fierce indignation can no longer injure the heart. Go forth, voyager, and copy if you can this vigorous champion of liberty.

The epitaph was later translated into English by the poet W B Yeats:

> Swift has sailed into his rest.
> Savage indignation there
> cannot lacerate his breast.
> Imitate him if you dare,
> world-besotted traveller.
> He served human liberty.

In his will he left all his possessions to the founding of a hospital for mental illness. John Ruskin named him among the three people in history by whom he was most influenced.

Jonathan Swift quotes

"A lie does not consist in the indirect position of words, but in the desire and intention of false speaking, to deceive and injure your neighbour."

"A man should never be ashamed to own that he has been in the wrong, which is but saying . . . that he is wiser today than yesterday."

"A tavern is a place where madness is sold by the bottle."

"A wise man should have money in his head, but not in his heart."

"Every man wishes to live long, but nobody wishes to be old."

"He was a bold man that first eat an oyster."

"I never wonder to see men wicked, but I often wonder not to see them Ashamed."

"Interest is the spur of the people, but glory that of great souls. Invention is the talent of youth, judgement of old age."

"Although men are accused of not knowing their weakness, yet perhaps few know their own strength. It is in men as in soils where sometimes there is a vein of gold which the owner knows not of."

"Men are happy to be laughed at for their humour, but not for their folly."

"No man was ever so completely skilled in the conduct of life, as not to receive new information from age and experience."

"Power is no blessing in itself, except when it is used to protect the innocent."

Leo Tolstoy (1828–1910)

Novelist, dramatist, essayist and philosopher, Tolstoy is regarded as one of the giants not only of Russian, but of world literature. His masterpieces, *War and Peace (1869),* and *Anna Karenina (1877)* are considered the peak of realist fiction. Other important works included *A Confession (1879)* and *My Beliefs* (1881). His ideas on non-violence were influenced by the Sermon on the Mount, and in turn influenced both Mahatma Gandhi and Martin Luther King. In his earlier days, however, he considered himself as a non-believing rationalist.

Early years

Count Leo Tolstoy came from a family steeped in wealth and privilege in the days of the Czars. Although a baptised member of the Russian Orthodox Church, his own personal understanding of Christianity was to be far from orthodox. His extreme interpretation of the gospels, especially the moral teachings of Jesus, was to cause great controversy, and bring much pain to his wife and family. Towards the end of his life he took the gospel so seriously that gave up all his possessions. He turned his estate over to his family and lived on it as a poor, celibate peasant. Tolstoy looked back on his early years as years of perverse wickedness. In his *Confession,* he sadly reflected on the failure of his religious upbringing to make much difference to his life:

> "...religious doctrine, accepted on trust, and supported by external pressure, thaws away gradually under the influence of knowledge and experience of life which conflict with it, and a man very often lives on, imagining that he still holds intact the religious doctrine imparted to him in childhood whereas in fact not a trace of it remains."

His grim reflection on his own former behaviour helps us to measure the astonishing change he underwent later on:

> "I cannot recall those years without horror, loathing and heart rending pain. I killed people in war, challenged men to duels with the purpose of killing them, and lost at cards; I squandered the fruits of the peasants' toil and then had them executed; I was a fornicator and a cheat. Lying, stealing, promiscuity of every kind, drunkenness, violence, murder—there was not a crime I did not commit... I tried to perfect my will... and perfect myself physically... (I desired) to be better not in my own eyes or the eyes of God, but in the eyes of other people. And very soon this effort again changed into a desire to be stronger than others: to be more famous, more important and richer than others... Every time I tried to express my innermost desires—a wish to be morally good—I was met with contempt and scorn, and as soon as I gave in to base desires I was praised and encouraged."

Pacifist and troublemaker

Clearly stung by the memories of his early degenerate life, Tolstoy decided to change his ways. From the young man who was boorish, violent and cruel, he resolved to pursue the values of love, courtesy and tolerance. From a belief in the methods of violence he came to believe in the values of conciliation and peace. These were beliefs that he would publicly defend and publicly practice. But as an energetic advocate of justice for the poor he took the dangerous road of attacking the state for being degenerate and corrupt. A state that supported violence and brutality to further its aims and protect its authority had lost, in his view, any claim to the obedience of its citizens. He called people instead to find moral solutions within themselves. This was an approach difficult for rulers to contain, but which brought him many admirers.

Return to Christianity

Rejecting his earlier life of self-indulgence through the arrogant use of power and privilege, Tolstoy eventually returned to the Christianity of his upbringing. Although he felt that Christianity could not be defended rationally, he came to see it as the character Levin did, in his famous book *Anna Karenina*, as the only credible source of answers to the questions he had wrestled with: What is the meaning of life? What will come of *my* life? Levin had met a peasant who convinced him that the way of faith was the way to human goodness and truth. It was not an insight that could be defined or measured or defended intellectually, but it convinced Tolstoy that the big issue in life was "to live for the soul and not for the self". Those who chose the latter ended up, like Anna, unable to face a meaningless life and, like Anna, doomed to commit suicide.

> I read *Anna Karenina* with a deepening sense of the author's unrivalled greatness... the book is a sort of revelation of human nature... concerning an illicit love. When you have once read this book you know how fatally miserable and essentially unhappy such a love must be. But the character of Karenin himself is quite as important as the intrigue of Anna and Vronsky. It is wonderful how such a man, cold, philistine, even mean in certain ways, towers in sublimity... when he forgives, and yet knows that he cannot forgive with dignity. There is something crucial, something triumphant, not beyond the power... but hitherto beyond the imagination of men in this effect, which is not solicited, not forced... but comes naturally, almost inevitably from the make of man.
>
> W.D. Howells, author

Extreme moral and religious views

His highly personal understanding of Christianity as a strict moral programme for living was admired by many. But others found his brand of Christianity impractical and embarrassing. Giving up all one's possessions might be alright in some circumstances but not for someone with dependents. Tolstoy seemed so preoccupied with his own ideals that he forgot the consequences for those closest to him. His wild generosity made him a nuisance to his family.

Trouble with the Church

He also found himself in trouble with the Russian Orthodox Church which found his rejection of traditional Christian beliefs unacceptable. Tolstoy rejected all traditional "religious" aspects of the faith, reducing it to a challenging moral programme designed for the betterment of humanity. He rejected such key beliefs as the divinity of Christ, the Trinity, the Resurrection, the reality of sin, and the need for a Church. In doing so he eliminated not only the heart of the Christian message but the whole idea that the Christian faith was a message, a source of good news, a gospel. In doing so he was on collision course with the body entrusted to keep that message alive, the Church. As a result he was excommunicated, and his books declared misleading and dangerous.

Tolstoy's God

Tolstoy's religious critics found fault with his ideas on faith and the pursuit of goodness. They wondered why he saw no connection between faith in God and the will to do good rather than evil. This connection, they pointed out, was made especially clear by Christ (who in other respects was Tolstoy's inspiration). Others ask how Tolstoy could concentrate on Jesus' teachings about renouncing material things, turning the other cheek and loving our neighbour, and at the same time reject Jesus' related teachings about love, faith, forgiveness and the afterlife. It is difficult to believe that Tolstoy did not see this, especially in the light of what he puts into the mouth of Levin in *Anna Karenina:*

> "I shall still go on in the same way, losing my temper with Ivan the coachman, falling into angry discussions, expressing my opinions tactlessly . . . I shall still go on scolding (my wife) for my own terror, and being remorseful for it; I shall still be unable to understand with my reason why I pray, and I shall go on praying; but my life now . . . is meaningless no more . . . it has the positive meaning of goodness, which I have the power to put into it."

Tolstoy and non-violence

One of Tolstoy's outstanding principles was the use of non-violence. But religious commentators have pointed out that Tolstoy's view on non-violence and non-retaliation, which he received from the Sermon on the Mount, is not quite the same as that of Jesus. For Tolstoy non-violence is a *practical* or *commonsense* philosophy, one that can be defended rationally as the best way for human beings to relate to each other. For Jesus, non-violence was part of an overall spiritual vision of man and the world, a vision based on a supernatural understanding of man's value and dignity. In Jesus' view, they point out, self-sacrifice and love of neighbour were not natural drives. They needed the dynamism of divine inspiration and grace.

In praise of Tolstoy

Others have defended Tolstoy, arguing that although he rejected many of the religious teachings of the church, he was not lacking in a religious spirit. They point out that:

> "Tolstoy doesn't give readers the answers to life's vexing questions, but he gives you something even more valuable. He gives readers such an appreciation of the truth and totality of life that you feel enlarged as a human being. After you read Tolstoy you feel spiritually uplifted and intellectually empowered to seek out the answers to life's vexing questions on your own."
>
> Andy Kaufman www.professor andy.com

Goodness as inspiration

Tolstoy clearly believed that love and goodness seen in others were genuine sources of moral inspiration, a view defended by Christian theologians. They argue that examples of goodness in others can be real sources of a divine impulse, capable of being revelations of grace even to people who are not necessarily orthodox believers. Besides, they point out, Tolstoy made no secret of his debt to Christ for the inspiration he received in changing his life. For him the good meant peace and the end of conflict, violence and brutality. It was above all the way of Jesus, as he reminds us:

> "The movement of humanity towards the good takes place, not thanks to the tormentors, but to the tormented. As fire does not put out fire, so evil does not put out evil. Only the good meeting the evil, and not becoming contaminated by it, vanquishes the evil. Every step in advance has been made only in the name of non-resistance to evil. And if this progress is slow, it is because the clearness, simplicity, rationality, inevitableness, and obligatoriness of Christ's teaching have been concealed from the majority of men in a most cunning and dangerous manner; they have been concealed under a false teaching which falsely calls itself his teaching."
>
> Leo Tolstoy

Death of Tolstoy

But for all the controversy he caused and the number of people he upset so deeply, Leo Tolstoy has gone down in history not only as a supreme literary genius, but a great moral leader whose heart was in the right place, and publicly so. But for many, especially in his church, this was not enough. At the time of his death he officially remained excommunicated, and when he died his burial was not attended by the church's sacramental rites. Yet his large popular following said something about him. Why did people flock in such numbers to his funeral? No doubt to show their admiration and reverence for a man whose life had indeed made a difference. As his biographer put it, in this poignant account of his burial:

> It could not be described as a secular funeral. The huge crowd was full of reverence. They defied their priests by singing the ancient Russian funeral hymns. When the coffin passed by them, everyone except the police removed their hats and many fell on their knees. No novelist has ever been given such a funeral, but it was not for his novels that they honoured him. It was for the deeds which now seem to us half mad and quixotic ... And they went on singing "Eternal Memory".
>
> A. N. Wilson, Tolstoy's biographer

Leo Tolstoy quotes

> "Man is a fraction whose numerator is what he is and whose denominator is what he thinks of himself. The larger the denominator the smaller the fraction."

"Even if some men succeed in dulling their conscience, they cannot succeed in dulling their fears."

"Whether he be master or slave the man of today cannot help constantly feeling the opposition between his conscience and actual life, and the miseries resulting from it."

"Everyone thinks of changing the world, but no one thinks of changing himself."

"The hero of my tale, whom I love with all the power of my soul, whom I have tried to portray in all its beauty, who has been, is, and will be beautiful, is Truth."

"One would have thought that the efforts of all men of the present day who profess to wish to work for the welfare of humanity would have been directed to strengthening (the) consciousness of Christian truth in themselves and others."

"Not without good reason was Christ's only harsh and threatening reproof directed against hypocrites and hypocrisy."

"Historians are like deaf people who go on answering questions no one has asked them."

"Art is a human activity having for its purpose the transmission to others the highest and best feelings to which men have risen."

> Tolstoy's life has been devoted to replacing the method of violence for removing tyranny, or securing reform by the method of non-resistance to evil. He would meet hatred expressed in violence by love expressed in self-suffering. He admits of no exception to whittle down this great and divine law of love. He applies it to all the problems that trouble mankind.
>
> Mahatma Ghandi (1909)

Fyodor Dostoevsky (1821–1881)

Noted for his profound insights into the human psyche, Dostoevsky was a major influence on later novelists (like Hemmingway, Joyce and Virginia Wolff), with his emphasis on the deeper and darker sides of human nature. He joins Tolstoy as one of Russia's greatest novelists. In his writings he raised important religious, moral and philosophical questions that continue to be of universal significance. Questions about God, the problem of evil, and the suffering of the innocent haunt the majority of his novels, many of which stand as classics of world literature.

Early years

Born in Moscow the second of six children of Russian Orthodox parents, Dostoevsky spent much of his early life with his frail mother and violent, alcoholic father. In his occasional wanderings around the neighbourhood where his father worked as a hospital surgeon, the young Dostoevsky had an early familiarity with the morbid aspects of human nature. Near the hospital stood a lunatic asylum, a cemetery for criminals and an orphanage for abandoned children. Along with this mix of influences he also had a Christian upbringing. He recalled:

> "I descended from a pious Russian family... We, in our family, have known the gospel from our earliest childhood."

Questionings and concerns

After his mother's death in 1837 he entered the Academy of Military Engineering in St. Petersburg. Although he successfully graduated, his interest was less in engineering that in his reading of Shakespeare, Pascal, and Victor Hugo. During this time he underwent a period of serious questioning and abandoned his faith, a decision not unconnected with his tortured upbringing. His father, though outwardly respectable and a believer, was a drunk and a wastrel who had a despotic relationship with his sons. A rumour that he was eventually murdered by serfs on the family farm would add to Dostoevsky's life-long obsession with patricide, a subject that would form a major theme in one of his greatest novels.

The experience of prison

In 1846 he was sentenced by the Czar to four years of hard labour in a Siberian penal colony where he was compelled to wear fetters. During this harrowing period he suffered great physical and mental pain, including repeated attacks of epilepsy. The prison experience worked a profound change in him. He abandoned his belief in the liberal atheistic ideologies that had become dominant in his time, and turned to the religious faith of his upbringing. In the following passage he captures the old feelings aroused by his first Christmas in prison:

> **MEMORIES OF CHRISTMAS**
> At last the holidays arrived. On Christmas Eve very few convicts went out to work... The day that would come tomorrow was a real holiday, which the convicts could not be deprived of—it was formally recognised by law... And really, who can tell how many memories must have stirred in the souls of these outcasts as they rose to meet such a day! The days of the great feasts are sharply imprinted on the memory of the common people, beginning in childhood. These are the days when they rest from their strenuous labours, days when families gather together. In prison they must have been remembered with torment and anguish. At last it arrived. Early, before it was light, as soon as reveille had been sounded on the drum, the barracks were unlocked and the duty sergeant wished them all a merry Christmas. The men did likewise, replying in a friendly, affectionate tone... They all knew that it was a day of great importance, a religious holiday of the first magnitude. There were some who went round the other barracks to give their greetings to men from their part of the country...
>
> Fyodor Dostoyevsky (*House of the Dead*)

The only book he was allowed in prison was a copy of the gospels, a copy he retained all his life. His experience of living with those convicted of serious crimes led him to contemplate the nature of human failure and human salvation. He felt he could "compel people to admit that ideal Christianity was not an abstraction, but a vivid reality, possibly near at hand, and that Christianity is the sole refuge of Russia from all its evils".

The existence of God

Dostoevsky famously raised the question of how far the existence of evil and suffering counts either for or against the existence of God:

> "Now assume there is no God or immortality of the soul. Now tell me why I should live righteously and do good deeds if I am to die entirely on earth? And if that is so why shouldn't I (provided I can get away with it) cut another man's throat, rob and steal...?"

But he knew that the situation was never simple. Even if God existed, his face could be clouded by the actions of human beings. This included so-called Christians, and even the Church itself. Yet his underlying conviction was that God did exist, and is able to forgive the hypocrisy he encounters among humans.

Personal troubles

In Dostoevsky's own case there were financial troubles, as well as a turbulent love affair and a passion for roulette. This was part of a nightmarish period in Germany, described in his novel of 1866, *The Gambler*. His gambling left his family in financial peril and his eventual marriage ended unhappily with the death of his wife. Dostoevsky later remarried and found much solace in his later years.

> "The writer's own troubled life enabled him to portray with deep sympathy characters who are emotionally and spiritually downtrodden and who in many cases epitomise the traditional Christian conflict between the body and the spirit."
>
> Google. F Dostoevsky Biography

The Brothers Karamazov

One of his greatest novels was *The Brothers Karamazov* in which he dealt with the universal themes of crime, guilt, faith, doubt and salvation. The book is written on two levels. At face value it is a story of how three brothers are in varying degrees involved in the eventually killing of their father. Historically, the event echoed the author's obsession with one of the greatest of human crimes, patricide, something that he felt people could be driven to do.

Faith and unbelief

But on a deeper level it is a moral drama that deals with human questions of faith, doubt and unbelief, and how far reason and freewill are capable of dealing with life's problems. The brothers represent thee aspects of a human being: Ivan (reason), Dimitri (emotion) and Alesha (faith). It is Dostoevesky's style as an author of fiction to allow his atheistic characters to give full voice to questions of God and religious unbelief. The main character is Ivan who has lost his religious faith. This is not because he simply disbelieves in God, but because he cannot believe in a God who is responsible for the world as it is: "It is not God that I don't accept, understand this, I do not accept the world, that he created, this world of God's, and cannot agree with it."

Standing in opposition to Ivan is his brother Aloysha, a devout believer who has joined a religious order. His faith is inspired by the holy Elder Zosima who lives in a nearby monastery. The saintly monk preaches reconciliation to the brothers and reminds them that each one is guilty of each other's sins. But this begs a lot of questions.

Christ and the Grand Inquisitor

Ivan says that God is no help either when it comes to morality, since Christ has allowed himself to be long ignored. This is the point of one of the most famous sections in the book, Ivan's imaginative poem about *The Grand Inquisitor* where he imagines Christ making an appearance to him during the dark days of the Inquisition. Ivan had been discussing God and immortality with the devout Aloysha who tells him that although God and suffering cannot be comprehended, their connection can be understood—by one man, Jesus Christ. But Ivan is not satisfied, believing that Christ is an enigma.

The evil of freewill

In the scene, the Inquisitor reproaches Christ for causing so much trouble in the world, telling him that it was all caused by the intolerable burden he has placed on man by giving him freewill. As a result, he says, it is the same devil (who once tempted Jesus) that now takes control of the world with his ancient temptations. Tantalisingly, all during the lengthy inquisition Jesus says nothing, as if half in sadness, half in agreement. For Ivan, the ideals Christ taught were beyond reproach, but their practice was beyond the ability of mortal beings once they were mistakenly given the freedom to be evil:

> He saw that the Prisoner (Christ) had listened intently and quietly all the time looking gently into his face and evidently not wishing to reply. The old man longed for Him to say something, however bitter and terrible. But He suddenly approached the old man in silence and softly kissed him on his bloodless aged lips. That was all His answer.
>
> Dostoyesky, The Brothers Karamazov

Faith and life

Yet Dostoevsky was not completely pessimistic about man achieving goodness. Commentators have pointed outh that in all Dostoevsky's novels the most attractive, most sympathetic, most moral characters all seem to be those who are aided by religious faith. The most disagreeable, most devious, most unattractive ones are those who reject it. In fact all the principal atheists in his novels, including Ivan, commit suicide, suggesting that the meaning of life is somehow beyond the powers of reason to grasp.

Dostoevsky's realism

But Dostoevsky remained a realist. He knew that faith is not easy to acquire: in real life it is always being undermined by doubt and temptation. This, he felt, was his novel's principal message, a statement of how faith often fares in real life, not how it is supposed to fare. Reacting to the poor reception of the novel when it first appeared, Dostoevsky showed little patience in trying to explain what he was really getting at:

> "The dolts have ridiculed my obscurantism and the reactionary character of my faith. These fools could not even conceive so strong a denial of God as the one to which I gave expression... The whole book is an answer to that. You might search Europe in vain for so powerful an expression of atheism. Thus it is not like a child that I believe in Christ and confess him. My hosanna has come forth from the very crucible of doubt."

The tragic figure of man

The question of God and suffering as voiced by Ivan reflects the author's own torments about God's existence. In his treatment of the human condition Dostoevsky reflects the traditional Christian understanding of sin as the result of a fundamental tension within man. Like Adam, man is a tragic figure, banished from paradise but longing to return. The desire to return is the recognition that there can be no paradise on earth. The stark alternative is the path of reconciliation, forgiveness and love. But not everyone is able to find it.

His death

Despite the fact that during his life he was always wrestling with some of the faith's most difficult questions, Fyodor Dostoevsky ended his life as a devout Christian. He was buried in the Alexandr Nevsky monastery in St. Petersburg where his funeral was attended by thousands. His tombstone bears the words of Christ: "Unless the grain of wheat goes into the ground and dies it remains only a grain of wheat. But if it dies it produces rich fruit" (John 12:24)

Dostoevesky quotes

"To be a human being among human beings and remain one forever, no matter what misfortunes befall . . . this is what life is, herein lies its task."

"Life is in ourselves, and not in the external."

"Nothing is more seductive for a man than his freedom of conscience. But nothing is a greater cause of suffering."

"Happiness does not lie in happiness, but in the achievement of it."

"Compassion is the chief law of human existence."

"Beauty is mysterious as well as terrible. God and devil are fighting there, and the battlefield is the heart of man."

"It is not possible to eat me without insisting on singing the praises of my devourer."

"If God does not exist everything is permitted."

"Atheists (when discussing religion) always talk outside the subject."

"Atheism . . . seeks to replace in itself the moral power of religion, in order to appease the spiritual thirst of parched humanity and save it; not by Christ, but by force."

"To live without Hope is to Cease to live."

"To love someone means to see him as God intended him."

"Love a man even in his sin, for that love is a likeness of the divine love, and is the summit of love on earth."

"If you want to be respected by others the great thing is to respect yourself. Only by that, only be self-respect will you compel others to respect you."

"Much unhappiness has come into the world because of bewilderment and things left unsaid."

"It is not brains that matter most, but that which guides them—the character, the heart, generous qualities, progressive ideas."

"The soul is healed by being with children."

"The secret of man's being is not only to live but to have something to live for."

"Man is fond of counting his troubles, but he does not count his joys. If he counted them up as he ought he would see that every lot has enough happiness provided for it."

"What is hell? I maintain it is the suffering of being unable to love."

"You can know a man from his laugh, and if you like a man's laugh before you know anything of him, you can confidently say he is a good man."

"Lying to ourselves is more deeply ingrained than lying to others."

"Without some goal and some effort to reach it, no man can live."

"with no other scale but the legal one is not quite worthy of man either."

"You are told a lot about your education, but some beautiful, sacred memory, preserved since childhood, is perhaps the best education of all. If a man carries many such memories into life with him, he is saved for the rest of his days. And even if only one good memory is left in our hearts, it may also be the instrument of our salvation one day."

"A real gentleman, even if he loses everything he owns, must show no emotion. Money must be so far beneath a gentleman that it is hardly worth troubling about."

"Men do not accept their prophets and slay them, but they love their martyrs and worship those whom they have tortured to death."

G. K. Chesterton (1874–1936)

One of the most colourful and larger-than-life of English writers, he is ranked as one of the great Edwardian men of letters. His vast output included journalism, history, biography, poetry and, what he became particularly famous for, Christian apologetics. With regard to the latter he never tired of defending, always with a strong dose of good humour, Christianity in general and, after his conversion, Catholicism in particular. His book *The Everlasting Man* had a particular influence on C. S. Lewis (see below), who acknowledged his debt to Chesterton for helping him to renew his own Christian faith. His style in the epic poem *Ballad of the White Horse* was a major influence on J. R. R. Tolkien's *Lord of the Rings* (see below). The writer Dorothy L Sayers was equally impressed. "To the young people of my generation", she wrote, "GKC was a kind of Christian liberator."

Early years

Gilbert Keith Chesterton was born in Kensington into a middle class family. He was educated at St. Paul's School; University College, London; and the Slade School of Art. Of his upbringing he said with typical wit:

> "I regret that I have no gloomy or savage father to offer to the public gaze as the true cause of all my tragic heritage . . . and that I cannot do my duty as a true modern, by cursing everybody who made me whatever I am."

His attraction to journalism made him abandon his degree studies before completion. In 1902 he was given a weekly column in the *Daily News,* followed in 1905 with a weekly column in the *London Illustrated News* which he kept up for the next thirty years. Already a convinced Christian during this time, in 1922 he converted to Roman Catholicism. Much of his writing was to contain many references to Christian beliefs, themes and symbolism. As befitted a man who liked life, and who always tried to spread good cheer around him, it was well said that his preference was for "merry" rather than "puritan" England.

Humorist and jovial debater

A man of immense bulk (he was 6 feet 4 inches and weighed 21 stone) he matched his physical presence with an equal dominance when it came to words and opinions. But sometimes he met his match. When he told the skinny George Bernard Shaw with whom he had many friendly exchanges, *"to look at you any one would think there was a famine in England",* Shaw retorted, *"to look at you any one would think you caused it."* He became famous for engaging in radio and other debates with Shaw and other notable figures of the time, such as H G Wells, Charles Darrow, and Bertrand Russell. All were in some way sparring with whom he liked to take on in lively and good-natured debate. During this time also he formed a firm friendship with Hilaire Belloc. He endeared himself to the public by his hopeless ability to dress, by his famous absentmindedness, and by his ability to laugh at himself. Once he sent a telegram to his wife saying "I'm at Market Harborough. Where should I be?" To which she replied dryly, "at home".

Christian writer

Before he embarked on his defence of Christianity, Chesterton went through a crisis of doubt, uncertainty and depression around the age of twenty leading him to experiment with the Ouija board and other forms of the occult. But in 1922 he converted from Anglicism to Roman Catholicism. He went on to produce a vast literary output which included biographies of St. Thomas Aquinas, St. Francis of Assisi, Chaucer, and Tolstoy. In 1908 his book *Orthodoxy* appeared, a defence of Christianity. In it he shrewdly disclaimed trying to show why his faith should be believed by others, only why *"I personally have come to believe it."* In the book he stated his basic conviction that the Christian faith was not an arbitrary set of beliefs that may or may not be true, but a definitive solution to the mystery of human existence, or as he put it "the riddle of life".

Chesterton's Christ

In the *Everlasting Man (1925)* he deals with the person of Christ, a figure seen by many as a man of his time, but in Chesterton's view this is an illusion. A man from the moon who might have met other humans would have problems working out what sort of person Christ was. Not a man of his time, certainly, because his ideas and teachings bore no relation to the ideas current during his life. His understanding of life and the difference he taught between good and evil was something new and strange to the ancient world. As Chesterton put it: "Aristotle was rational and logical, Jesus was something entirely new".

Comfort and discomfort

Chesterton sees many of Christ's utterances to be sublime, some mysterious, some terrifying. While ordinary mortals are prisoners of time, place, culture and circumstance, Jesus seems to appear from nowhere with a message that both comforts and chills. In the message of Christ man is destined to be saved, and invited to be saved; but he is also threatened to be damned. Neither word is fully explained, but each one conveys something easily understood. Everyone has an idea of what it is to be saved and what it is to be damned. One term comforts, the other chills.

> **THE EVERLASTING MAN**
> Considered to be Chesterton's masterpiece, this is his whole view of world history as informed by the Incarnation. Beginning with the origin of man and the various religious attitudes throughout history, Chesterton shows how the fulfilment of all human desires takes place in the person of Christ ...
>
> The Boston Transcript

Provocative sayings

Chesterton was famous for his witty, thought-provoking and illuminating aphorisms, like:

> "The man who does not believe in God will believe in anything... Thieves respect property. They merely wish property to become their property so that they may more perfectly respect it... Misers get up early in the morning; and burglars, I am informed, get up the night before... To be smart enough to make money you must be dull enough to want it... I believe in getting into hot water; it keeps you clean"...

It was no doubt his reputation for such provocative and often paradoxical (contradictory, challenging conventional wisdom) observations that made him one of the most quotable figures of his time. Some found his fondness for paradox worthy of satire:

"O Gilbert, I know there are many who like
Your talks on the darkness of light,
The shortness of length
And the weakness of strength
And the one on the lowness of height."

But he described his faith defiantly in typical tongue-in-cheek fashion, as in this extract from his autobiography:

> "So far as a man may be proud of a religion rooted in humility, I am very proud of my religion: I am especially proud of those parts of it that are called superstition; I am proud of being fettered by antiquated dogmas and enslaved by dead creeds (as my journalistic friends repeat with so much pertinacity), for I know very well that it is the heretical creeds that are dead, and it is only reasonable dogma that lives long enough to be called antiquated."

His death

G. K. Chesterton died at his home in Beaconsfield, near London, on June 14, 1936. His death was national news. His large funeral was held in Westminster Cathedral with a eulogy given by his distinguished friend and writer Ronald Knox. The poet and novelist Walter de la Mare wrote kindly of him:

> "Knight of the Holy Ghost, he goes his way,
> Wisdom his motley, Truth his loving jest;
> The mills of Satan keep his lance in play,
> Pity and innocence his heart at rest."

The following wistful extract from one of his poems could well be his epitaph:

> People, if you have any prayers
> Say prayers for me:
> And lay me under a Christian stone
> In that lost land I thought my own,
> To wait till the holy horn is blown
> And all poor men are free.
>
> From *Ballad of the White Horse*

Chesterton quotes

"If a thing is worth doing, it is worth doing badly."

"The Christian ideal has not been tried and found wanting; it has been found difficult, and left untried."

"Pessimism is not in being tired of evil, but in being tired of good. Despair does not lie in being tired of suffering, but in being weary of joy."

"Pride is the falsification of fact by the introduction of self."

"Existence is still a strange thing to me; and, as a stranger, I gave it welcome."

"War is not the best way of settling differences; it is the only way of preventing them being settled for you."

"The Bible tells us to love our neighbours, and also to love our enemies; probably because they are generally the same people."

"To have a right to do a thing is not the same as to be right in doing it."

"Literature is a luxury, fiction is a necessity."

"The true soldier fights not because he hates what is in front of him but because he loves what is behind him."

"My country right or wrong; my mother drunk or sober."

"Art, like morality, consists in drawing the line somewhere."

"The object of opening the mind, like opening the mouth, is to close it on something solid."

"An old don with a D. D. after his name may have become the typical figure of a bore; but that was because he himself was bored with his theology, not because he was excited about it."

"The relations of the sexes are mystical, are and ought to be irrational. Every gentleman should take off his head to a lady."

"A dead thing can go with the stream, only a living thing can go against it."

"Impartiality is a pompous name for indifference, which is an elegant name for ignorance."

"To have a right to do a thing is not at all the same as being right in doing it."

"All exaggerations are right, if they exaggerate the right thing."

"If there were no God there would be no atheists."

"The thing I hate about an argument is that it interrupts a discussion."

"The reformer is always right about what is wrong. He is generally wrong about what is right."

"Man is always something worse or something better than an animal; and a mere argument from animal perfection never touches him at all. Thus, in sex no animal is either chivalrous or obscene. And thus no animal invented anything so bad as drunkenness—or so good as drink."

"The philanthropist says, with a modest swagger, "I have invited twenty five factory hands to tea." If he said, "I have invited twenty five chartered accountants to tea," everyone would see the humour of so simple a classification."

"The opponents of marriage . . . have invented a phrase free love—as if a lover had ever been, or could be, free. It is the nature of love to bind itself, and the institution of marriage merely pays the average man the compliment of taking him at his word."

"This whole world is a work of art, though it is, like many great works of art, anonymous."

"Every great literature has always been allegorical ... The Iliad is only great because all life is a battle, the Odyssey because all life is a journey, the Book of Job because all life is a riddle."

"Reason is always a kind of brute force; those who appeal to the head rather than the heart, however pallid and polite, are necessarily men of violence. We speak of "touching a man's heart", but we can do nothing with his head but hit it."

"All healthy men, ancient and modern, Western and Eastern, hold that sex is a fury that we cannot afford to inflame; and that a certain mystery must attach to the instinct if it is to continue delicate and sane."

"Reason itself is a matter of faith. It is an act of faith to assert that our thoughts have any relation to reality at all."

"It is the reality that is often a fraud."

(Of Thomas Hardy) "He is like the village atheist brooding over the village idiot."

Francois Mauriac (1885–1970)

Major French author with a massive literary output (published works: 12 volumes); he was elected to the *Acadamie Francaise* in 1933; became winner of the Nobel Prize for Literature in 1952, and was awarded the Grand Cross of the *Legion d' Honneur* in 1958. Besides his novels he also wrote plays, and worked as a journalist and editorial writer for some leading Paris newspapers such as *Le Monde* and Le *Figaro*. Mauriac was a staunch Catholic who publicly supported national reconciliation in France in the aftermath of the war. In a column in *Le Figaro* he opposed Albert Camus who wanted action taken against all who collaborated with the Nazis during the occupation. Later Camus conceded that Mauriac had shown the greater wisdom.

He belonged to the lineage of French Catholic writers who examined the ugly realities of modern life in the light of eternity. His major novels are sombre, austere psychological dramas set in an atmosphere of unrelieved tension. At the heart of every work Mauriac placed a religious soul grappling with the problems of sin, grace and salvation ... His native city of Bordeaux and the drab and suffocating strictures of bourgeois life provide the framework for his explorations of the relations of characters deprived of love ... *Le Noeud de Vipers* (The Vipers Tangle,1941) is often considered Mauriac's masterpiece. It is a marital drama, depicting a lawyer's rancour towards his family, his passion for money, and his final conversion. In this, as in other Mauriac novels, the love that his characters seek vainly in human contacts is fulfilled only in love of God.

Encyclopedia Brittanica Online

Early years

Francois Charles Mauriac was born in Bordeaux. His father, who was a banker, died when he was eighteen months old leaving his mother to bring up the five children of whom Francois was the youngest. During World War I he served as a Red Cross hospital orderly in the Balkans. After university he moved to Paris for post-graduate studies, but abandoned these to work in journalism. He became a figure of controversy for his moral stand in opposing French rule in Vietnam, and for criticising the use of torture by the French army in Algeria.

Writer and journalist

When he worked for *l'Express* he threatened to resign over the paper's support for Roger Peyrefitte, an outspoken critic of the Vatican, because it had carried advertisements for his hostile books. The dispute became bitter and personal with Peyrefitte accusing Mauriac of being a homosexual. But Mauriac became highly respected as a writer of great stature in his native France and beyond, receiving important national and international awards. His novels have been praised for their treatment of human life with all its frustrations and failures, set forth in a distinct prose style that revealed important moral and psychological insights into the human condition.

Human rather than religious themes

Although Mauriac had a strong Catholic faith, he avoided any direct use of it in his carly novels (like Graham Greene below, with whom he was familiar). Although his main characters were usually believers, he never went beyond seeing religious faith as one solution among many to the bleakness of human existence as perceived by his characters. Like Greene, Mauriac portrayed his characters as children of the world, victims of greed, jealousy, hate and selfishness. In his earlier books his characters find no happy solutions to their problems. Mauriac portrays life as he imagines it to be, a struggle involving people whose moral characters incline, at least to human eyes, more to ruin than salvation. As one critic has written:

116 P. J. Clarke

> "All in all there are more sinners than saints in his stories . . . it is the subtle, inward betrayals that interest him . . . His early novels display the tensions within the family—a son oppressed by his mother, a daughter-in-law who is acquitted of poisoning her husband, the brood of vipers who gather like vultures while the patriarch dies . . . Mauriac's novels take place in half-light, his characters are troubled and by and large joyless, their Catholicism is a judgement on them. *A Kiss for the Leper, Viper's Tangle, The Desert of Love, Therese,* are perhaps the ones most familiar . . . Mauriac is interested in the drama of salvation, the deeds whereby human agents decide their eternal lot."
>
> Ralph McInerney (2005) http://ethics enter.nd.edu.

He claimed that no unbeliever was ever harder on Catholic characters than he was. By which he meant that conventional faith is no guarantee of either happiness or unwavering virtue. Equally the absence of faith is similarly no guarantee of an unhappy ending. To human eyes there is always the enigma of life's unpredictability, but in the end it is only God who can judge who is worthy and who is not.

The tragedy of Therese

This seems to be the message of one of his most famous books, *Therese.* Therese Desqueyroux is a young woman imprisoned in the social conventions of a respectable marriage, who is driven to overdose her husband with the medicine he takes for an illness. The attempt fails, but she is doomed to a shame from which there is no escape. After her trial, during which her husband lies to defend her innocence, she returns with him and her child to the remote town of Argelouse in the Landes, a symbolic landscape of unrelieved pines that suggest the loneliness and isolation of her life.

Prejudice and victimisation

Damned by her extended family and husband as a wicked woman, she is not even allowed to caress or care for her own child. But even though she was free to go to church, she was far from impressed by the cure's *"impersonal"* sermons, *"on points of dogma and morals"*. As a result she decided she would never go to confession or communion. *"For her to have done so would have seemed odd to the members of her family, and to the good people of the town"*. They would never have believed one so wicked could ever be converted. Here the author credits Therese with the courage of her natural convictions: she was not prepared to conform to religious conventions for the sake of an empty respectability.

Therese's early innocence

The poignancy of Therese's fall from grace is highlighted by the purity of her childhood. Therese began life "like the early stages of an unsullied stream fed by pure snow". At school she was held up as an example. One of her teachers had said:

> "Therese asks no reward other than the joy which comes of knowing that one has achieved superior virtue. Her conscience is the light by which she lives, and it is enough. Her pride in belonging to an elite has more power to control her conduct than any fear of punishment."

Here we see the typically human progression of virtuous beginnings eventually leading to a lost goodness. But also visible are the roots of her inner moral strength which prevails throughout the novel, and allows the author to leave the judgement of her life to God, not to those who are only too ready to judge by conventional or outwardly religious standards.

The absence of love

Therese in many ways symbolises a major theme in Mauriac's novels, how the absence of love affects the lives of his characters. It is this absence of love that bears down on them to marr their lives with frustrations and unhappiness. Ironically, it is those who set themselves up as moral judges that are usually the one's who refuse their love to those they criticise, thus fulfilling their own criticisms. Therese was one such victim. Had she been surrounded by love and affection her fate might have been different. The novel ends on a half note, with Therese finding a symbolic freedom, at last, in the streets of Paris.

No happy ending

In the preface, Mauriac later said that he refused to provide her with a happy ending, a salvation depicted in the terms expected by the religious and the pious. In his view it was more true to life to leave her final state unresolved, at least to human eyes. In real life not everyone who conforms to the requirements of religious piety is a saint; and not everyone who refuses to conform is a sinner. Mauriac explains with a depth of religious understanding:

> "Many, Therese, will say that you do not exist . . . I could have wished, Therese, that sorrow might have turned your heart to God . . . but had I shown you thus redeemed there would have been no lack of readers to raise a cry of sacrilege, even though they may hold as an article of Faith the Fall and Ransom of our torn and twisted natures. I take my leave of you upon a city's pavements hoping, at least, that you will not forever be utterly alone." At the end of *Therese* Mauriac wrote: "Why, someone may ask, do I break off this story before it has reached the point at which Therese might have found pardon and the peace of God? Let me make a confession. The pages dealing with that ultimate consolation were in fact written, but I destroyed them. I could not see the priest with the qualifications necessary if he was to hear her confession with understanding." Later he admitted that "some day, perhaps, I may tell the story of how Therese entered into the eternal radiance of death."

Worries about his novels

Later, Mauriac became worried that the apparent pessimism of his novels might give bad example to his readers (a worry incidentally felt by Chaucer after writing his somewhat bawdy, if highly amusing, *Canterbury Tales*). In 1928 he went through a religious crisis which made him resolve to be more open and direct as a Catholic writer. The result was another landmark novel *Le Noeud de Viperes,* the vipers tangle.

Greed versus spirituality

This novel, a family drama, depicts an old lawyer's bitter relations with his family and his self-absorbed passion for money. His determination to keep his wealth from his wife and children absorbs all his moral and spiritual energy. But they on their part behave like vipers obsessed with getting a share of the inheritance. In the end the old man sees the light, and through a religious conversion becomes reconciled to his family. Here Mauriac changes his moral approach to show the direct influence of faith. What people look for in material success is only fulfilled when they turn to others, and to God.

Nobel laureate

In 1952 Mauriac was awarded the Nobel Prize for Literature. The Prize was awarded, significantly:

> For the deep spiritual insight and the artistic intensity with which he has in his novels penetrated the drama of human life.
>
> The Nobel Foundation 1952

François Mauriac quotes

> "If there is a reason for the existence of the novelist on earth it is this: to show the element which holds out against God in the highest and noblest of characters—the innermost evils and dissimulations; and also to light up the secret sources of sanctity in creatures which seem to us to have failed."

> "No love, no friendship Can cross the path of our destiny Without leaving a mark on it forever."

> "We do not know the worth of one single drop of blood, one single tear. All is grace. If the Eternal is Eternal, the last word for each of us belongs to him. This is what I should have told this Jewish child. But I could only embrace him weeping."

> "If you would tell me the heart of a man tell me not what he reads, but what he rereads."

> "To love someone is to see a miracle invisible to others."

> "Human love is often but the encounter of two weaknesses."

> "Where does discipline end? Where does cruelty begin? Somewhere between these two thousands of children inhabit a voiceless hell."

> "The man who partakes in the breaking of bread dares to build his house on the very core of love. He becomes, as it were, Godlike, but regardless of the strength he derives from it, his freewill remains . . . The Greatest Love may be betrayed. Fed on the Living Bread, we nevertheless conceal part of ourselves which longs for swine's food."

> "We who still live beneath a sky still streaked with the blood of crematoriums have paid a high price to find out that evil is really evil."

> "However sullied the stream there is always snow at its source."

C. S. Lewis (1898–1963)

As a young student Lewis decided to interrupt his Oxford studies to fight for his country. Arriving on the Somme on his nineteenth birthday he soon experienced the horrors of trench warfare and the shattering effects of enemy bombardment. Some months later he was wounded in the Battle of Arras by a British shell that fell short of its target. During his convalescence he suffered from homesickness and depression. He was discharged in 1918 and returned to Oxford where he had the distinction of obtaining three firsts: in Classical Literature (1920), Philosophy and Ancient History (1922), and English (1923). At Oxford he became a close friend of J. R. R. Tolkien, author of *Lord of the Rings*. Although baptised into the Church of Ireland, Lewis abandoned his faith early on and turned to atheism. He said one of the strongest arguments against God's existence was put forward by Lucretius:

"Had God designed the world, it would not be,
As frail and faulty as we see."

He returned to Christianity under the influence of his friendship with J. R. R. Tolkien, and G. K. Chesterton's, *The Everlasting Man*. Like both men, he was to become a highly influential moral leader and defender of Christianity both in his writings and in his radio broadcasts. In 2008, *The Times* ranked him eleventh of the best British writers since 1945.

Early years

C. S. Lewis was born in Belfast. His father was a solicitor, and his mother who was the daughter of a Church of Ireland priest and a promising mathematician, died of cancer when he was ten. After a series of schools, one of which he named unkindly, but seriously, "Belsen", he enrolled at Malvern College in England at the age of fifteen. By then he had abandoned his faith and turned to atheism, mythology and the occult. He was appalled at the competitive spirit of Malvern where pupils were encouraged to achieve high social status at all costs. But he believed that close personal relations between the pupils (sometimes homosexual) helped to offset the materialist outlook of the school. In a highly perceptive judgement on behaviour many considered perverse, he saw as a much needed form of redemption:

"The one oasis (though green only with weeds and moist only with fetid water) in the burning desert of competitive ambition . . . a perversion was the only thing left through which something spontaneous and uncalculated could creep."

Religious conversion

Once he said he was "angry with God for not existing!" When he became fellow and tutor at Magdalen College in 1925, he found himself under a strange but irresistible compulsion to question his atheism:

> "You must picture me alone in my room at Magdalen (Oxford) feeling... the steady, unrelenting approach of Him whom I so earnestly desired not to meet. That which I greatly feared had at last come upon me. In the Trinity term of 1929 I gave in, and admitted that God was God, and knelt and prayed: that night the most reluctant and dejected convert in all England."

The Chronicles of Narnia

Lewis achieved great fame for his *Chronicles of Narnia,* a series of 7 fantasy novels for children written between 1949 and 1954. Although the books contain many references to Christian ideas they are universally popular with readers of all backgrounds. Children are presented as playing central roles in the unfolding history of the fictional realm of Narnia, a mystical place where animals talk, things happen by magic, and good is set against evil with the help of the lion *Aslan,* whose virtuous character suggests a divine figure. Under later examination many have found fault with some of the assumptions in the stories, seeing evidence of sexism, racism and the like. Yet their popularity has survived.

Other works

Lewis is also remembered for his imaginative work *The Screwtape Letters,* about a demon who suggests the best way to tempt humans and lead them to damnation. Later he became more openly concerned with showing the truth of Christianity against popular attack. His *Mere Christianity; The Problem of Pain;* and *Miracles* were attempts to justify Christian beliefs in these areas. Christian faith for him was more appealing because its truths were unlikely, and because of that, more likely to be true:

> Reality is something you could not have guessed. That is one of the reasons I believe Christianity. It is a religion you could not have guessed. If it offered us just the kind of universe we had always expected, I should feel we were making it up. But, in fact, it is not the sort of thing anyone could have made up. It has just that queer twist about it that real things have.
>
> From *Mere Christianity*

His death

After a series of painful illnesses, Lewis resigned his post at Oxford and later died of renal failure on 22 November 1963. The coverage of his death was overshadowed by the shocking assassination of John F. Kennedy, President of the U S. which happened on the same day. His lasting legacy was his books for children which are still popular. His memory is also kept alive by the C. S. Lewis Foundation which aims "to advance the renewal of Christian thought and creative expression throughout the world of learning and culture at large".

C. S. Lewis quotes

> "Aim at heaven and you will get earth thrown in. Aim at earth and you will get neither."

> "A young man who wishes to remain a sound atheist cannot be too careful about his reading."

> "Affection is responsible for nine tenths of whatever solid or durable happiness that we find in our lives."

> "Christianity, if false, is of no importance. If true, it is of infinite importance. The only thing it cannot be is moderately important."

> "Courage is not simply one of the virtues, but the form of all the virtues at the testing point."

> "Education, without values, useful as it is, seems rather to make man a more clever devil."

> "Eros will have naked bodies; friendship naked personalities."

> "Experience: that most brutal of teachers. But you learn. My God do you learn."

> "Failures are finger posts on the way to achievement."

> "Friendship is unnecessary, like philosophy, like art . . . It has no survival value; rather it is one of those things that give value to survival."

> "I believe in Christianity as I believe that the sun has risen; not because I see it but because by it I see everything else."

> "Lets pray that the human race never escapes from Earth to spread its iniquity elsewhere."

> "You don't have a soul. You are a soul. You have a body."

> "With the possible exception of the equator, everything begins somewhere."

J. R. R. Tolkien (1892–1973)

The name J. R. R. Tolkien is immediately associated with his two famous fantasy books, *The Hobbit (1937),* and its sequel *The Lord of the Rings (1954–55)*. The latter is an epic story describing the battle between good and evil for the fate of Middle Earth. The target is to destroy the One Ring, a weapon of mysterious power forged by the evil lord Sauron. The books however are not meant to be an allegory of reality (a coded picture of the real world) or to contain any hidden references to God or religion. In his writings Tolkien rarely mentions religion. Instead, he offers revealing insights into the human condition, while dealing with universal problems that inevitably bear on whatever vision of life a person chooses to have.

Early years

John Ronald Reuel Tolkien was born on January 3, 1892 in Bloemfontein of expatriate parents who had moved to South Africa to follow a banking career. Soon afterwards his father died in exile when Tolkien was 3. His mother and two sons later moved back to their origins near Birmingham. Although his parents were Baptists, his mother, Mabel, converted to Catholicism much to the disapproval of her family which, as a result, withdrew all financial assistance to her. She meanwhile arranged with Father Xavier Morgan, a priest of the *Oratory Retreat,* to be her son's guardian. Sadly, she died prematurely of diabetes at 34 when Tolkien was only 12. Humphrey Carpenter wrote that:

> "the death of his mother filled him with a sense of impending loss . . . it taught him that nothing is ever safe, that nothing will ever last, that no battle will be won forever."

Looking back, Tolkien paid touching tribute to the sacrifices she made for her sons, especially their religious upbringing:

> "My own dear mother was a martyr indeed, and it is not to everybody that God grants so easy a way to his great gifts as he did to Hilary and myself, giving us a mother who killed herself with labour and trouble to ensure us keeping the faith."

Wartime experience

In 1916, shortly after his marriage to Edith (with whom he had four children), Tolkien was sent to France where he fought with his regiment in the Somme offensive. Although he escaped the butchery unscathed he came home invalided with trench fever. He remained greatly affected by the loss of most of his friends in the war. He wrote: "Junior officers were being killed off, a dozen a minute ... Parting from my wife then ... it was like a death".

Teacher and writer

Some have argued that the fearsome scenarios that filled his books were echoes of his wartime experiences. But before he turned to writing Tolkien took up a post in English Literature at Leeds University where he taught from 1925 to 1929. He then obtained a post of Professor at Oxford in 1945 which he held for the next 34 years. In 1997 he came top of three literary polls (Channel 4, Waterstones, the Folio Society), confirming what *The Daily Telegraph* had said: that he was the greatest writer of imaginative fiction of the 20th century.

Lord of the Rings

Tolkien's most famous book, *Lord of the Rings,* set in a fictional prehistoric era, is regarded as "one of the most-printed and most-read books in history". The book was composed of three parts and took 14 years to write. On face value the book is a fantasy appealing especially to children. But fantasy has a way of representing reality, some would say the best way. Critics of his books have claimed that such fairy tales have no significance for mature adults, being merely a form of escape from reality. But for Tolkien fantasy was not only derived from reality but could enrich our view of it. "*The Lord of the Rings*", said Tolkien should be read as a fantasy tale, not an allegory, or parable, or instructive tale of good and evil.

Fantasy and Reality

Tolkien had no intention of letting reality (as understood in the 20th century with all its religious and political baggage and symbolism) interfere with his imaginative fantasies, or of inserting some hidden meaning or message to serve a naïve moral purpose. Rebutting the idea that he was in some way putting forward religious beliefs, he said that as a mere mortal he could not presume to speak for God, or how he deals with the world. The fantasies do however contain contrasting universal principles such as courage and cowardice, fidelity and betrayal, truth and falsehood, good and evil. As he put it: "That is why I have . . . cut out practically all references to anything like "religion", to cults and practices, in the imaginary world".

Moral and spiritual values

For one thing the world of the *Rings* is too primitive to allow for what we today call religion. Yet the moral and spiritual values belonging to religion and life do permeate this world of elves, wizards, trolls, orcs (goblins), dwarves, magicians, evil monsters and, of course, hobbits. Life, it seems, even in a fantasy world revolves around universal values and their anti-theses, such as truth and lies, the ugly and the beautiful, loyalty and treachery, bravery and cowardice, good and evil, right and wrong, life and death. There was no need therefore to interpret these things in the light of later happenings in the real, historical world.

Religious beliefs

As a devout Catholic, Tolkien was a firm defender of Christian beliefs and moral values. Yet despite his unhappiness with the direction he saw his church going during the sixties in its efforts to become more modern, he felt that its essential mission was still to preserve the Christian story. As he put it:

> "There is no other tale ever told that men would rather find was true, and none which so many sceptical men have accepted as true on its merits."

Political and moral critic

Tolkien adopted a fierce moral stand against many of the events of his time. He was an outspoken critic of Stalin, Hitler and the anti-Semitism that was rampant in his day. He lamented the setback to German culture caused by unrepresentative Hitler who merely turned upside down what Germany had always stood for. He was also critical of the ferocity of Allied bombing in Europe and the unnecessary destruction and loss of life that it caused. He was also strongly opposed to the dropping of the atomic bombs in Hiroshima and Nagasaki. Yet he refused to give in to pessimism, preferring to see the future as a time when the unexpected would happen:

> **PARADOXICAL VISION**
> All that is gold does not glitter,
> not all those who wander are lost,
> the old that is strong does not wither,
> deep roots are not reached by the frost.
> From the ashes a fire shall be woken,
> a light from the shadows shall spring;
> renewed shall be the blade that was broken,
> the crownless again shall be king.
>
> Tolkien poem

Last years

After the success of his works Tolkien spent his latter years suffering the discomfort of being a celebrity. He was invited to speak, give interviews and accept awards. The unwanted adulation he received drove him to seek a more private life in the seaside resort of Bournemouth. He died on September 2, 1973 and was buried beside his wife in a plain grave in the Catholic section of the Wolvercote cemetery in Oxford. Several blue plaques were erected to his memory, including one's at Birmingham and Harrogate. In 2008, the Times ranked him sixth on a list of the 50 greatest writers since 1945.

J. R. R. Tolkien quotes

"There is nothing like looking if you want to find something. You certainly find something if you look, but it is not always quite the something you were after."

"The world is full of hurts and mischance without wars to multiply them."

"To crooked eyes truth may wear a wry face."

"The wise speak only of what they know, Grima son of Galmud. A witless worm have you become. Therefore be silent and keep your forked tongue behind your teeth. I have not passed through fire and death to bandy crooked words with a serving-man till the lightning falls."

"Those who break a thing to find out what it is have left the path of wisdom."

"Faithless is he who says farewell when the road darkens."

*"Still round the corner there may wait
A new road or a secret gate."*

"If more of us valued food and cheer and song above hoarded gold, it would be a merrier world."

"I do not love the bright sword for its sharpness, nor the arrow for its swiftness, nor the warrior for his glory. I love only that which they defend."

"Let him not vow to walk in the dark who has not seen the darkness fall."

"It needs but one foe to start a war; but those who have not swords can still die upon them."

"Fair speech may hide a foul heart."

"I have no help to send, therefore I must go myself."

"We have sworn, and not lightly. This oath we will keep. We are threatened with many evils, and treason not least: but one thing is not said: that we shall suffer from cowardice, from cravens or the fear of cravens. And therefore I say that we will go on, and this doom I add: the deeds that we shall do shall be the matter of song until the last days of Arda."

Hilaire Belloc (1870–1953)

One of the dominant figures in English literary life during the first half the 20th century, Belloc was born in France but spent the greater part of his life in England. He went to the Newman Oratory school in Birmingham but was still undecided whether to settle in England or France. In the end his great love was England where his greatest work was done as a speaker, writer and one-time parliamentarian.

Early years

Hilaire Belloc was born near Versailles of a French father and English mother who was also a writer. Following a stock-market crash that devastated the family, his father died young, and the young Hilaire was brought up by his mother who took him back to England. As a young man he lost his faith, but following an experience he was never prepared to discuss he became a confirmed Catholic for the remainder of his life. His love of his Church was expressed in the warm belief that it provided "hearth and home for the human spirit".

Oxford

As a French citizen, Belloc joined the army and served with the French artillery as a gunner at the garrison town of Toul. But fed-up to read in his report *"Gunnery, mediocre"*, he returned to England and entered Balliol College Oxford. There he became a distinguished student, receiving a first class honours degree in History. His love for Balliol was never in doubt, as he recalled:

> *"Balliol made me,*
> *Balliol fed me*
> *Whatever I had*
> *She gave me again."*

Member of Parliament

After graduating from Oxford he became a British subject in 1903. Three years later he became a candidate for Parliament for the unlikely seat of Salford, an industrial town near Manchester. It was strongly non-conformist, and as a Catholic he was presumed to be a liability. To improve his chances he was told not to mention his religion. It was typical of him to ignore the advice. Instead, at his first meeting he held up a rosary and said he went to Mass as often as he could. He then told them that if he was barred from election because of his Catholic faith he would thank God from sparing him the indignity of representing so narrow-minded a constituency! After a stunned silence he got a rousing applause. He was elected with a big majority.

Disillusioned with politics

But after serving only two terms in Parliament he became bored with politics and turned his attention to writing and lecturing. This decision was to cost him dear in terms of material comforts and financial security, but it was a mark of his personal integrity. Being part of what he saw as the selfserving and hypocritical system of politics was a moral deficit he was not prepared to pay. In a prophetic disclosure he admitted being appalled by the easy conscience of politicians in regard to fees and expenses!

Distinguished writer

His only alternative was to turn to writing, a profession that he would never find financially rewarding, and at times frustrating and unfulfilling. Yet he went on to have an impressive output, with books on

Catholicism, the Reformation, Politics, History, Poetry, Travel, Art, and a series of biographies of important figures in European history such as Napoleon, Joan of Arc, Milton, Cromwell and others. As a prose writer he could reach impressive heights, as in this stirring extract from his study of Danton:

> **THE DEATH OF DANTON**
> It was close on six, and the sun was nearly set behind the trees of the Etoile; it reddened the great plaster statue of Liberty that stood on the Place... it sent a level beam on the vast crowd that filled the square, and cast long shadows, sending behind the guillotine a dark lane over the people. The day had remained serene and beautiful to the last, the sky was stainless and the west shone like a forge. Against it, one by one, appeared the figures of the condemned... Danton was the last. He had stood unmoved at the foot of the steps as his friends died. Trying to embrace Herault before he went up, waiting his turn without passion, he heard the repeated fall of the knife in the silence of the crowd. His great figure, more majestic than in the days of his triumph, came against the sunset... They say that a face met his and a sacramental hand was raised in absolution... When Sanson put his hand upon his shoulder the ghost of Mirabeau stood by his side and inspired him with the pride that had brightened the death-chamber of three years before. He said "show my head to the people, it is well worth it." Then they did what they had to do, and without any kind of fear, his great soul went down the turning of the road.
>
> Extract from *Danton*, by Hilaire Belloc

Apologist and debater

Belloc was always prepared to defend religious faith as the most valid solution to the meaning of life. He famously engaged in a series of debates with H G Wells over his book *Outline of History,* in which Wells takes a secular stance, expressing anti-religious views about evolution and natural selection. Belloc, of course, rebutted such views, leaving the exasperated Wells to say: "debating with Mr. Belloc is like arguing with a hailstorm." Later, Belloc produced a more detailed reply to Wells, defending religion as central to Europe's civilisation and achievements.

Some accused him of bias and intolerance, suggesting that his over-zealous defense of religion might conceal inner doubts:

> Always without philosophical preoccupations, he was nonetheless haunted by the temptation that at bottom there is no answer to the riddle of human existence. His conquest of that aberration made his faith something hard, crystal clear, without compromise. Of religions other than the Catholic he had an Olympian contempt and an impatience barely disguised and then imperfectly. He would not have fared well in these days of ecumenical tea-parties, and the so-called New Church would have bewildered him.
>
> Frederick Wilhelmsen www.catholiceducation.org

Convivial companion

Such accusations, however, were easier to make than to prove. Those who knew him always vouched for his sincerity in expressing his deeply-held beliefs about the religious, moral and social issues of the day. But despite his robust approach, whether as a writer or debater, and his strict Catholicism, Belloc also had a human, convivial side to his character which comes out in his writings, poems and verses. This can be glimpsed in the following examples, beginning with one of the joke verses he once composed for Christmas:

> *"May all good fellows that here agree,*
> *Drink Audit Ale in heaven with me,*
> *And may all my enemies go to hell!*
> *Noel, Noel, Noel, Noel."*

His love of good company comes out in:
> *"From quiet homes and first beginnings*
> *Out to the undiscovered ends,*
> *There's nothing worth the wear of winning*
> *But laughter and the love of friends."*

And his mischievous sense of humour in:
> *"The Devil, having nothing else to do,*
> *Went off to tempt My Lady Poltagrue,*
> *My Lady, tempted by a private whim,*
> *To his extreme annoyance, tempted him."*

His strong affection for the Sussex countryside comes out in:
> *"The great hills of the South Country*
> *They stand along the sea;*
> *And it's there walking in the high woods*

That I could wish to be,
And the men that were boys when I was a boy
Walking along with me."

A contemporary who saw him as a "provocative personality" balanced this with another, much kinder, assessment:

> "Of course Belloc was prejudiced, but there were few who knew him who did not love his prejudices, who did not love to hear him fight for them, and who did not honour him for the passion and sincerity with which he held to them. Once the battle was joined all his armoury was marshalled and flung into the fray... Yet he was a courteous and a chivalrous man. A deeply sensitive man, his was the kindest and most understanding nature I have ever known. In spite of a rollicking and bombastic side he was as incapable of the least cruelty as he was capable of the most delicate sympathy with other people's feelings. As he himself used to say of others in a curiously quiet and simple way, "He is a good man, he will go to heaven."
>
> Lord Sheffield

Epitaph

The following words might well be his epitaph, echoing both his convictions as well as his wit and inherent humanity:

> Heretics all, whoever you be,
> In Tarbes, or Nimes, or over the sea,
> You never shall have good words from me,
> *Caritas non conturbat me.* (Charity does not bother me)
> But Catholic men that live upon wine,
> Are deep in the water, and frank, and fine;
> Whenever I travel I find it so,
> *Benedicamus Domino.* (Let us bless the Lord)
> On childing women that are forlorn,
> And men that sweat in nothing but scorn;
> That is on all that ever were born,
> *Miserere Domine.* (Lord have mercy).
> To my poor self on my deathbed,
> And all my dear companions dead,
> Because of the love that I bore them,
> *Dona Eis Requiem.* (Grant them rest)

Hilaire Belloc quotes

"When friendship disappears then there is a cold space left open to that awful loneliness of the outside world which is like the cold space between the planets. It is an air in which men perish utterly."

"All men have an instinct for conflict: at least, all healthy men."

"Child! Do not throw this book about, refrain from the unholy pleasure of cutting all the pictures out."

"Wherever the Catholic sun doth shine, there's love and laughter and good red wine."

"We wander for distraction, but we travel for fulfilment."

"Loss and Possession. Death and Life are one."

"There falls no shadow where there shines no sun."

"The moment a man talks to his fellows he begins to lie."

"Of three in One and One in three
My narrow mind would doubting be
Till Beauty, Grace and Kindness met
And all at once were Juliet."

"Every major question in history is a religious question. It has more effect in moulding life than nationalism or a common language."

Graham Greene (1904–1991)

Greene was a renowned English writer whose novels were perceived to have a universal significance because they deal with many of the moral and religious dilemmas that face everyone. Greene became a Catholic convert, but preferred to call himself "a Catholic who wrote novels rather than one who wrote Catholic novels."

Early years

Henry Graham Greene was born in Berkhampsted near London, the fourth of six children, many of whom become distinguished in their own right. He had a difficult time at boarding school where he confessed to once being desperate enough to think about suicide. In 1925 he went up to Balliol college Oxford to study history. After graduation he worked as a sub-editor with the Times, a job he disliked. Soon he turned to writing and produced a series of successful novels.

Writer

Of his many novels perhaps there were four in particular that established his reputation as a Catholic writer. These were *The Power and the Glory (1940), The Heart of the Matter (1948), The End of the Affair (1951),* and *A Burnt out Case (1961).* His characteristic tendency was to deal with the way moral and religious issues impinge on people's lives. In these novels Greene focuses on Catholic characters whose lives and moral choices often sharply conflict with their assumed religious convictions. It was Greene's conviction that people are never predictable, and that life is never clearcut.

The realities of life

In doing this, Greene typically deals with life as it is rather than how it should be. He portrayed the reality gap between the ideal and the real, between virtue and sin, between supposed holiness and the need for forgiveness. For Greene, life was a moral minefield full of uncertainty, with disasters difficult to foresee but always waiting to happen. Above all, he was optimistic about the effects of grace, which he saw as a spiritual dynamism that could work in whoever was open to it. But in a secular age it needed to be portrayed not in religious but in more humanitarian ways. He saw grace at work wherever there was sympathy, compassion or a willingness of human beings to help each other.

Judging the heart

Grace was that which, more often than not, came from a human, compassionate understanding of the plight of others, and in that compassion came spiritual transformation. The purpose of religion, and religious practice, was to make a difference to the heart. Otherwise it was humanly artificial, and spiritually empty. Above all, what mattered was that which elevated the character, not the label (religious or otherwise) which it went under. In the end only God is the judge: and he judges what humans cannot see, the heart.

The Burnt out Case

His novel *The Burnt out Case* encapsulates many of Greene's ideas about the true nature of morality and spiritual development. The story centres on Querry, the burnt-out case of the title, who is a well-known successful architect, but abandons his opulent Western lifestyle to seek refuge in a remote leper colony in Africa. A victim of loss of faith in himself and his life, he is a *"spiritually-empty hero"* suffering now from the effects of years of public fame and the egotism it created. The buildings he designed, including churches, now seemed to be his accusers, as seen in this dialogue with the mission doctor:

> "The use of what I made was never important to me. I wasn't a builder of council houses or factories. When I made something I made it for my own pleasure. Your vocation is quite a different one, doctor. You are concerned with people. I wasn't concerned with the people who occupied my space—only with the space."

Involvement with people

Querry gradually begins to realise what it is that brings human fulfilment. It is involvement with people in their deepest needs, like the Superior of the *leprosie*, and the doctor, even though the latter is not a believer. Eventually Querry himself becomes involved with the *leprosie*, and is given care of one of its victims, Deo Gratias. By caring for him he regains a new sense of what is really important in life. Later, by helping to design badly-needed new buildings for the lepers he feels a new sense of direction, and finds new fulfilment.

Fundamental beliefs

In this novel Greene brings out some of his own most fundamental beliefs about religion, faith and life. Christianity, he was convinced, is not to be confined to explicitly religious things or actions, and is not limited to those who might claim to be initiated into church membership. It is often expressed better by non-believers in the showing of *agape* (love expressed in help) for those in need, than so-called "Klistians" whose boast of official membership of a spiritual organisation can often appear hollow. As the Superior put it in his sermon to the congregation at the leprosie:

> "There is a doctor who lives near the well beyond Maria Akimbu's house and he prays to Nzambe and he makes bad medicine ... but once when a *piccin* was ill and his father and mother were in hospital he took no money ... I tell you then he was a Klistian, a better Klistian than the one who broke Henry Okapa's bicycle ... There is no man so wicked he never once in his life show in his heart something that God made."

The nature of life

Many see the problems he raises, such as forbidden love, marital infidelity, the temptation to suicide, the corrosive effect of pride, the ultimate emptiness of worldly fame, as reflecting problems in his own life and make-up. Greene himself lived a tortured, complex and somewhat uneasy life, one that he felt was hard to reconcile with his public reputation as a Catholic novelist. But like the characters in his books, he seems only too aware of the possibility that personal success, while temporarily gratifying, is not in the end the greatest of human achievements.

> "Graham Greene is perhaps the most perplexing of all the literary converts... His visions of angst and guilt, informed and sometimes deformed by a deeply felt religious sensibility, make his novels, and the characters that adorn them, both unforgettable and fascinating."
>
> Joseph Pearce

Graham Greene quotes

"It is impossible to go through life without trust: that is to be imprisoned in the worst cell of all, oneself."

"There is always a moment in childhood when the door opens and lets the future in."

"In human relationships, kindness and lies are worth a thousand truths."

"There is always hope until one is completely and utterly dead."

"Those modernist writers who have lost a religious sense result in dull, superficial characters who wander about like cardboard symbols through a world that is paper thin."

"We all make mistakes, we all make people we love suffer in one way or another—c'est la vie, and luckily people don't love us for our virtues or we'd be in a bad way."

Malcolm Muggeridge (1903–1990)

One of the most colourful public figures of the early television age, Malcolm Muggeridge was a provocative thinker who was never slow to express himself either in writing, lecturing or in discussion on radio or television. He was especially critical of the liberal culture of his day which he saw as a new gospel being greedily absorbed by the masses tired of the post-war austerities. This was the hey-day of the swinging sixties, when "sex, drugs and pop" threatened to replace the sedate values of marriage and family, hard work and moral respectability. In the sixties this world was being challenged, replaced by a new appetite for fun and self-indulgence that threatened to make the old values of restraint and moral correctness appear out of fashion.

Early years

Thomas Malcolm Muggeridge was brought up a socialist in South London and, although a baptised Christian, inherited the prevailing attitude to religion as something antiquated and out of touch with modern society. He went on to Cambridge, from where he graduated in 1924. Initially he went to teach in India but returned to England in 1927 and married Katherine Dobbs, his companion for the rest of his life. After a short spell as a supply teacher in Egypt he joined the *Manchester Guardian* in 1932, and shortly afterwards moved to Moscow as its Russian correspondent. During the war he served as a spy for MI6, stationed in Mozambique. After the war he returned to journalism and wrote for most of the leading English dailies. Later he rose to become editor of the London satirical magazine *Punch*. But his greatest popular impact was on television, where he became a celebrity in a medium that was still in its infancy.

Public celebrity

His views were always very highly sought after, so that he became a regular contributor on many programmes that dealt with the issues of the day: modern life, teenage sex and drugs, permissive living, and politics. Living during the emergence of the so-called permissive society, he made no secret of his fears about the new tide of liberal–secular thinking that was sweeping Britain and other western democracies. Issues such as drugs, contraception, divorce, pornography, and sex before marriage, were frequently making the headlines. His articulate and searing criticism of these modern mores earned him the nickname *St. Mugg*, an indulgent title that belied an earlier life not particularly noted for its sanctity.

Moral conversion

In fact it was the moral change that he underwent in his middle years that later made him so fascinating. People who heard the new Muggeridge pontificating on the evils of sex and drugs could hardly recognise the one-time heavy drinker, chain smoker and rampant womaniser. But far from coming across as hypocritical or insincere, he seemed to speak with authority because, like St. Augustine whom he admired, people knew that he spoke from experience. He also spoke in a language that entertained as well as instructed, as when he once warned that there could be no future "in joining the Gadarene swine and going on LSD trips over the hills and far away".

> Critical interest in Muggeridge rests on three bases: his personal story as a self-indulgent intellectual who slowly develops a passionate religious faith; his iconoclastic scourging of the famous and powerful; and his Christian apologetics (defence) ... But the contradictions of his personality and career ... renders (him) as a whole a subject of enduring critical interest.
>
> TDA Notes Internet

Defining experience

While he was correspondent in Moscow he heard rumours of a famine in the Ukraine and decided to go there to see for himself. What he saw was to have a profound effect on his outlook, ending his faith in communism. Instead of evidence of the Soviet dream utopia he was brought up to believe in, he saw instead a country being victimised by the Stalinist terror, riddled with social inequality, party indifference, government hypocrisy and state brutality. The miseries of the people, he discovered, were not accidental but part of a deliberate Stalinist plan to starve and liquidate the peasants. In a powerful passage, he described attending a church service where he received a depressing insight into the realities faced by the ordinary people:

> "In Kiev, where I found myself on a Sunday morning, on an impulse I turned into a church. It was packed tight ... young and old, peasants and townspeople, parents and children, even a few in uniform—it was a variegated assembly. The bearded priests, swinging their incense, intoning their prayers, seemed very remote and far away. Never before, or since, have I participated in such worship: the sense conveyed of turning to God in great affliction was overpowering. Though I could not, of course, follow the service, I knew from Klavia Lvodna little bits of it: for instance where the congregation say there is no help from them save from God. What intense feeling they put into these words! In their words, I knew, as in mine was a picture of those abandoned
>
> (continued)

> villages, of the hunger and the hopelessness, of the cattle trucks being loaded with humans in the dawn light. Where were they to turn to for help? Not to the Kremlin, and the Dictatorship of the Proletariat, certainly; nor to the forces of progress and democracy and enlightenment in the West... Every possible human agency was found wanting. So, only God remained, and to God they turned with a passion, a dedication, a humility, impossible to convey. They took me with them; I felt closer to God then than I ever had before, or am likely to again."
>
> From *The Green Stick* (1972)

Return to Christianity

One of the effects of his moral dissatisfaction was a growing attraction to the Christianity of his upbringing. In 1969 he published *Jesus Rediscovered*, a collection of essays, articles and sermons on faith. This was followed in 1976 with *Jesus: The Man who Lives*. While describing his change from agnostic to believer as a true conversion, he denied that there was anything spectacular about it: it was simply the outcome of how he felt about the way the world, and he himself, was going. He wrote:

> "What then is conversion?... Some, like St. Paul have a Damascus Road experience. No such experience has been vouchsafed me; I have just stumbled on, like Bunyan's pilgrim, falling in the Slough of Despond, locked up in Doubting Castle, terrified at passing through the Valley of the Shadow of Death; from time to time relieved, by God's grace from my burden of sin, only, alas, soon to acquire it again."

Search for truth

In his book *A Third Testament* he revealed his admiration for the people he called "God's Spies", who included St. Augustine, William Blake, Blaise Pascal, Soren Kierkegaard, Leo Tolstoy, Fyodor Dostoyevsky, and Dietrich Bonheoffer. He saw them as earnest souls whose writings reflected his own troubled search for truth and meaning. He saw their testimonies making up a new "Third Testament", a later witness to the working of God's grace throughout the centuries. He once said that Christianity was not destroyed by Stalin or Hitler (or the Archbishop of Canterbury!), but by the materialism and decadence that has spread through western society.

Mother Teresa

A futher influence on his inner beliefs was his meeting in1971 with Mother Teresa in the slums of Calcutta. During the visit he got a first hand experience of her work among the poor and destitute of the city. Later, in 1983, he was to embrace the Catholic faith, admitting the impact of that visit:

> "Mother Teresa is, in herself, a living conversion; it is impossible to be with her, to listen to her, to observe what she is doing and how she is doing it without being in some degree converted."

> The aim of the Malcolm Muggeridge Society, founded in 2003, is to "perpetuate the ideas and beliefs of a St. Augustine figure who became famous for abandoning a libertine lifestyle to proclaim the growing dangers of what he plainly saw as the godless moral escapism of modern western society."

Malcolm Muggeridge quotes

"An orgy looks particularly alluring seen through the mists of righteous indignation."

"Every happening, great and small, is a parable whereby God speaks to us, and the art of life is to get the message."

"How do I know that pornography depraves and corrupts? It depraves and corrupts me."

"I can say that I never knew what joy was until I gave up pursuing happiness, or cared to live until I choose to die. For these two discoveries I am beholden to Jesus."

"Sex is the mysticism of materialism and the only possible religion in a materialistic society."

"St. Teresa of Avila described our life in this world as a night in a second-class hotel."

"The orgasm has replaced the cross as the focus of longing and fulfilment."

"This horror of pain is a rather low instinct . . . and if I think of human beings I've known and of my own life such as it is, I cannot recall any case of pain which didn't, on the whole, enrich life."

"If the greatest of all, incarnate God, wished to be the servant, who would wish to be the master."

"There must have been a resurrection because Christ is alive now, 2000 years later. There is no question at all about that."

"I want God to play tunes through me. He plays, but I, the reed, am out of tune."

Alexander Solzhenitsyn (1918–2008).

Outspoken Russian writer who fell foul of Stalin for daring to criticise him in a letter to a friend, he was summarily sentenced to a labour camp for eight years. During that time he set about gathering the evidence that would expose to the world the inhumanity and brutal methods of communism, a system that many believed would lead the world to the promised land of peace and prosperity. As a result he was expelled from his native land as a traitor and troublemaker.

In his later years, Solzhenitsyn emerged as a man of profound spiritual ideas, taking a public stand against what he saw as the moral decadence of the West. This, he believed, was greatly due to the replacement of religious faith with a misguided belief in material prosperity and progress.

Champion of the individual

Later, under a more tolerant regime, he was pardoned and allowed back into Russia. Through his actions, writings and lectures he set out to address the question of what makes man unique. In challenging the communist answer, which reduced the individual to relative insignificance, he became one of the most daring moral voices of the 20th century. For his work in standing out as a champion of man's spiritual nature, capacities, and destiny, he was awarded the Nobel Prize for Literature in 1974.

Early years

Alexandr Solzhenitsyn was born in Rostov-on-Don, Russia on December 11, 1918 to an intellectual father who, six months before his son's birth, was killed in action while fighting as an artillery officer on the German front. He was brought up as a Christian by his devout mother who worked as a short-hand typist in Rostov. In 1941, a few days before Russia became involved in the war, he graduated from Rostov University with a degree in physics and mathematics. But he confessed from an early age his interest in writing. A year later he joined the Red Army where he rose to the rank of artillery captain. He served faultlessly on the front line, only to find himself branded a traitor for writing critical remarks about Stalin in a private letter to a friend. "I served the army without a break until I was arrested in 1945 because of certain disrespectful remarks about Stalin", he wrote.

The Gulag Archipelago

He was sentenced in his absence and given eight years in a labour camp where he suffered all the hardships reserved for traitors: oppression, isolation, lack of food and contempt. After his release he vowed to pay tribute to the nameless millions who had been treated (many were killed, or to use the favourite Soviet term, *liquidated*), like animals, often ending up in the *gulags* which dotted the Siberian landscape like thousands of tiny islands in a geographical archipelago. Hence the title of his great work *The Gulag Archipelago (1973–1978),* in which he set out to provide not only a detailed account of the inhuman treatment of those he met in the slave camps, but the actual names of as many of those he met as he could. His literary and moral aim was to ensure that prisoners were identified and named as individual persons. In doing so he sought to emphasise that each individual had a unique human identity that followed from their unique dignity. These they were robbed of in the cruel environment created by an inhuman system that saw everyone as merely a number, and treated as such.

> He was one of the first to speak of the inhumane Stalinist regime and about the people who experienced it but were not broken.
> Mikhail Gorbachev, former Soviet leader

Mystery of the human spirit

An earlier book, *One Day in the Life of Ivan Denisovich (1962)* was a compressed chronicle of life in a freezing labour camp in Kazakhstan set within the time-frame of a single day. It highlighted the power of humans to transcend sub-human conditions where hardship, tyranny and unbearable cold tested men to the limit. He wanted to show the indomitable power of the human spirit to overcome all attempts to crush it. This gave him an admiration for men who had to endure the limits of what others could do to them. It also made him ponder the mystery of how some could become degraded and bestial, while others maintained their dignity and their spirit in the most deplorable conditions.

The good and the bad

Solszhenitsyn was especially struck by the way circumstances determined how people behaved. Those in authority usually acted with cruelty and inhumanity. The most despicable were the guards, many of whom had gained positions of authority by lies and deception, often betraying their comrades. Religious symbols or badges meant nothing. Once he remembered ethnic guards wearing crosses round their necks who acted with the same brutality as the rest. But he saw reasons for optimism: when circumstances changed so could people's characters and personality. Goodness, it seems, is always trying to get out, and at worst can only be suppressed, but not forever. The human spirit is never so dead that it fails to respond to the light that shines from the good of others. This was equally applicable to the oppressors as well as the oppressed and was, he felt, equally applicable to himself:

> "It was granted to me to carry away from my prison years on my bent back, which nearly broke beneath its load, this essential experience: how a human being becomes evil and how good. In the intoxication of youthful successes I had felt myself to be infallible, and I was therefore cruel. In the surfeit of power I was a murderer and an oppressor. In my most evil moments I was convinced that I was doing good, and I was well supplied with systematic arguments. It was only when I lay there on rotting prison straw that I sensed within myself the first stirrings of good. Gradually it was disclosed to me that the line separating good and evil passes . . . right through every human heart . . . This line shifts. Inside us it oscillates with the years. Even within hearts overwhelmed by evil, one small bridgehead of good is retained; and even in the best of all hearts there remains a small corner of evil."

Help from beyond man

Solzhenitsyn transcended his sufferings only with the help, he believed, of an inspiration and grace that came from beyond him. He was inspired to see that communism was profoundly wrong in reducing human beings to the level of animals and material commodities. If man is only a material object in a universe that is itself material, then the conclusion can only be depressing: life can have no final meaning, and human beings will behave accordingly.

Sense of right and wrong

But given the chance, man is a profoundly spiritual being who is always open to a meaning that is awoken by, and matches, his spiritual instincts. He is aware deep down that his real destiny is not to be defined by fortune or misfortune here and now. This is because he has, in the end, a spiritual capacity to recognise two things. What is outrageous, inhuman and unjust, as opposed to what is noble, sublime and uplifting. The ability to recognise the difference is the ability to know good from bad, right from wrong.

> Solzhenitsyn's old Russian ideals were already explicit in the character of Matryona, in his book *Matryona's House*. Its narrator meets a saintly woman whose life has been full of disappointments but who helps others. "We have lived side by side her and had never understood that she was the righteous one without whom, as the proverb says, no village can stand."
>
> AS Biography/ Internet

Return to Christianity

After a growing interest in the religious faith of his upbringing which steadily developed during his years in the labour camps, Solzhenitsyn abandoned his atheism and returned to Christianity in the belief that it contained the solution to life's problems. He wrote:

> "Over half a century ago, while I was still a child, I remember hearing a number of old people offer the following explanation for great disasters that had befallen Russia: "Men have forgotten God; that is why all this has happened." Since then I have spent well nigh 50 years working on the history of our revolution; in the process I have read hundreds of books... But if I were asked today to formulate as concisely as possible the main cause of the ruinous revolution that swallowed up 60 million of our people, I could not put it more accurately than to repeat: "Men have forgotten God; that's why all this has happened."

He believed that many of the ills of recent centuries, including regional and world wars, have ultimately resulted in what he called:

> "the calamity of an irreligious, humanistic consciousness . . . that has made man the measure of all things on earth, imperfect man, who is never free of pride, self-interest, envy, vanity and other defects . . . On the way from the Renaissance to our days we have enriched our experience, but we have lost the concept of a Supreme Complete Entity who used to restrain our passions and our irresponsibility."

Moral voice

But many found his moral outbursts against both East and West too sweeping. In particular, his frequent judgements on social and political developments made him a controversial figure in both Europe and America. At the same time his own tragic life, and the integrity he brought to his opinions made him one of the most listened to moral voices of the twentieth century.

Tributes and awards

After the collapse of the Soviet Union in 1994 Solzhenitsyn returned to Moscow to live the rest of his life. While his award of the Nobel Peace Prize in 1974 was, at first, badly received in Russia, he now enjoyed a new status. His citizenship was restored, and treason charges were dropped. He received praise from Russian leaders, and was eventually allowed to address the *Duma*, the Russian parliament in 1994. In 2007 he received a Russian State Award from President Vladimir Putin for "humanitarian achievement".

Death

Solzhenitsyn died of a heart condition in Moscow on August 3, 2008. A burial service was held at the Donskoy monastery, Moscow, where the author requested to be buried. His burial was accompanied by a military band and three-gun salute. "His coffin was borne to his grave by an honour guard of Russian soldiers as the words of the Orthodox hymn *Eternal Memory* echoed round the monastery" (The Times, London).

> Alexander Solzhenitsyn, who has died aged 89 was not only a great, but a passionately committed writer—he believed it was his moral duty, in the face of systematic totalitarian obfuscation, to record Russia's 20th century experience for posterity.
>
> Daily Telegraph, London 3 August 2008

Solzhenitsyn quotes

"Do not pursue what is illusory—property or position: all that is gained at the expense of your nerves decade after decade and can be confiscated in one fell night. Live with a steady superiority over life—don't be afraid of misfortune and don't yearn after happiness; it is after all, all the same; the bitter doesn't last forever, and the sweet never fills the cup to overflowing."

"If one is forever cautious, can one remain a human being?"

"Our envy of others devours us most of all."

"Hastiness and superficiality are the psychic diseases of the 20th century."

"Pride grows on the human heart like lard on a pig."

"You only have power over people so long as you do not take everything away from them. But when you've robbed a man of everything he is no longer in your power—he is free again."

"We have placed too much hope in political and social reforms, only to find out that we were being deprived of our most precious possession: our spiritual life."

"Even if we are spared destruction by war, our lives will have to change if we want to save life from self-destruction. We cannot avoid revising the fundamental definitions of human life, and human society. Is it true that man is above everything? Is there no Superior Spirit above him? Is it right that a man's life and society's activities have to be determined by material expansion in the first place? Is it permissible to promote such expansion to the detriment of our spiritual integrity?"

"Justice is conscience, not personal conscience but the conscience of the whole of humanity. Those who clearly recognise the voice of their own conscience recognise also the voice of justice."

"The Universe has as many different centres as there are living beings in it."

"Not everything has a name. Some things lead us into a realm without words."

"Even the most rational approach to ethics is defenceless if there isn't the will to do what is right."

"The salvation of mankind lies only in making everything the concern of all."

"It is time in the West to defend not so much human rights as human obligations."

"One should never direct people to happiness, because happiness too is an idol of the marketplace. One should direct them towards mutual affection. A beast gnawing at its prey can be happy too, but only human beings can feel affection for each other, and this is the highest achievement they can aspire to."

"I have spent all my life under a Communist regime, and I will tell you that a society without any objective legal scale is a terrible one indeed."

"So long as a man remains free he strives for nothing more incessantly and painfully as to find someone to worship."

"If it were desired to reduce man to nothing, it would be necessary only to give his work a character of uselessness."

"The socialist who is a Christian is more to be dreaded than the socialist who is an atheist."

"The most pressing question on the problem of faith is whether man as a civilised being . . . can believe in the divinity of the Son of God, Jesus Christ, for therein rests the whole of our faith."

"Everything you add to the truth subtracts from the truth."

Modern Leaders

John Wesley (1703–1791)

One of the outstanding figures of his time, John Wesley dedicated his life to bringing Christianity to what he saw as the lost sheep of the Church of England. His reforming approach brought him both popularity and contempt, success and opposition. It all began when he came to realise that the kind of faith represented by the established church (the Church of England) had ceased to appeal to ordinary people. He believed that its cold, intellectual and detached form of worship had become too closely identified with the upper classes. Besides, on the pastoral side the Church had become sidelined as the conditions of the poor workers of the industrial towns were being forgotten.

Appeal to the emotions

A visit to a Moravian Community during a missionary trip to America convinced him that a more heartfelt, or emotional brand of Christianity was needed to appeal to ordinary people. On returning to England in 1738 he attended a religious meeting in London's East End. It was at this meeting that he had a profound religious experience that changed his life. He wrote:

> "I felt my heart strangely warmed . . . I felt I trusted in Christ, Christ alone."

Inspired with this intense feeling of new-found faith he resolved to devote his life to taking Christianity to the people of the industrial towns and cities, the forgotten souls of the Industrial Revolution.

Early years

John Wesley was born in Epworth, Lincolnshire, the son of a Church of England Rector. In 1720 he went to Oxford where he became involved in a group of devoted Christians that were later called "Methodists" because of their highly organised methods. He decided to become a clergyman like his father, and spent a short time working as a curate at the rectory at Epworth. Later he returned to teach at Oxford but the dry academic life left him dissatisfied. He yearned instead to return to parish work where he would meet real people with real problems to solve. He had become keenly aware of the distance that had arisen between the Church and the ordinary working classes.

The Industrial Revolution

England at the time was in the grip of the Industrial Revolution. Large crowds had flocked to the industrial centres which were ill equipped to cope with their needs, either material or spiritual. Overcrowded slums, poor housing and despotic factory owners left many people struggling to cope. Poverty and despair led many to seek solace in alcohol, gambling and other diversions. Those who became addicted to drink inevitably became trapped in further poverty.

Loss of worth and dignity

Wesley saw that there was an urgent need to reach out to such people. There was an urgent need to raise their morale by restoring their sense of personal worth and dignity. Wesley knew that two problems needed to be addressed. One was a dire absence of spiritual care. The other was an equally dire level of material poverty. But he knew that the first solution was to provide material assistance to the poor. The second was to communicate a new spiritual vision that would uplift their spirits and restore a sense of their lost dignity. The two, of course, were intertwined.

Poverty relief

Wesley was particularly aware that much needed to be done about the social problems he encountered in his travels. It was not enough to encourage people with his spiritual message, although he knew that this too was important. Many were poor and hungry and needed material support. Food, shelter, clothing and medicines were an urgent priority. He recruited and trained aid workers and preachers to assist him in his work. Longer term aid was also needed to consolidate the process of first aid. So Wesley went on to organise schools, set up orphanages and learning centres, and later, meeting places for worship and the practice of the faith.

Spiritual solace

The "Meeting Houses" would eventually evolve as Methodist chapels, a more permanent symbol of his mission to the poor. These stood as witnesses to his first commitment, spreading the Christian message. Although he still belonged officially to the Church of England, he was now effectively outside it. His new mission to the poor, as well as his liking for a more democratic, people-centred form of Christian faith and worship made him an outsider, a renegade. The Methodist chapels that now sprang up all over England were churches with a difference. They were geared to appeal to the ordinary people, providing spiritual solace to those weighed down by the social problems that others had ignored.

A sense of brotherhood

What Wesley aimed to achieve was to create a sense of brotherhood among his worshippers. This meant creating a strong social, spiritual and emotional bond among people united in hardship and neglect. The result would be a sense of communal fellowship in which people would feel at home, knowing that their problems were recognised and that somebody cared. Only against this kind of background would prayer and worship make any sense. So Wesley drew up a heart-warming spiritual programme that focussed on communal prayer, hymn-singing (he and his brother Charles was a noted writer of hymns), the preaching of a rousing message together with the inspirational power of Holy Communion to forge a new sense of communal unity.

Traveller and preacher

For the next 53 years John Wesley travelled throughout England, often on horseback, to preach a gospel of liberation rooted in the original vision of "good news for the poor". Wesley saw the need to replace the established and less appealing gospel of rules and obligations with a gospel of hope and compassion. He took his message to the tin-miners and smugglers of Cornwall; the dockers of London, Bristol and Liverpool: the "dark satanic" mills of Yorkshire and Lancashire; and the coal mines of South Yorkshire, Durham and Northumberland. By making God's love and forgiveness more tangible, he called on the people to rise up and better themselves both materially and spiritually.

> Liberty is the right of every human creature as soon as he breathes the vital air; and no human law can deprive him of that right which he derives from the law of nature.
>
> John Wesley (on the slave trade)

Rebel and outcast

But his efforts on behalf of the poor were not always met with appreciation. Trying to speak up for the poor meant that he incurred the wrath of the mill owners, the factory directors and other industrial groups. Often he was attacked by secret agents who were sent to disrupt his meetings. Seen as a revolutionary and a trouble-maker, he also encountered opposition from within the established Church. Parish church leaders made sure that he was forbidden to preach, celebrate worship, or make use of church facilities. As a result he was forced to hold meetings in halls and schools and other places—and frequently in the open air. This was in the early days, before he had established his chapels and meeting houses.

Legacy

John Wesley's main legacy is the Methodist Movement with its continuing dedication to popular worship, the promotion of personal holiness and care for the poor. Vibrant Methodist and Wesleyan Churches exist across America, Africa and Australia dedicated to keeping alive the spirit of their founder. It was fitting that he was recognised as an authentic champion of the gospel that he preached and the poor that he served. The following is a handsome tribute to the great leader he was:

> "Because of his charitable nature he died poor... As an organiser, a religious leader and a statesman, he was eminent. He knew how to lead and control men to achieve his purposes. He used his power, not to provoke rebellion, but to inspire love. His mission was to spread "scriptural holiness"...
>
> Wikipedia

John Wesley quotes

"Passion and prejudice govern the world, only under the name of reason."

"No circumstances can make it necessary for a man to burst in sunder all the ties of humanity."

"I had the quintessential liberal arts experience. I came out of college not having a clue of what to do."

"I was of the 60's and there was an idealistic motivation I had at the time that one could make an impact on the social justice system by having a life within the law . . . at the risk of sounding flowery, I still believe that."

"Catch on fire with enthusiasm and people will travel for miles to watch you burn."

"When I have money I get rid of it quickly lest it find a way into my heart."

"Every one, though born of God in an instant, yet undoubtedly grows by slow degrees."

"The Bible knows nothing of solitary religion."

"Beware you be not swallowed up in books! An ounce of love is worth a pound of knowledge."

"You may be as orthodox as the devil, and as wicked."

"My ground is the Bible. Yea, I know I am a Bible-bigot. I follow in it all things, both great and small."

"When I was young I was sure of everything . . . At present, I am hardly sure of anything but what God has revealed to me."

"The Church recruited people who had been starched and ironed before they were washed."

"Justifying faith implies, not only a divine evidence or conviction that 'God was in Christ reconciling the world to himself', but a sure trust and confidence that Christ died for my sins, that He loved me and gave Himself for me."

"God buries his workmen, but carries on his work."

> "I'll praise my Maker while I've breath,
> And when my voice is lost in death,
> Praise shall employ my nobler pow'rs;
> My days of praise shall ne'er be past,
> While life, and thought, and being last,
> Or immortality endures."
>
> John Wesley hymn

Angelo Roncalli (Pope John XXIII) (1881–1963)

Pope John, as he was popularly known, is remembered for his efforts to make Catholicism look in two important directions. To look outward, and become more accessible to the secular world; and look sideways, in order to forge new links with the Christian churches she had become separated from at the Reformation. Pope John was credited with letting a "new wind of fresh air" blow through the Catholic Church. In contrast to previous popes who had continued to adopt a defensive, even critical, stance not only in relation to other Christian churches but also to the world. John emerged with a new approach that effectively called time on old attitudes and old hostilities. He saw that in a world of fast advancing secular ways of thinking it was high time for Christians to close ranks and give a new unified witness to what was distinctive about the Christian message: its spiritual world vision. To this end he called a world council of all Catholic bishops to address these problems.

Early years

Angelo Roncalli was born in a farming community in Sotto il Monte, near Bergamo in northern Italy. He was third in a family of thirteen, brought up in a community that had to eke a living in small farms from soil that was far from fertile. He decided early to enter the priesthood, and devote his life to holiness and pastoral work among the poor. But to his disappointment he ended up working in the Church's diplomatic corps, a way of life far removed from the work he yearned to do among the ordinary people. In the interim he served as private secretary to the local bishop of Bergamo, before entering the first world war as a stretcher bearer and chaplain.

Cultured diplomat

Although not regarded as a scholar, he was a highly cultured man with a love of literature, art and music, as well as a fluency in many languages. Above all he possessed great personal charm which made it easy for him to get on with people. His motto, *obedientia et pax,* (obedience and peace) probably to his own annoyance, marked him as an ideal candidate for the Church's diplomatic service.

Papal representative

Shortly after the war he was appointed papal nuncio to Bulgaria. After ten years there he took up similar posts in Turkey (see box below), and later Greece. In 1944, with the war still on, he was appointed Nuncio to France. There he was given the sensitive and difficult task of bringing about peace and reconciliation between hostile factions that had taken opposing sides during the war. This included the thorny task of making bishops retire who had collaborated with the Nazi rulers during the occupation.

> During his time in Turkey in the war years he was instrumental in helping Jews to flee the Nazis. He also worked to provide food, shelter and safety for countless Jewish refugees.
>
> Encyclopedia Brittanica

Election as Pope

In 1953 he came closer to realising his pastoral ambitions when was named Cardinal Patriarch of Venice, a post that finally offered him a chance to fulfil his dream of being a "shepherd of souls". There he became renowned for his pastoral zeal by visiting parishes and meeting ordinary people. Five years later, he found himself facing a new challenge: he was elected Pope. At the age of 76 he was judged to be merely a "caretaker" figure for a daunting post that required much energy and dynamism. But he soon showed he had the very qualities that were needed for the leader of the Church in the mid-twentieth century.

Pooling of wisdom

His first move was a decision that nobody had foreseen. He was the first pope in over one hundred years to call General Council of the Church in 1962. Previous popes had assumed all power to themselves, ignoring the need for general councils that might dilute, or threaten, their authority. But John saw that the time had come for the Church to draw on the wisdom of its world-wide leaders, the bishops. The result was the convening of a General Council in Rome to discuss the Church's role in the modern world, and how it could be better equipped to carry out its God-given mission.

Facing a new world

The aim of the Council was to arrive at a better understanding of how the Church could fulfill its mission as a world-wide religious institution that embraced nearly all the languages and cultures of the world. There were a number of critical issues. One, the need to open up new avenues of dialogue with other churches. Two, the need for a new openness to other cultures and religions. Three, to find new ways to address the problems of world poverty. Four, the need to find ways to ease world tensions created by the cold war and the proliferation of nuclear weapons. The Council lasted for over two years, and during its sessions other religious leaders were invited to attend as observers, already a sign of a new approach to "outsiders".

> From the Second Vatican Council, or Vatican II, came changes that reshaped the face of Catholicism: a new ecumenism (relations with other churches) and a new approach to the world.
>
> Knowledgerush.com

Justice and peace

Pope John died one year after the Council had begun, but he had issued two major encyclicals (letters) before his death. These reflected his political, social and humanitarian concerns about two critical issues plaguing the world. The first, *Mater et Magister, (1961)* addressed the issue of social justice, and the growing problem of world poverty. The second, *Pacem in Terris (1963)* dealt with the continuing "cold war", the dangers of nuclear weapons, and the urgent need for world peace.

New respect for papacy

Pope John's easy-going approach, personal warmth and endearing way with people both high and low, religious or not, made him a landmark holder of the papal throne. Before him the papacy had been seen as remote, formal and unapproachable. After him it was seen as more accessible to the outside world and, in consequence, began to enjoy a new recognition as a focus of religious and moral leadership.

Death

Pope John died after a brief illness in his Vatican apartment on June 3, 1963. Unusually, his death became an international event covered widely in newspapers, radio and television. From the simple priest he wanted to be, he had become a world figure. His burial with other Popes in the crypt below St. Peter's Basilica was a long way from his rustic beginnings. In the year 2000 he was raised to the rank of "Blessed".

Angelo Roncalli quotes

"The feelings of my smallness and nothingness always kept me good company."

"Anyone can be Pope; the proof of this is that I have become one."

"Men are like wine. Some turn to vinegar, but the best improve with age."

"You know its rough being a papal nuncio. I get invited to these diplomatic parties where everyone stands around with a small plate of canapés trying not to look bored. Then in walks a shapely woman with a low-cut, revealing gown and everyone turns around and looks. At me!"

"Italians come to ruin most generally in three ways, women, gambling and farming. My family chose the slowest one."

"It often happens that I wake up at night and think of a serious problem and decide I must tell the Pope about it. Then I wake up completely and remember that I am the Pope."

"It is easier for a father to have children than for children to have a real father."

"A peaceful man does more good than a learned one."

"Mankind is a great and immense family . . . This is proved by what we feel in our hearts at Christmas."

"Born poor, but of honoured and humble people, I am proud to die poor."

"You could not come to me, so I came to you" (to inmates of Roman prison).

Jose Escriva (1902–1975)

Josemaria Escriva de Balaguar was born in Barbastro, Spain of a devout Catholic family. Impressed after once seeing the bare footprints of a friar left in the snow he was drawn to dedicate himself to the religious life. He was ordained a priest in 1928 and began his ministry as a curate in a rural parish before moving to Saragossa, where he had once been a student at the University. In 1927 he was moved to Madrid to begin studies for a doctorate in law.

Man of energy and spiritual devotion

When the civil war broke out in 1936 he was still in Madrid, but caught up in the religious persecution against clerics he had to flee across the Pyrenees to the safety of France. When the war ended he returned to Madrid and finished his law degree. In 1946 he was moved to Rome to study for a doctorate in theology. Known for his energy and capacity for organisation he sensed a new need within the Church. This was the need to raise the spiritual intensity of ordinary believers without interrupting their work in the world. His vision resulted in the founding of an organisation that came to be known as Opus Dei.

> "The first impression one gets from watching Escriva "live" is his evervescence, his keen sense of humour. He cracks jokes, makes faces, roams the stage, and generally leaves his audience in stitches in off-the-cuff responses to people in the crowd."
>
> John L. Allen Jr.

Opus Dei

Opus Dei was a behind-the-scenes, but not secret, organisation that aimed to help its members to come closer to the ideals of the gospel. Escriva believed that the path to holiness had been too closely identified with the "official" religious life of priests and nuns. He felt that lay people, living in the circumstances of secular life (working in the professions and in industry, raising families), could achieve true holiness without resorting to other traditional forms of dedication, such as serving as priests or nuns, or living in monasteries. Although his vision seemed new and innovative, there were many who questioned the need for any extra disciplines within the Church.

> Opus Dei is a Catholic institution founded by Saint Josemaria Escriva. Its mission is to spread the message that work and the circumstances of everyday life are occasions for growing closer to God, for serving others and for improving society.
>
> Opus Dei website

Spiritual support

In Escriva's view, to make the most of their opportunities in the world, men and women needed a communal framework that would provide them with spiritual and moral support. This was to be the function of Opus Dei. Its aim would be to help its members to progress together in living by the gospel ideals of goodness and holiness. This is achieved by following a daily programme of prayer, spiritual reading, worship, and occasionally doing specific acts of mortification as penance for sins. The aim of each member is to absorb and transmit the love of God by showing charity towards others. Each member therefore sets him or her self as a model of Christian living.

Charge of elitism

One of the problems faced by Opus Dei was the charge of elitism: its members pretending to be better than others. Although its members see themselves as simply following a more single-minded form of the Christian life, others were not so sure. Many questioned whether such a strict form of the Christian life was really necessary. Some expressed the worry that its emphasis on penance and mortification, for instance, has often been taken too far. Opus Dei, however, denies this and insists that its programme and aims are beyond reproach, being clearly in line with Church traditions and gospel ideals:

> "Opus Dei's mission is to help people integrate their faith and the activities of their daily life, so its spiritual education and counselling help members to be more ethical than less so" ... "Opus Dei members make limited use of (self) discipline ... types of mortification that have always had a place in the Catholic tradition because of their symbolic reference to Christ's passion."
>
> Opus Dei website

Conspiracy theories

Inevitably Opus Dei has become the subject various conspiracy theories in which its members are cast as secretive, scheming and pursuant of power and self-interest in the name of faith. Such allegations recently became the subject of a well-known fictional work called the *Da Vinci Code* in which a supposed Opus Dei "monk" becomes involved in a murder plot. The organisation has protested strongly against such charges being made under the cover of fiction, and insist that such allegations are outrageous and without foundation. Besides, they point out, such charges are absurd, considering the good moral standing in which the order is held within the normally strict and censorious Catholic Church.

Canonised a saint

Jose Escriva inevitably became tainted by the reputed faults of the movement he founded. Yet his defenders have spoken strongly of his sincerity and personal holiness. For these qualities he was canonised a "saint of the ordinary people" on October 6, 2002. Despite the controversy that has surrounded his person and Opus Dei, he is considered by many to be one of the most edifying religious leaders of the 20th century.

Jose Escriva quotes

> "Holiness is not something for the privileged few . . . all the ways of the earth, all the professions, all honest tasks can be divine . . . we tell each one—all men and all women that there where you are you can acquire Christian perfection."

> "We bear the only flame capable of setting fire to hearts made of flesh."

> "The baptised are enlightened by Christ regarding a knowledge of the truth, and they are impregnated by him with an abundance of good works through the infusion of faith."

> "It is in the midst of the most material things of the earth that we must sanctify ourselves, serving God and all mankind."

> "The laity, by their very vocation seek the kingdom of God by engaging in temporal affairs, and by ordering them according to the plan of God . . . In this way they can make Christ known to others, especially by a life resplendent with faith, hope and charity."

> "You want to be a martyr. I'll place martyrdom within your reach: to be an apostle and not call yourself an apostle, to be a missionary—with a mission—and not call yourself a missionary, to be a man of God and seem to be a man of the world: to pass unnoticed."

Brother Roger of Taize (1915–2005)

Brother Roger was one of the most highly respected figures within the Christian Church until his tragic death during a service at his beloved Taize in eastern France one summer's evening in 2005. In spite of all efforts to save him he was stabbed to death by a woman of unsound mind, an event that caused widespread shock.

Centre for world youth

Brother Roger did more than any other religious leader to reach out to the youth of the world and invite them to the remote village of Taize. It was to be a place of pilgrimage to ponder the meaning of life in the light of their own experiences and the wisdom of the Christian gospel. His method was simple: to welcome and show hospitality. The throngs who came to Taize were asked for nothing except their goodwill in being there. Year after year thousands of young people have travelled from all corners of Europe and beyond to the hillside of Taize, making it a household name.

> "Very few people in a generation manage to change the whole climate of a religious culture, but Brother Roger did just this. He changed the image of Christianity for countless young people."
> Dr Rowan Williams, Archbishop of Canterbury

Poor but rich in spirit

In an age when everything has a price, when the spirit of the age is to always seek ways of making a profit and cashing in on a "brand", Taize under his stewardship wanted nothing to do with such worldly opportunism. Its outward shabbiness and poverty, symbolised more than anything by the rows of tents erected to accommodate the visitors, was meant to speak loudly of the contrasting richness of the human spirit. It is the values of the spiritual life, encapsulated in the sincerity of the pilgrim, that Taize's bells and loudspeakers still proclaim to the youth of Europe and the world who still go there in vast numbers.

Early years

Roger Louis Schutz-Marsauche was the youngest child of a Lutheran pastor and a French mother from Bachs in Switzerland. During his recovery from a severe bout of tuberculosis in adolescence he reflected on two problems that had divided Europe: the savagery of the first world war, and the divisions that existed between the churches. This left him with a sharp sense of the need for a new order of peace and reconciliation. After studying Reformed theology in Strasbourg and Lausanne he was ordained a pastor like his father. During his studies he became Leader of the Swiss Youth Movement, so beginning a lifelong interest in the welfare of young people.

A place called Taize

One day in 1940 he cycled from Geneva to Taize in search for a site to build a monastic community. What he had in mind was a monastery with a difference. One that would embrace men of different Christian backgrounds to become a beacon and symbol of human reconciliation in a world split asunder by conflict and war. But after buying a derelict property in Taize his first task was to help Jewish refugees fleeing the Gestapo in nearby occupied France. Word had got around that help could be found "in a place called Taize". This work occupied him for two years before he was forced to go back to Geneva for his own safety. When the war was over he returned to Taize to lay the foundations of his ground-breaking community.

Ecumenical community

In 1949 seven men had come forward to join Brother Roger in realising his vision. They committed themselves together to a community life based on celibacy that would be a model of harmony and human reconciliation. The community drew from different Christian denominations that crossed Catholic-Protestant boundaries to build a bridge across centuries-old divisions. In so doing he became one of the earliest pioneers of the ecumenical movement (the bringing together of divided Christians). Today it numbers 100 men from Protestant, Catholic and Orthodox backgrounds.

> "Since my youth I think that I have never lost the intuition that community life could be a sign that God is love . . . a community where kindness of heart and simplicity would be at the centre of everything."
>
> Brother Roger

TAIZE SUMMARY
Modern Christian, but non-denominational, centre of pilgrimage appealing to the young in search of the meaning of life. Noted for its stark poverty and physical bleakness (on approach the tented landscape makes it look like a refugee camp, which in a sense it is), it provides a symbolic environment in which material cares can be forgotten and spiritual values pondered. The keynote is organised reflection on gospel passages in groups based on similarity of language and culture. No charges are made for food or accommodation. Volunteers help with catering for visitors and with organising spiritual discussions and communal worship that embrace a multiplicity of languages.

Taize's appeal

The appeal of Taize to thousands of visitors (mainly young people) over several decades since the war owes nothing to the comforts and conveniences of modern life. The accommodation is austere and the food simple and basic. In the absence of luxuries taken for granted elsewhere young people find a welcoming atmosphere that makes no demands on them religiously or financially. No charges are made and no donations accepted.

Self-supporting community

The running costs of Taize are borne by the brothers who work to support themselves, and by volunteers who work as co-helpers. Some like Brother Roger earn royalties from writings. Other earnings come from tapes and videos of sacred music (especially the famed *Taize chants*), and from art-works sold in the community shop. To support themselves the community own a farm co-operative, a printing press and studios for painting and pottery.

> The charisma of this frail and sensitive Swiss pastor ... has attracted more young people than any other religious leader in Europe, Catholic or Protestant.
>
> The Times, obituary 2005

Taize worship

Communal worship takes place takes place every evening in the rather functional Church of Reconciliation, built in the 1962 with help from German Christians. Originally it was thought to be too large, but soon after its completion the back wall had to be demolished for the addition of a marquee to cater for overspills. Taize has gained a wide reputation for providing an unique experience of Christian worship. Nowhere else does an act of worship have to be so multi-lingual. At any one time it is normal to have worshippers present from most of the languages of Europe. Part of the solution is to have short prayers and readings in languages selected for the occasion, with languages chosen in rotation.

Taize chants

The other part of the solution is the use of *Taize chants*. These are usually short arrangements, in Latin or other language, which can easily be understood across different language groups. Because the melodies and words lend themselves to easy repetition they are quickly picked up by the worshippers. The result is a moving experience where visitors from diverse backgrounds join together to form a microcosm of a united world. (Taize chants have become famous across the Christian world and are widely available in DVD).

> **VISITORS TO TAIZE**
> Accompanied by his wife and several co-workers (the Archbishop of Canterbury, Dr Rowan Williams) began his 3 day visit on August 6, 2009 by attending the midday prayer. Upon his arrival he reminded the brothers that he came to Taize when he was young, and told them that Taize had always played a very important role in his life. During the evening prayer he spoke to the thousands of young people from many countries ... He prayed at the tomb of Brother Roger and met young people from Britain who were present, with volunteers who spend time in Taize, and with the sisters who help with the welcome. By coming to Taize he revived an old tradition. He is the third archbishop of Canterbury to make such a visit. Michael Ramsey visited the community in 1973, and later George Carey brought with him a thousand Anglicans for a week in 1992.
> Taize website news

Taize international youth gatherings

Because of its reputation as a beacon of peace and brotherhood, Taize has extended its influence to become an organising centre for youth gatherings in all five continents. Taize brothers travel to these international gatherings to meet young people and encourage them to share the Taize experience in their search for peace and understanding. Through these meetings Taize continues to proclaim its core message that spiritual values unite a world too often divided by the material values of greed, power and the enjoyments of wealth and status. In this way Taize has become a significant educational and cultural force in raising awareness of both the causes and effects of an unequal and divided world. In 1988 Brother Roger was awarded the UNESCO Prize for Peace Education.

> Roger's visits to cities were astonishing. He drew thousands of young people to London in 1981 and 1987. By miracles of efficiency and goodwill, St. Paul's, Westminster Abbey, Westminster Cathedral, and cathedrals

> in Southwark and Methodist Central Hall were linked, so that prayers, hymns and words could be relayed from each to the others. St. Paul's had its largest congregation since VE Day—more than 9000 worshippers with simultaneous translation in several languages. The sense of reconciliation between visitors from the East and the West was personal and moving.
>
> The Times, August 18, 2005

Brother Roger quotes

> "We have come here to search, or to go on searching through silence and prayer, to get in touch with our inner life."

> "I have found my own identity as a Christian by reconciling within myself the faith of my origins with the mystery of the Catholic faith, without breaking fellowship with anyone."

> "Faith must always involve an investment of trust . . . Jesus said 'do not worry'."

> "We are not called by God to be on a mountain top, but to be with others."

> "We are all seekers in regard to the realities of God . . . but one day we shall understand."

> "Human beings are sometimes severe. God, for His part, comes to clothe us in compassion."

> "Sometimes you say to yourself: the fire in me is going out. But you were not the one who lit that fire. Your faith does not create God, and your doubts cannot banish Him to nothingness."

> "For whoever knows how to love, whoever knows how to suffer, life is filled with supreme beauty."

> "What matters most is discovering that God loves you, even if you think that you do not love God."

> "Prayer is a serene force at work in human beings. It keeps them from growing unfeeling in the face of turmoil experienced by whole sectors of humankind. From it are drawn vital energies of compassion."

> "I repeated to a girl from Belgium who spoke of her deep unhappiness: anyone who looks only at themselves will inevitably sink into melancholy. Open your eyes to creation all around you and the shadows already begin to disperse."

Modern Humanitarians

William Wilberforce (1759–1833)

Widely regarded as the greatest of the slave trade abolitionists, William Wilberforce combined his Christian faith with political influence to bring about a new social awareness of the slave trade and, later, legislation that would eventually see its end. His approach was one of outrage that so patent an evil was allowed to continue, saying "slavery is a sin for which Britain must repent or be damned". In one of his last letters before his death John Wesley wrote to encourage him, telling him to press ahead with his efforts: "Unless God has raised you up for this very thing, you will be worn out by the opposition of men and devils. But if God be for you, who can be against you?" In 1807 a new law was passed ending slavery, but criminal elements and entrenched business interests involved in the profitable trade made it another 25 years before all slaves were freed.

Early Life

William Wilberforce was born into a privileged family in Hull in 1759, a port which, ironically, saw little of the slave trade that he would later oppose. His upbringing was complicated by weak health and poor eyesight; his father's death when he was eight led to further unhappiness. In a move intended to help his struggling mother he was taken in by prosperous relatives in South London. Sensing himself displaced, he took advantage of his new surroundings where normal family controls were absent. Known more for enjoying recreation than study he eventually received a place at St. John's College, Cambridge, where his lax life-style continued to be funded by his wealthy background. In his own words he was "more idle than studious", yet he managed to pass his examinations, leaving with an MA in 1788.

Member of Parliament

While still a student Wilberforce decided to go into politics, becoming a member of parliament for Hull at 21 standing as an independent. But after an indulgent tour of Europe he was introduced to a spiritual book by the evangelical Philip Dodderidge. This led to his becoming an evangelical Christian in 1785, a decision that brought him much ridicule from his friends. His unyielding conviction was the country's urgent need for social and moral reform, and as a parliamentarian he was in an ideal position to use his influence.

> **BUSY SCHEDULE**
> On one chair sat a Yorkshire constituent, on another a petitioner for charity, or a House of Commons client; on another a Wesleyan preacher; while side by side with an African, a foreign missionary, or a Haitian professor sat perhaps some men of rank who waited for a private interview . . .
> Description of waiting room by his son.

The slave trade

Wilberforce's opposition to slavery was boosted when he joined the Clapham Sect, a leading group of Christian activists led by Thomas Clarkson, which had begun to campaign against slavery. Clarkson had visited the slave ships and brought back examples of the chains, handcuffs and leg-irons used on the victims. He persuaded Wilberforce to use his parliamentary influence to lobby against the evil. In his first anti-slavery motion in 1788 Wilberforce concluded his speech with an appeal to morality and justice:

> "Sir, when we think of eternity and the future consequences of all human conduct, what is there in this life that shall make any man contradict the dictates of his conscience, the principles of justice and the law of God!"

> So enormous, so dreadful, so irremediable did the (slave) trade's wickedness appear that my own mind was completely made up for abolition. Let the consequences be what they would: I from this time determined that I would never rest until I had effected its abolition.
> William Wilberforce

End of slave trade

As events proved, after 18 years of introducing anti- slavery motions the trade in slaves was finally brought to an end. When it did end, the government had to pay compensation to the plantation owners and slave merchants. At the end of his life Wilberforce recognised this material cost. He said: "Thank God that I have lived to witness a day in which England is prepared to give twenty million sterling for the Abolition of Slavery".

Social reformer

Wilberforce's Christian faith also prompted him to engage in other social reforms, such as improving factory conditions and ending child labour. He also set out to "renew society" by working on the moral climate of the time. Firstly he became involved in the Association for the Better Observance of Sunday. Its aim was to provide children with better education in reading, personal hygiene and religion. Secondly, in 1802 he helped to organise the Society for the Suppression of Vice, aimed at the poverty-related evils of alcoholism and prostitution.

Tributes

> "A passionate man of God, a rarity today."
> Catholic News Service
>
> "A true believer, a crusader, a man of action ... He's at once pure and seductive ... a dashing romantic figure ... unfailingly attractive."
> NY Times
>
> "Every school boy knows the name of William Wilberforce."
> Abraham Lincoln

At the end of his life William Wilberforce was recognised as a national hero. He was buried in Westminster Abbey, and later honoured with numerous memorials and monuments to his memory.

William Wilberforce quotes

> "Can you tell a plain man the road to heaven? Certainly, turn at once to the right, then carry straight on."

> "The objects of the present life fill the human eye with a false magnification because of their immediacy."

"God Almighty has set before me two great objects, the supression of the slave-trade and the reformation of manners."

"Of all things guard against neglecting God in the secret place of prayer."

"Is it not the great end of religion, and, in particular, the glory of Christianity, to extinguish the malignant passions; to curb the violence, to control the appetites, and to smooth the asperities of man; to make us compassionate and kind, and forgiving to one another; to make us good husbands, good fathers, good friends; and render us active and useful in the relative social and civic duties?"

John Bosco (1815–1888)

Remembered for his outstanding service to abandoned young people in the teeming suburbs of northern Italy, he laid the foundations for their care and education that others would build on. Today he continues to be revered not only as a pioneering figure in the rescue of homeless youth, but an enlightened educator whose ideas have perennial relevance to modern schooling. At a young age he had a dream of being told by an important person that he must fight a great battle. The battle appeared to be on behalf of a multitude of poor, abandoned and unruly young people. He was told in the dream that he had the skills and ability to change these unfortunates and make them his friends. But he was warned:

> "not through rude control, but through charity and gentleness must you draw these young ones to the path of virtue."

Early years

John Bosco was born of poor parents in a farming community near Piedmont, Italy. His father died when he was two years old, leaving the upbringing of three brothers to his mother. Gifted with a ready wit and a retentive memory he missed much of his early schooling because he was needed on the family farm. Later he proved intellectually capable enough to gain a place in the seminary at Chieri. After six years there he was ordained priest in 1841.

Abandoned youth

After his ordination he was sent to take up work in the slum areas of one of the most glamorous cities in Italy, Turin. The city was then in the grip of the industrial revolution, but its glamorous façade concealed a darker reality. The teeming quarters where the factory workers lived were rife with all kinds of social problems: poverty, poor housing, prostitution, alcoholism and crime. A visit to the local prison left him horrified. But the sight of so many young people already prisoners made him resolve to do something to help them. As he said: "To see so many children from 12 to 18 years of age, all healthy, strong, intelligent, lacking material and spiritual nourishment . . . I must by any available means, prevent children from ending up here."

Early efforts

At first he set up makeshift centres to cater for children on the streets. He first aim was to provide basic food and lodgings and later to set up centres for night school. Many of the young had long ceased to attend local schools, preferring to do odd-jobs in factories and workshops. He knew that many others indulge in lives in petty crime. But it took time for his work to be accepted, both by the young people he tried to help, and the better-off citizens who considered them both beyond help and a social nuisance. But Bosco was undaunted.

Education and shelter

He went on to found a religious Society called the Salesians (named after Bosco's favourite saint, Francis de Sales, a noted teacher and spiritual director). Its aim was to attack the roots of poverty and destitution, which he believed lay above all in lack of education. He was instrumental in starting technical schools where young people could learn the skills to get jobs and make a better future.

> The boys were given all the freedom compatible with discipline and good conduct. When the bell summoned they were not required to line up; in the hot season they could remove coats and ties. Teachers often reminded John Bosco that order and decorum demanded otherwise, but he was loath to yield to this, so anxious was he to avoid all regimentation.
>
> Don Ruffino, colleague

Prevention rather than repression

Although he had little time for educational theories, John Bosco had a simple principle that he always tried to follow. This was what he called the principle of prevention. Its opposite he called repression: the use of punishment, and reliance on fear. Bosco was aware of how punishment, especially corporal punishment, can cause bitterness and resentment both then and later on. But he knew that prevention, as he understood it, was the more demanding approach. Prevention is something that is slowly built up. It is based on trust between teacher and pupil. For it to work the teacher must show friendship, tolerance, compassion and fairness. The pupil must be given a chance to respond in kind and understand that the learning process calls for his willing cooperation. As he put it:

> The repressive system may stop a disorder, but can hardly make the offenders better. Experience teaches that the young do not easily forget the punishments they have received, and for the most part foster bitter feelings ... and even seek revenge ... But the preventive system stresses inter-personal relationships, and pupils acquire a better understanding.
>
> John Bosco

The Salesian Order

The Order founded by John Bosco today carries on his work of education and childcare. Salesian Sisters concentrate on the welfare and education of girls. The Salesian Order is the third largest missionary organisations in the world, with houses, schools and orphanages in Europe, South Africa, India, China, the US and Latin America. Its aim is to care for the young and underprivileged by offering shelter and education under the motto:

> Reason, Religion and Kindness.

Teacher Saint

In 1934 John Bosco was canonised a saint, the only saint ever called Father and Teacher of Youth. Today numerous schools and colleges throughout the western world are called after him in memory of his work for young people and education.

John Bosco quotes

> "Everything and everyone is won by the sweetness of our words and works."

> "Every virtue in your soul is a precious ornament which makes you dear to God and to man."

> "Teaching is not about methods; pupils are not automatons. It is about style, tolerance and encouragement. Discipline must always come last."

Henri Dunant (1828–1910)

A young Swiss businessman and social activist, Henri Dunant became the founder of the organisation that bears one of the world's most recognisable symbols, the Red Cross. Following an experience in Italy where he witnessed the aftermath of a bloody battle he was struck by the gross inhumanity of each side having to fend for itself in treating the wounded. At that moment he resolved to set up an organisation that would impartially help the wounded on either side, regardless of race, colour, creed or any military considerations. His sunsequent fame earned him the first ever Nobel Peace Prize in 1901.

Early years

Born in Geneva, Henri Dunant was greatly influenced by his Calvinist upbringing. He was particularly inspired by the example of his parents, both of whom were actively involved in humanitarian work among the city's poor and deprived. As he grew up he often used his free-time visiting orphanages, prisons and other centres serving the needy. However he was not doing well at school and found himself having to leave the *College Calvin* because of poor grades. He turned instead to banking (for which Switzerland was famous) and became a financial apprentice.

Battle of Solferino

After a business trip to Algeria where he ran into problems over land rights, he decided to appeal to the French emperor Napoleon III who at this time was in Italy where the French were fighting against Austria. Dunant arrived at the town of Solferino where, unknown to him, a bloody battle had just been fought betweem the two sides. He was little prepared for the sight he saw of the bloodbath left behind on the battlefield. As many as 38,000 lay wounded with nobody to care for them. Shocked, he set about doing what he could to organise the civilian population to help tend the wounded and sick soldiers. He organised the purchase of basic materials and set up an emergency field hospital. His guiding principle was to help the needy regardless of which side they were on. Borrowing the local expression *tutti fratelli* (all are brothers), he directed the rescue effort.

The Red Cross

The experience of Solferino made a deep impression on Dunant, inspiring him to write a book exposing the urgent need for an organisation that would stand outside all conflicts and warring factions and be solely dedicated to helping the wounded in battle. With five important figures from the military and medical fields, he set up a committee to oversee the new movement. It was the first International Committee of the Red Cross (ICRC), founded in 1863. Following from this came an agreement among twelve states which led to the Geneva Convention, an agreement on the treatment of war-victims, prisoners and refugees, as well as the recognition that all victims of war had certain human rights.

Period of eclipse and decline

Following these events, however, Dunant's influence began to decline. His business operations began to go downhill, probably as a result of his humanitarian involvements. He was also bitterly opposed by other leading figures in the Red Cross who disageed with him on policies that they considered too idealistic. Eventually becoming backrupt, he left Geneva in 1867, never to return. He eventually moved to Paris, and later, London where, although experiencing hard times, he continued to work for better conditions for prisoners and for other humanitarian causes. But that was not the end. In 1895 an article appeared in a German newspaper lauding his earlier efforts on behalf of the Red Cross. This led to a revival of his memory and new recognition of what he had achieved.

Nobel Peace Prize

In 1901 Henri Dunant was awarded the first ever Nobel Peace Prize for his efforts in founding the Red Cross and the Geneva Convention. He shared the prize with the French pacifist Frederic Passy. The citation highlighted Henri Dunant's humanitarian achievement:

> "There is no man who more deserves this honour, for it was you, forty years ago, who set in foot the international organisation for the relief of the wounded on the battlefield. Without you, the Red Cross, the supreme humanitarian organisation of the 19th century, would probably never have been undertaken."

The Red Cross today

Today the Red Cross is one of the most prominent relief organisations in the world. It works not only in the field of man-made disasters such as war and conflict, but also in the field of natural catastrophies, such as earthquakes, hurricanes, floods, droughts, and the relief of illness and disease. Although its emblem of a red cross against a white background suggests a Christian connotation, this was never intended. Possibly inspired by the Swiss flag whose colours it reverses, its highly visible emblem and outstanding significance is medical rather than religious. It is simply dedicated to helping human beings regardless of colour, class, creed or nationality. Its counterpart in the Muslim world, the Red Crescent, is testimony to the far-reaching embrace of Henri Dunant's original inspired vision.

Albert Schweitzer (1875–1965)

A profound religious and ethical thinker, and an established philosopher, theologian, New Testament scholar, pastor, medical doctor and musician, Albert Schweitzer was a multi-talented figure who could have had a successful career in whatever field he chose. But his religious convictions were to be the deciding factor. Shunning the life of fame and fortune that lay ahead of him as an academic or professional in his native Germany, he felt his mission was to work abroad as a missionary "to serve humanity". His destiny was to go to a poverty stricken region in the jungles of French Equatorial Africa called Lambarene.

Early years

Born in German occupied Alsace of cultured parents, he was destined to seek success by following in his father's footsteps either as a musician or an educated professional in another field. His father was a Lutheran minister who was keen for his son to study the organ, an instrument he would master. He went to Paris to study music and philosophy, but decided he also wanted to become a church minister in order to do something practical for people in the pastoral field. To prepare himself he became a brilliant student of theology, first, at the University of Strasbourg, then at the Sorbonne in Paris, and later at Tubingen where he obtained his Ph.D. in 1899.

Pastor, theologian and organist

For a while he served as a Lutheran minister in Strasbourg. During this time he became a renowned theologian and scripture scholar, writing books that were held in high regard by other scholars and academics. But his genius for music made him an internationally distinguished organist, specialising in concert recitals of the music of Bach (recordings of his recitals are still available). Yet in spite of his gifts, and much to the disapproval of his family and friends, he decided to use his earnings from playing and writing to fund a seven year course in medicine, qualifying as a doctor in 1911.

Medical missionary

Schweitzer believed that he could serve humanity best by using his talents as a doctor working as a Christian missionary. He therefore persuaded the Paris Missionary Society to send him to Africa as a missionary doctor, but at his own expense. He was posted to the Society's mission in Lambarene (present day Gabon) where he began his work, not surprisingly, under conditions far removed from those he was used to in the more developed world of the west.

Albert Schweitzer Hospital

Beginning his work under basic conditions he soon realised the need for a hospital to make possible the medical care which the people needed, especially those suffering from leprosy. Financing the project with his own funds from his writings and organ recordings, the Albert Schweitzer Hospital eventually became a reality. With his fame increasing the former scholar and musician began to receive donations from many countries to support his efforts in the treatment of tropical ailments and diseases. Newspaper reporters and cameramen went there to record interviews and send back photographs and film records. He became, in modern terms, an international celebrity.

Nobel Peace Prize

With the help of the additional donation he expanded the original hospital until it was capable of housing 500 patients at any one time. In

1952 he was awarded the Nobel Peace Prize for his "reverence for life", a tribute to his life-saving work. He used the $33,000 prize money from his Nobel prize to invest in the treatment of one of the most critical diseases he had to deal with, leprosy. The result was the building of a new leprosy centre, or leprosarium, next to the hospital.

Sacredness of life

Albert Schweitzer developed a particular attachment to the principle of the sacredness, or sanctity of life, something he believed had long been ignored by western civilisation, partly evidenced no doubt by the carnage of two world wars that he had witnessed. His basic premise was that "I am life that wants to live, in the midst of life that wants to live". This led to his ethical conviction that man's true calling was respect for other creatures, animal as well as human, and a willingness to help ease the distress of all living things. He was later criticised for taking his reverence for life too far. He refused to kill harmful pests and was often accused of compromising hospital rules on cleanliness and hygiene. But despite what many regarded as his later eccentricities, his remained a powerful ethical voice that gained the respect given to those who practice what they preach.

Albert Schweitzer quotes

> "The tragedy of life is what dies inside a man while he lives."
>
> "Life becomes harder for us when we live for others, but it becomes richer and happier."
>
> "Happiness is nothing more than good health and a bad memory."
>
> "A man does not have to be an angel in order to be a saint."
>
> "In everyone's life, at some time, our inner fire goes out. It is then burst into flame by an encounter with another human being. We should always be thankful to those people who rekindle the inner spirit."
>
> "It is not Jesus as historically known, but Jesus as spiritually arisen among men, who is significant for our time and can help it ... He comes to us as One unknown, without a name, as of old by the lakeside he came to those men who knew Him not. He speaks to us the same word: "Follow thou me!" and sets us to the tasks He has to fulfil for our time."
>
> "Humanitarianism consists in never sacrificing a human being to a purpose."

"Do something for those who have need of a man's help, something for which you get no pay but the privilege of doing it."

"I wanted to be a doctor that I might be able to work without having to talk because for years I had been giving myself out in words."

"Impart as much as you can of your spiritual being to the people on the road with you, and accept as something precious what comes back to you from them."

"Man must cease attributing his problems to his environment, and learn again to exercise his will—his personal responsibility in the realm of faith and morals."

"Serious illness doesn't bother me for long because I am too inhospitable a host."

"An optimist is a person who sees a green light everywhere, while the pessimist sees only the red stoplight. The truly wise person is colourblind."

"Anyone who proposes to do good must not expect people to roll stones out of his way, but must accept his lot calmly, even if they roll a few stones upon it."

"As soon as a person does not take his existence for granted, but beholds it as something unfathomably mysterious, thought begins."

"By respect for life we become religious in a way that is elementary, profound and alive."

"Constant kindness can accomplish much. As the sun makes ice melt, kindness causes misunderstanding, mistrust and hostility to evaporate."

"Day by day we should weigh what we have granted to the spirit of the world against what we have denied to the spirit of Jesus, in thought and especially in deed."

"Ethics is the activity of man directed to secure the inner perfection of his own personality."

"Revenge . . . is like a rolling stone, which when a man has forced up a hill will fall on him with greater violence, and break those bones whose sinews gave it motion. The purpose of human life is to serve, and to show compassion and the will to help others."

"Example is not the main thing in influencing others. It is the only thing."

William Booth (1829–1912)

One of the most earnest religious and moral thinkers of his time, William Booth became distinguished for his perceptive awareness of how the social problems of his day often underlay more serious problems affecting people's moral and spiritual development. Even in today's welfare state the organisation that he founded, the Salvation Army, continues to play an important role in helping to meet the needs of a society whose social and moral needs are not altogether far removed from what they were in Booth's day.

Early years

Born in Nottingham, William Booth was part of a well to do family, but his father later fell on hard times and became bankrupt. At the age of 13 he was apprenticed to a pawnbroker, a position he later left because he considered it "ungodly". In the 1840's he was converted to Methodism. He decided to become a lay preacher to the "sinners" of Nottingham, stressing simple "evangelical" beliefs and values. He taught that eternal salvation meant belief in Jesus Christ, and that every believer should order their lives to reflect this. But he also believed that poor social circumstances can seriously hamper this achievement. He saw that such circumstances as poverty, squalor, and other inhuman living conditions were unfavourable to human moral progress. He saw that these things were regrettably common, but that people could be helped to overcome them.

The Christian Mission

In 1865, he moved to London he set up, with the help of his wife Catherine, the *Christian Mission* in the East End . This was a part of London rife with the well-known social and moral problems usually expected in an area of dense population and high immigrant intake. The *Mission* had two functions, one spiritual, the other material. It was dedicated to helping the poor and the wayward; in particular alcoholics, criminals and prostitutes. Booth's conviction about the way poverty and deprivation barred the way to spiritual development underlay all his work. Unless people are helped to improve their living conditions moral decadence tends to follow. He was therefore committed to providing soup kitchens and other forms of material relief as part of his mission.

Defence of women workers

Despite his good intentions he was not always well received in the tougher part of the East End. Although he was providing significant forms of material help he was also well-known on the streets as a fiery preacher. As a result, the *Christian Mission* he represented came in for mockery and derision. But, to his credit, some of the hostile abuse he received was organised by factory owners who resented his criticism of local factory conditions where, in one case, women workers developed health problems. This was the match factory of Bryant and May which used match tips of the damaging yellow phosphorus that caused serious facial injuries. Booth was successful in forcing the company to change to the less harmful red phosphorus.

The Salvation Army

In 1878 Booth decided to change the image of his *Mission* to one that openly took on the fight against sin and crime. He named it The Salvation Army. The idea of an army fighting against sin caught the imagination of the people, attracting them to enlist as soldiers in his new battle against evil and injustice. It was modelled on military lines with its own flag, a general (Booth was the first) and lesser ranks called officers, all wearing the distinctive uniform of the Army. His book *In Darkest England and the Way Out* became a bestseller. In its introduction Booth wrote words that summed up his belief not only that human misery is a serious obstacle to personal or religious salvation, but that such relief is only a temporary step to spiritual regeneration. A battle still needs to be fought:

> My only hope for the permanent deliverance of mankind from misery, either in this world or the next, is the regeneration or remaking of the individual by the power of the Holy Ghost through Jesus Christ. But in providing for the relief from temporal misery I reckon that I am only making it easy where it is now difficult, and possibly where it is now almost impossible, for men and women to find their way to the Cross of our Lord Jesus Christ.
>
> William Booth

Recognition and honours

At first Booth was looked on with hostility and derision not only for his out-spoken evangelical views and his so-called poverty relief efforts, but also for his enlightened views on social justice which made others uncomfortable. He was criticised for "elevating women to man's status" and was even dismissed by some as the "Anti-Christ". But gradually his reputation grew. He was made a freeman of London, and given an honorary degree by Oxford University. In 1902 he was invited to attend the coronation of Edward VII. Numerous statues and monuments have since been built to his memory. He is buried with his wife in Stoke Newington. Today the Salvation Army that he founded is one of the largest humanitarian agencies in the world.

William Booth quotes

"In answer to your enquiry, I consider that the chief dangers which confront the coming century will be religion without the Holy Ghost, Christianity without Christ, forgiveness without repentance, salvation without regeneration, politics without God, and heaven without hell."

"While women weep, as they do now, I'll fight; while children go hungry, as they do now, I'll fight . . . while there is a poor lost girl upon the streets . . . I'll fight to the very end."

"I must assert in the most unqualified way that it is primarily and mainly for the sake of saving the soul that I seek the salvation of the body."

"To get a man soundly saved it is not enough . . . even to give him a university education. These things are all outside a man, and if the inside remains unchanged you have wasted your labour.

Look! Don't be deceived by appearances. All who are not on the rock are in the sea."

"A man's labour is not only his capital but his life."

"It is against stupidity in every shape and form that we must do battle."

"There are men so incorrigibly lazy that no inducement you can offer will tempt them to work; so eaten up by vice that virtue is abhorrent to them; and so inveterately dishonest that theft is to them a master passion."

"But what is the use of preaching the Gospel to men whose whole attention is given to keeping themselves alive?"

"The profession of a prostitute is the only one where the maximum income is paid to the newest apprentice . . . it is the ever-new embodiment of the old fable of the sale of the soul to the devil . . . nor does the other party forget to exact his due to the uttermost farthing."

Thomas Barnardo (1845–1905)

Thomas John Barnardo became renowned for his work of providing help, education and shelter for young people in London in the mid 1800's. Since the foundation of the first Barnardo home in 1870, some 60,000 children have been cared for, trained and placed in society.

Thomas Barnardo became one of the most famous Victorian humanitarian figures in England. He is buried in front of his village home complex in Barkingside, London. Today the charity, originally called *Dr. Barnardo's,* continues its work under the name *Barnardo's.*

Early years

Born in Dublin of a Jewish father and a mother who was a member of the Plymouth Brethren, a devout Christian group, he grew up at first without any strong sense of wanting to do good. His early schooling was less than successful, he being, as was said "an independent spirit", mischievous, and easily bored at lessons. Yet despite his negative reputation, he began to show positive signs, with an impressive ability to hold his own in argument and debate. At the age of seventeen he underwent a conversion, and became an evangelical Christian "impatient to convert others, and urgent for action", as he put it.

Medical studies

After hearing a talk by Hudson Taylor, the well-known missionary to China who was on a visit to Dublin, Banardo thought he might follow in his footsteps to take up missionary work in the far east. After deciding to become a medical missionary, he studied to be a doctor, first at the London Hospital, and later at the Royal College of Surgeons in Edinburgh where he qualified in 1860.

Problems in London

But while working as a doctor in London's East End he became keenly aware of the number of abandoned and destitute children roaming the streets. Many others were working in harsh conditions as chimney sweeps and in factories. To make matters worse London had just endured a severe plague of cholera which hit the East End particularly hard. He realised then that his vocation was to the deprived youngsters around him, and not to the foreign fields of China.

Shelter and education

Barnardo began to search the streets for destitute children and teenagers, first offering them shelter and later education. Although a grounding in Christian education was one of his priorities, he was equally concerned to provide the youngsters with training in various trades. As a result of his efforts, many young people later went abroad to find success in various British colonies, especially in the remoter parts of Canada and Australia. Barnardo's conviction was that circumstances, especially the social environment, was crucial in shaping the future of the young. As he put it:

> "if children of the slums can be removed from their surroundings early enough, and can be kept sufficiently long under training, heredity counts for little, environment for almost everything."

Resistance and help

Barnardo's good intentions were often tested when he discovered that many of the youngsters under his care were not completely persuaded about the benefits of the free education he was offering. Many turned away from his offer, while others treated him with ridicule and scorn. But Barnardo persisted in his rescue efforts, persuading others to respond, as many did with interest and gratitude. When knowledge of his work spread, he was helped financially by the well-known Earl of Shaftesbury, another Christian philanthropist; and Lord Cairns, who provided housing for his projects. One immediate effect of such welcome aid was that Londoner's became aware of the scale of child-neglect in the city, aided by the publicity provided by Fleet Street newspapers. In a reference to the primitive conditions under which Barnardo worked, and the lack of so-called "security" that is a priority today, one religious leader recently reflected wryly:

> Can you imagine the problems Thomas Barnardo would face today? His attempts to rescue the homeless and destitute children would have to be accompanied by a health and safety audit. His homes would never get planning permission ... and at every turn he would be subjected to CRB (criminal record) checks.
>
> Dr George Carey, NOW, July 2010

Barnardo Homes

In 1867 Barnardo set up a *Ragged School* for deprived youngsters where poor children could get a basic education. This was the beginning of his involvement with young people, and by 1870 he had begun to provide them with housing and shelter. The first *Barnardo Home* was opened in Stepney Causeway. An unfortunate incident happened involving a young boy who was refused admission because the house was full. When it was later found he had died, Barnardo made a resolution that from then on that "no destitute child would ever be refused admission". Later, he and his wife Syrie were given property that eventually became a *Girls' Village Home* in Barkingside, near Ilford. His vision was to build a collection of cottages around a green which would provide a feeling of village life, to offset the earlier bleak experiences of his homeless youngsters. The village eventually grew to house 1,500 girls. He always tried to make sure that girls left with domestic skills, and boys with a trade or craft.

> In the space of forty years, starting without patronage or influence of any kind this man . . . had established a network of Homes of various kinds such as never existed before for the reception, care and training of homeless, needy and afflicted children, and had rescued no fewer than sixty thousand destitute boys and girls.
>
> A. E. Williams, Barnardo's secretary

From Homes to fostering

However, Barnardo was aware from an early stage that his efforts were no substitute for the real thing. He knew that the best environment for a child to be brought up was in a loving, secure family. For this reason he began a fostering scheme to place as many children as possible in willing families. Today *Barnardo's* is completely committed to fostering, rather than providing rescue accommodation for young people. Yet he knew the importance of his original mission: to pick up the pieces left behind by a broken society. Those who were part of secure families had no need of his help; his job was saving those who had no such luck. As a result his name will ever be associated with the *Homes* he provided for the disadvantaged young.

> When Dr Barnardo died there were nearly 8000 children in the 96 residential homes he had set up. Around 1300 of these children had disabilities. More than 4000 children were boarded out, and 18,000 had been placed in Canada and Australia.
>
> Mark K. Smith (2002)

Thomas Barnardo quotes

"Character is better than ancestry, and personal conduct is better than highest parentage."

"Young people need to be cared for. An untended garden runs wild."

"I am a strong believer in training and discipline. I would throw every rule overboard and send them to the bottom of the sea tomorrow, if I thought there was a more excellent way."

"There is no greater gratification than knowing that you have taken someone off the streets and steered them towards a profitable life."

"I think our work has pleased the Lord."

Damien of Molokai (1840–1899)

The Hawaiian islands are usually shrouded in a romantic mist, attracting tourists to their sandy beaches where waving palm trees look down on surfers as they ride the rolling waves of the blue Pacific. But there was nothing romantic about the island of Molokai which is one of those islands. It was a notorious human dumping ground, ideal for use as a leper colony. It was to here that Father Damien came in 1873 and devoted his life to caring for the inhabitants, eventually contracting leprosy himself. Described by Robert Louis Stevenson as not only a man of "heroic virtue", but a man of "rugged honesty, generosity and mirth", he is recognised as the spiritual patron of Hansen's Disease (leprosy), HIV and AIDS. Canonised by the Pope on October 11, 2009, he is the patron saint of the Catholic diocese of Honolulu and Hawaii.

Early years

Born Joseph de Veuster in the Belgian village of Tremelo into a devout family and the seventh son of a Flemish corn merchant, he went on to become a member of the missionary Congregation of the Sacred

Hearts of Jesus and Mary. The order was based in Louvain and had missions abroad including Hawaii. Originally considered fit only to be a "brother" because of his poor studies record, he was eventually allowed to go to Hawaii in place of his brother who had fallen ill. After further studies and preparation he was ordained priest in 1864 in Honolulu.

Island health crisis

Father Damien began to serve in various parishes in the island of O'ahu when a growing health crisis began to develop due to the influx of foreign traders and sailors. For the first time many islanders contracted influenza, syphilis and other ailments they had never heard of. One was Hansen's Disease, also called leprosy. The authorities, fearful of its spread, decided to segregate some 700 lepers and confine them to an isolated settlement called Kalaupapa on the island of Molokai. When a missionary chaplain was required to minister to their needs, Father Damien volunteered, knowing from local wisdom that it was a "sentence of death". The local bishop Louis Maigret presented Damien (rather presumptuously) to the inhabitants of "the colony of death" as "one who will be a father to you, and who loves you so much that he does not hesitate to become one of you; to live and die with you".

Working in Molokai

When Damian arrived on Molokai it is said that he was so distressed to see the state of the lepers that he lay down under the shelter of a native *pandanus* tree and wept. His first tasks were not offering spiritual assistance but in bandaging wounds and helping to ease the sufferings of the afflicted. With no financial assistance or medical supplies forthcoming from the Hawaiian authorities, the conditions under which he worked were primitive and inadequate. On top of everything there was a certain lawlessness and unrest among the hopeless unfortunates that only made conditions worse.

Living conditions improved

He soon realised the importance of some basic infrastructure. Under his leadership basic laws were enforced to prevent violence, stealing and other crimes. Housing was built, mostly in the form of wooden shacks, and other structures were planned to include a community centre and a primitive hospital. Basic farming was implemented and markets organised. Yet because of the poor health of the people, physical work was beyond many of them and progress was slow and sporadic. In the midst of such problems Damien continued with his efforts, refusing to give in to what seemed a hopeless task.

> For a long time Father Damien was the only one to bring (the lepers) the succour they so greatly needed. He not only administered the consolations of religions, but also rendered them so little medical service and bodily comforts as were within his power. He dressed their ulcers, helped them erect their cottages, and went so far as to dig their graves, and make their coffins. After twelve years of this heroic service he discovered in himself the first symptoms of the disease. He nevertheless continued his charitable ministrations, being assisted in this period by two other priests and two lay brothers.
>
> The Catholic Encyclopedia

Damien's affliction and death

In December 1884, eleven years after his arrival, his worst fears were realised when he found that he had contracted leprosy. That was when he put his foot in scalding water and felt nothing. The first his parishioners knew of it was on Sunday morning when he began his sermon, not with the usual greeting "my dear brethren" but with the words "my fellow lepers". Residents say that despite this discovery Damien worked feverishly to build more houses and community facilities, sensing that his time was short:

> With help from only the few lepers that were not ready for the grave, he built cottages, an aquaduct, schools, a church, a dispensary. A husky peasant, the missionary dressed the rotting sores of his wards.
>
> Time magazine (1936)

During the next five years his leprosy got worse, leaving his face with what is described as the lepers look: leonine, patchy, with fierce eyes and thick lips. A Japanese doctor, Masanao Goto, came to Honolulu in 1885 and was visited by the ailing priest, but to no avail. Father Damien died of leprosy on April 15, 1889, aged 49. He was buried by his parishioners under the pandanus tree where he lay when he first arrived.

Attack on Damien

While Father Damien was working in Molokai he was subjected to a dismissive attack by a local religious minister from Honolulu, a Reverend C.M. Hyde, who was himself living in comfortable circumstances. The poet Robert Louis Stevenson, then on holiday in Hawaii, replied to his critical attack on Damien as "an uncouth, strong-headed and bigoted peasant" with an open letter hotly defending Damien's courage in living and working in a place that others, preferring their comforts, shunned. Calling Damien "one of the world's heroes and exemplars", his letter included the following moving testimony:

> We are not all expected to be Damiens:a man may love his comforts better... when we have failed, and another has succeeded; when we have stood by, and another has stepped in under the eyes of God, and succours the afflicted and consoles the dying, and is himself afflicted in his turn, and dies upon the field of honour it is easy to be critical... When I was pulled ashore (on Molokai) one early morning, there sat in the boat with me two sisters bidding farewell (in humble imitation of Damien) to the lights and joys of human life. One of these wept silently; I could not withhold myself from joining her... I never recall the days and nights I spent on that island promontory without heartfelt thankfulness that I am somewhere else.
>
> Robert Louis Stevenson

Mahatma Ghandi

Father Damien also received a remarkable commendation for his heroism from Mahatma Ghandi, who admitted that the leper priest was one of his inspirations. He wrote:

> "The political and journalistic world can boast of very few heroes who compare with Father Damien of Molokai. It is worthwhile to look for the sources of such heroics."

Tributes to Damien

In 2005, Damien was ranked "The Greatest Belgian" by the country's two leading public broadcasters. The story of his life was found to be so dramatic that several films have been made of his work. Father Damien has also inspired a number of organisations around the world concerned with the care of victims of diseases like AIDS and Hansen's Disease. Many, like the Damien Centre in Minneapolis, are named after him. Damien House in Cootehill, Ireland is another example.

> Damien House is a place of welcome, acceptance and peace for families and individuals affected by bereavement, stress, violence and other difficulties... Damien House takes its name from Father Damien de Veuster, a missionary who lived and worked with the lepers of Molokai, who brought hope where there was despair and acceptance where there was rejection.
>
> Damien House website

Veneration and sainthood

In 1936, in a joint move involving the Hawaiian authorities and the US and Belgian governments, the remains of father Damien were dug up and prepared for transfer to his native Belgium. They lay in state in Honolulu before boarding a US transport which transferred them to the Belgian schoolship *Mercator* bound for Antwerp. Following years of veneration Father Damien was canonised a saint on October 11, 2009 by Pope Benedict XVI in the presence of the King of Belgium and government ministers. Known today as Saint Damien of Molokai, his shrine is in Pater Damienplein in the centre of Louvain (Leuven). A statue of the leper priest stands outside the entrance of the Hawaii State Capitol Building on the island of O'ahu as a lasting recognition of his life and sacrifice.

Abbe Pierre (1912–2007)

The charity priest Abbe Pierre became one of the most loved and respected religious figures in France for over 70 years for his work on behalf of the poor and destitute. The *Emmaus Community,* now called *Emmaus International,* which he founded in 1949 is a legacy that will long outlive his memory. His fundamental humanity and transparent humility endeared him to millions, especially the homeless, the poor, the displaced and the rejected. When, after a series national polls, Abbe Pierre topped the list of the most popular figures in France, he asked to have his name deleted.

Early Life

Henri Groues was born in Lyon to a wealthy family of silk traders. During a school trip with his scout group to Assisi he became impressed by the life of St. Francis. The trip, he said later, brought "the process of my transformation to a head". At seventeen he entered the Capuchin's, a strict branch of the Franciscan Order. He marked his entry by renouncing his inheritance and giving all his possessions away to various charities.

Health problems

He stayed there for seven years but was advised to leave because of a lung infection and related ailments. The severity of the monastic life was not suitable for anyone in weak health, but he had already been spiritually influenced by his experience and knew that he wanted to give his life to the service of the poor. He wrote "those seven years in the cloister were the key to my life". After ordination as a priest in 1938 he began his clerical life as a curate in Grenoble just as war was breaking out.

French Resistance

By 1942 he became a local leader of the French Resistance in the area around Grenoble. His main task was to subvert Nazi operations. As a result he became a marked man and a local hero. Operating under several different names he was arrested twice by the Gestapo who, to their annoyance, each time allowed him to slip through their hands! After discovering that the Jews were being persecuted and sent off to labour and death camps (such as Auschwitz-Birkenau), he became actively involved in helping Jews to escape the terror. His biography states:

> "In July 1942, two fleeing Jews asked him for help. Having discovered the persecution taking place, he immediately went to learn how to make false passports. Starting in August 1942 he began guiding Jewish people to Switzerland."

War-time involvement

He eventually fled to Spain and Gibraltar before joining the Free French Forces of de Gaulle in Algeria, then part of France. Next he became a chaplain in the French Navy joining the battleship *Jean Bart* in Casablanca. His wartime experience was decisive in making him aware of the sufferings of the persecuted, and resolve to work actively, even at a political level, to improve the lot of the oppressed.

Political influence

Aware of the importance of political influence as a more effective way to get things done, Abbe Pierre decided to enter the political arena in the aftermath of the war. He eventually became an elected member of the National Assembly, much to the disapproval of his Church which normally forbade clerics to get involved in politics. In his new position be made friends with many notable figures such as the writers Albert Camus; Andre Gide; the theologian Teilhard de Chardin; the well-known Russian philosopher Nikolai Berdyaev; and the physicist Albert Einstein. His aim at all times was to seek the influence that would enable him to advance the cause of international peace and justice. In 1948 he met Einstein in Princeton where he succeeded in convincing him to pursue international nuclear disarmament.

Human rights activist

His colourful life continued in the the 1950's. In his travels as a determined advocate of human rights by peaceful means, he met the Colombian revolutionary Father Camilo Torres who was later killed; the US president Eisenhower; and King Mohammed V of Morocco. But he was also fortunate to escape two serious accidents. In 1950 he survived a plane crash on a visit to India, and in 1963 he survived shipwreck in the Rio de la Plata by clinging to flotsam while over 80 people perished.

Mission to the homeless

He eventually became disillusioned with all political work, and returned to his original vocation of helping the dispossessed. By 1949 he had in mind a charity that would provide shelter for homeless people. Two years later he bought a large run-down house in the outskirts of Paris and did all the repairs himself. This was to be the foundation of the organisation with which he would always be associated, the *Emmaus Community*.

Emmaus Community

> Our guiding principle is one which is essential to the whole human race if there is to be any life worth living, and any true peace and happiness either for the individual or society: serve those worse off than yourself before yourself. Serve the needy first.
>
> Universal Manifesto of Emmaus International

The name was derived from the village mentioned in the Gospel of Luke where two disciples offered hospitality to Jesus without recognising who he was. But despite its Christian inspiration the Emmaus Community was to be an all-embracing organisation aimed at offering hospitality to homeless people regardless of their colour, race or creed. Always on the lookout for opportunities to raise funds, Abbe Pierre entered a Radio Luxembourg game show and won the top prize of 850,000 francs! In the freezing winter of 1954 he used his fame by broadcasting the need to help homeless people, many of whom were dying on the streets. He immediately set up Fraternal Aid Centres, calling on people: "if you suffer, whoever you are, enter, eat, sleep, recover hope, here you are loved".

How Emmaus works

In 1954 *Emmaus Communites* were officially formed. The original idea was to have volunteers help groups of homeless people by offering them food, accommodation, and eventually, if possible, work. Later the emphasis was on helping the homeless to work for themselves, thus raising their own sense of worth. Communities began selling donated furniture and other used goods with a view to supporting themselves and enlarging their accommodation. By the end of the 1950's *Emmaus* had begun to spread worldwide. In 1959 the first *Emmaus* was founded in Beirut with the help of a Sunni Muslim and a Catholic Archbishop! Today there are Emmaus Communities throughout the world offering food, help and shelter to the homeless.

World influence

Throughout his life Abbe Pierre used his influence wherever he could to improve the lot of people who were deprived or oppressed. He saw that many of the evils of the world were caused by man-made conflicts that led to war and devastation, usually adding to the misery and destitution of the already poor. Seizing opportunities to help wherever he could, he often travelled to trouble spots as a mediator and peacemaker. In his later travels he met important national leaders including US Presidents Bush, and Iraq's Saddam Hussein. He spoke out frequently against the evils of racism, apartheid and anti-Semitism and called for a strengthening of the UN's work on behalf of refugees. As an international figure of respect, his work received patronage and support from many well-known figures.

Honours and awards

At the end of the war he was awarded the prestigious *Croix de Guerre,* and the *Medaille de la Resistance.* In 1988, in recognition of his work, he was made Grand Officer of the National Order of Quebec, and given the high French award of Grand Cross of the Legion of Honour. In 1991, he was awarded the prestigious International Balzan Prize for Humanity, Peace and Brotherhood:

> "For having fought, throughout his life, for the defence of human rights, democracy and peace. For having entirely dedicated himself to helping to relieve spiritual and physical suffering. For having inspired—regardless of nationality, race or religion—universal solidarity with the Emmaus Communities."

Rebel figure re-instated

Abbe Pierre was a controversial figure within his Church, coming in for severe criticism for his political and social involvement, activities considered unbecoming for a priest. Yet at the end, his sacrifices and achievements were recognised at the highest level. At his death, the Vatican sent this message:

> "Informed of the death of Abbe Pierre, the Holy Father gives thanks for his activity in favour of the poorest, by which he bore witness to the charity that comes from Christ. Entrusting to divine mercy this priest whose whole life was dedicated to fighting poverty, he asks the Lord to welcome him into the peace of His kingdom."

Death of Abbe Pierre

Abbe Pierre continued with an active life until his death on January 22, 2007. He died at the Val-de-Grace military hospital in Paris. With homage paid by international dignitaries, his funeral took place in Notre Dame Cathedral, Paris, attended by the French President, Ministers and members of the government.

Abbe Pierre quotes

> "After the war, prompted by the Cardinal Archbishop of Paris, I entered Parliament so that a priest could speak out for the poor."

> "Hope is not a matter of age."

> "Illness has always brought me nearer to a state of grace."

> "Providence was well aware of what lay ahead of me, and my Capuchin training was to prepare me for it."

"It's true that humanity has seen a succession of crises, wars and atrocities, but this negative side is offset by advances in technology and cultural exchanges."

"My family background was deeply Christian."

"People are needed to take up the challenge, strong people who proclaim the truth, throw it in people's faces, and do what they can with their own two hands."

"The process of my transformation came with my discovery of St. Francis of Assisi during a pilgrimage I went on with a scout group from my school."

"What I would say to young men and women who are beset by hopelessness and doubt is that they should go and see what is being done on the ground to fight poverty, not like going to the zoo but to take action, to open their hearts and their consciences."

"When they are assailed by despair, young people should let universal concerns enter their lives."

Leonard Cheshire (1917–1992)

Leonard Cheshire was a distinguished bomber pilot for the RAF, returning unscathed from more bombing sorties than any other pilot, with 102 missions. This was all the more remarkable considering his moral preference for the low-level bombing of enemy positions, which was always a higher risk to the pilot, but reduced the risk of unnecessary death of civilians. Cheshire ended up as the most decorated pilot of world war two, the highest of which was the prestigious Victoria Cross, awarded for: "an extended period of sustained courage and outstanding effort". This was to distinguish the award for repeated acts of courage in situations of danger, rather than for the normal single act of valour, making him one of the great war heroes of Great Britain. In a BBC poll of the 100 Greatest Britons he was voted number 31. His VC is on display in the Imperial War Museum in London.

> In one raid he flew his Lancaster bomber low over a factory in Limoges three times, to warn women workers, before dropping his marker on a fourth run. The factory was flattened but not one French worker died.
>
> Daily Mail article 2006

Early years

The son of an eminent professor of law, Geoffrey Leonard Cheshire was born in Chester, but was brought up in Oxford. During his student days he was no saint. Famed for his liking of drink, women and fast cars he believed in living life to the full. But this did not stop him from graduating in law from Merton College in 1939, just before the war broke out. The following year he joined the RAF and fought in the Battle of Britain, receiving the DSO for flying his badly damaged aircraft back to base. Rising steadily up the ranks, he became a Squadron Leader in 1942, and the following year rose to the rank of Group Captain.

Low level bombing techniques

When he was posted as commander of the legendary 617 "Dambusters" Squadron flying over Nazi Germany he developed the new, controversial, and risky strategy of low level bombing. This was the most humane form of bombing. In contrast to carpet bombing, which was indiscriminate, it limited casualties to specific targets and saved lives. He also developed low-level marking techniques which greatly increased bombing accuracy but which left the fighter pilot much more exposed to counter-attack.

> "In four years of fighting against the bitterest opposition he maintained a standard of outstanding personal achievement, his successful operations being the result of careful planning, brilliant execution, and supreme contempt for danger—for example on one occasion he flew his B-51 Mustang in slow figures of 8 above a target obscured by low cloud, to act as a bomb-aiming mark for his squadron. Cheshire displayed the courage and determination of an exceptional leader . . . Later over Munich he flew his Mosquito at low level against withering fire."
>
> Citation for the Victoria Cross

Observer of atom bomb

On the occasion of his 103rd mission he was the official British observer of the dropping of the atomic bomb on Nagasaki in 1943. The experience affected him deeply. Its destructive power left him with serious doubts about the future of war, and, understandably, about the future of civilisation. Soon afterwards it was time to leave the RAF and he returned to his home *Le Court* in Hampshire.

Religious conversion

After the war Leonard Cheshire underwent a religious conversion and joined the Catholic Church. He had already been a Christian of sorts but had abandoned any practical belief in religion. Some trace his changed views to a conversation with an apparently agnostic lady in the Vanity Fair Club in London in 1945. After telling her that "God existed only as a convenient figure of speech ... and was invented to explain the voice of conscience", she rebuked him for "talking such rot". Later he saw the Christian faith as having the much-needed potential to unite people in a new fellowship at a time of rising international tensions:

> I see no final solution to the problem of the world, except by establishing a Christian fellowship of mankind ... the forces of good both active and passive must be mobilized and encouraged to fight the forces of evil.
> Leonard Cheshire (1945)

Wounded ex-servicemen

After his retirement from active service he became aware of the number of wounded or ill ex-servicemen who had nobody to care for them. He decided it would be a small gesture to make his home at Le Court available to such people. A man of great practical awareness and attention to detail, he saw the need to acquire nursing skills in order to look after the people in his care. His first guest was Arthur Dykes who had terminal cancer. By the time he died in 1948 there were 24 people staying at Le Court.

Cheshire Homes

This was the beginning of the Cheshire Homes, a charitable organisation that would become worldwide, specialising in caring for people with disability regardless of its cause (many of its patients are the result of road accidents). Today, the organisation he founded is called *Leonard Cheshire Disability*. It supports 21,000 disabled people in the UK, and works in 52 countries worldwide. It is one of the top British charities.

> Leonard Cheshire Disability changes attitudes to disability and supports people with disabilities and their right to participate fully in society. Working with partners in over 50 countries, we support more than 250 independently managed disability organisations.
> LCD website

Sue Ryder Care

In 1959 Cheshire married Sue Ryder, an equally devout Christian, who herself became the founder of another humanitarian charity, Sue Ryder Care. They worked for many years together as well-known husband and wife devoted to their charities.

> Sue Ryder Care is dedicated to helping people get the best from life. We specialise in palliative care, neurological care and home care. We provide expertise where people need it, maximising and supporting their choices and independence.
>
> SRC website

Death and legacy

Leonard Cheshire was increasingly hampered by ill-health during the 1980's when he contracted Motor Neurone Disease. He died on 31 July 1992, and was buried in Cavendish in Suffolk. Despite his illustrious war record, he is mainly remembered today for his peacetime legacy.

> **OBITUARY**
> Leonard Cheshire was one of the most remarkable men of his generation, perhaps the most remarkable. A war hero and pioneer of the Cheshire Homes for sick people ... he had the priceless gift of appearing ordinary while accomplishing quite extraordinary achievements in war and peace ... Of warm and friendly personality, he was always quietly spoken but with a most compelling presence and an almost hypnotic gaze. His almost schoolboyish sense of humour never deserted him ... He will be profoundly missed but his memory and his work will live on.
>
> The Independent, 1 August 1992

Leonard Cheshire quotes

> "We need a vision, a dream. The vision should be the oneness, the essential organic solidarity of the human family. The dream, that each in our own way make our personal contribution towards building unity and peace among us."

> "As I reflect on the years I have spent among disabled people, I see them as men and women who are at the forefront of our common struggle, just as in a different way were those amongst whom I served during the war."

"Firstly, the most fundamental of all, the really important thing for us to do is to empty ourselves . . . it is the emptying of everything self-centred, even if it is a good thing. Your attachment to earthly things is dissolved so that God can fill you totally."

Jean Vanier (1928–)

Jean Vanier is a French Canadian Christian who has become renowned for his work on behalf of the mentally disabled in society. Rejecting the common view that the disabled are a burden on society, he sees them instead as an unappreciated asset, often showing insights into the human condition that the more able bodied and able minded are blind to. As a result of his own close association with the disabled by living amongst them, he has emerged as a modern-day prophet, broadcasting as often as he can how much they have to offer. In his writings and lectures he brings his great intellectual powers and spiritual insights to underline how much we can learn from the disabled about ourselves, our frustrations, our strengths and our weaknesses, the way we think, and above all what matters in life. He is renowned as a profound thinker on the human condition whose writings are widely read across many languages and cultures. His organization, *L'Arche,* is one of the leading humanitarian charities in the world dedicated to helping the mentally and intellectually disabled.

Early years

Jean Vanier is the son of the 19th Governor General of Canada, but he was born in 1928 in Geneva while his father was on diplomatic service in Switzerland. He was educated in England and lived for awhile in Canada where his family had settled. During world war two he served in the Royal Navy and the Royal Canadian Navy. In 1950 he resigned from the navy to study philosophy and theology at the Institut Catholique in Paris. There he met Thomas Philippe, a Dominican priest who was later to be chaplain to a small institution for men with disabilities in Trosly-Breuil, in northern France. In the meantime he returned to Canada to take up a teaching post at the University of Toronto. But he remained drawn to the vision of giving his life for the disabled. Vanier decided to leave the academic life and do humanitarian work with Thomas Philippe. They bought a house in Trosly-Breuil and named it *L'Arche*.

L'Arche

L'Arche reaches out to people with a range of "developmental" (physical, mental or intellectual) disabilities. At a practical level it is dedicated to the creation and development of homes, therapy programmes and support networks, all directed to the care and welfare of those with such disabilities. Vanier was resolved to find ways to get the disabled out of institutions, where they tended to be treated as insignificant and useless. His aim was raise their morale by giving them an experience of love and care in an environment where they could enjoy a level of personal independence that would enable them to flourish as human beings. The name "L'Arche" (the French for "ark"), was a clear reference to Noah's Ark, the archetypal haven of protection and safety in the midst of a hostile world. *L'Arche* represents a place of refuge for the weak and vulnerable of society, people who would otherwise find themselves cast aside as unproductive, and therefore useless, in the judgement of a materialistic and utilitarian age. In the philosophy of Jean Vanier, people should not be devalued for how useless they are, but valued for what they are, human beings with an inherent dignity and worth. But he also believes the disabled have much to teach the more able: the value of life, and a sense of what is important and what is not.

> Jean Vanier is first and foremost committed to the person with an intellectual disability. Indeed, it is his experience of a shared life with people with an intellectual disability that allowed him to develop his vision of what it means to become human.
>
> Jean Vanier website

Learning from the disabled

Vanier envisaged a community where the able-minded and the disabled are in partnership. This means that, wherever possible, the carers should live with the cared-for so that both can come to a better appreciation of their mutual dignity as human beings. Vanier, therefore, considers himself no great hero. Living with the disabled himself, he believes he has received more from them than he has given to them. He believes that the disabled can teach us much about ourselves, and much that stands in the way of our own development as human beings. He is especially convinced that learning from the disabled is a healing process in which we learn the importance of giving as the pathway to receiving. Aware that there is nobody who can consider themselves beyond improvement, and that many are indeed in need of some form of healing, Vanier believes that the disabled can be ignored only at cost to ourselves, that they are witnesses to a truth that applies in the outside world as well: nobody, however self-sufficient, can survive without the help of others. As he puts it:

> "Those we lock away and think worthless have the power to teach and even heal us... When you start living with people with disabilities you begin to discover a whole lot of things about yourself... To be human is to be bonded together, each with our own weaknesses and strengths, because we need each other."

Dignity and worth

The need for coming together in communities of mutual sharing is one of Jean Vanier deepest convictions, as he sees today's society dominated by selfish interest, worldly success and the cult of the useful. He sees the utilitarian trend of casting the disabled on the rubbish heap of society the result of a lost vision of the spiritual dignity of man, one which had prevailed in the past. He considers *L'Arche* an important witness to that dignity, but not in a patronising way as if the disabled were in some way inferior beings.

L'Arche International

Now heavily committed to the expansion of L'Arche, Vanier began giving lectures, conferences and retreats in various countries calling attention to the plight of the disabled. These became the inspiration for the various branches of L'Arche that now exist worldwide. From the original seminal community that Vanier founded, there are today 131 L'Arche communities scattered throughout Europe, Africa, Asia, Australia, and in North and South America offering shelter and support to disabled of every background, race and creed.

Supporting organisations

Not content to rest with L'Arche, in 1968 Jean Vanier became co-founder of Faith and Sharing, and Faith and Light, two organizations aimed at helping families with a disabled member. These groups meet once a month for prayer, mutual support, friendship and celebration. In the early 1990's he founded Intercordia, providing university students with an academically credited cross-cultural experience of social education and personal growth among marginalized people in the developing world. In this way young people come to realize the needs and value of the disabled in society as they stand on the threshold of their own professional lives.

Honours and awards

Jean Vanier has been showered with international honours and awards for his work, including the French Legion d'Honneur, the Companion of the Order of Canada , the Rabbi Gunther Plaut Humanitarian Award, the Chicago Catholic Theological Union "Blessed are the Peacemakers" Award, and many more. Despite his busy writing and speaking schedules (his books have been translated into 27 languages) and his widespread travels, he continues to live with the disabled in the original l'Arche community home at Trosly in France.

Jean Vanier quotes

"Envy comes from people's ignorance of, or lack of belief in, their own gifts."

"Growth begins when we begin to accept our own weakness."

"Life is a succession of crises and moments when we have to discover who we are and what we really want."

"But in another way community is a terrible place. It is a place where our limitations and our egoism are revealed to us . . . We discover . . . our insatiable desires, our frustrations and jealousies, our hatred and our wish to destroy."

"Community begins in mystery and ends in administration. Leaders move away from people and into paper."

"The Word became flesh to communicate to us human beings caught in the mud, the pain, the fears and the brokenness of existence, the life, the joy, the communion, the ecstatic gift of love that is the source of all love and life and unity in our universe and that is the very life of God."

"Courage is doing what you're afraid to do. There can be no courage unless you're scared."

"Those who cannot change their minds cannot change anything."

"Sometimes it is the smallest decisions that can change your life forever."

"What you leave behind is not what is engraved in stone monuments but what is woven into the lives of others."

"To be lonely is to feel unwanted and unloved, and therefore unloveable. Loneliness is a taste of death. No wonder some people who are desperately lonely lose themselves in mental illness or violence to forget the inner pain."

"Every child, every person needs to know that they are a source of joy; every child, every person needs to be celebrated. Only when all of our weaknesses are accepted as part of our humanity can our negative, broken self-images be transformed."

"When children are loved they live off trust; their hearts open up to those who respect and love them, who understand and listen to them."

Chad Varah (1911–2007)

Chad Varah is remembered today for the organisation he founded in the crypt of his London church in 1953, known worldwide as the Samaritans. Although inspired by Varah's Christian concern, Samaritans, the world's first telephone crisis hotline, is open to everyone regardless of colour, race or creed. Its purpose is to provide immediate counselling, understanding and support for those in serious mental distress, particularly those on the verge of suicide. Many were aware of the problem, but it took Chad Varah to do something to solve it.

Early years

Edward Chad Varah was born in Barton, Lincolnshire, eldest of nine children and son of the local vicar of the Anglican church of St. Chad's from whom he was said to inherit the inconvenient habit of blurting out unpopular truths. With a memory by which he was able to remember every poem he ever learnt, he shone academically and gained a scholarship to Keble College, Oxford. In 1833, he graduated in Philosophy, Politics and Economics, but did little work and earned a third. In 1936 he was ordained as Anglican priest, and in 1940 he married Doris, with whom he had four sons and a daughter. He served in various London parishes, making a name for his unconventionally permissive beliefs. Described by the *Telegraph* as "a dynamic, combative priest of generous disposition and immense compassion, especially for those with sexual problems, he was quite unshockable". But it was his understanding attitude to those in distress that inspired him. After his posting to the Church of St. Stephen Walbrook in 1953 he founded the Samaritans, which began operating from the crypt of the building, using the famous telephone number MAN 9000.

Samaritans

Chad Varah became aware of the problem of mental distress leading to suicidal feelings when he officiated at a funeral of a young girl who had taken her life because she had tragically misunderstood the onset of her menstruation. The incident was the culmination of his awareness that depression and despair were common problems in society at the time. He said: "Little girl, I didn't know you, but you have changed the rest of my life for good". From that moment he resolved to start an organisation to befriend "the suicidal and despairing". These were people, he knew, whose troubles were so profound that they had nobody to turn to in their direst moments.

Samaritans and Befrienders worldwide

Samaritans now has 202 branches in the UK and Ireland, with 15,000 volunteers providing emotional support around the clock. They do this by patiently listening (also nowadays corresponding through www.samaritans.org) to and with people in desperate straits, many of them contemplating suicide. Its international arm, *Befrienders Worldwide,* of which he was founder chairman and president for 12 years, works in more than 40 countries. The rise of the Samaritans was matched by a dramatic fall in the suicide rate, but the effect of its work is not so easily measured. By speaking to a Samaritan many are helped through difficult times and, in the normal case, if disasters are averted they make no news. Its many branches in Britain and around the world handle millions of calls every year.

Sexuality and relationships

Varah campaigned vigorously for better sex education, the rights of women, and other issues that cause human distress. He found that one of the greatest causes of distress were problems to do with sexuality and relationships: sexual exploitation, pregnancy, infidelity, desertion and divorce. He campaigned for greater tolerance towards drug addiction, HIV and AIDS suffers, was a supporter of gay rights, and was patron of the Terrence Higgins Trust, the AIDS charity.

Worldwide traveller

He also had other skills. To supplement his income he wrote the script for the spaceman Dan Dare of the Eagle comic for several years in the 1950's. He also travelled widely abroad, seeking ways to extend the work of offering solace to the depressed and despairing. Every year from 1974 to 1986 he travelled the equivalent of twice around the world encouraging the work of Samaritans overseas. Humorous by nature, he enjoyed sending letters to his friends from various locations. From the African country that bore his name he wrote: "Love from Chad, from Chad"!

> Chad was quite simply an extraordinary man, and his legacy is a strengthened Samaritans which seeks to make emotional health part of everyday conversation... Samaritans believe that offering people the opportunity to be listened to in confidence, and accepted without prejudice, can alleviate despair and suicidal feelings. Chad's vision—of a society in which people are able explore their feelings without fear or prejudice, in turn respecting the feelings of others—has touched millions of people in the 54 years since we started offering emotional support.
>
> Dominic Rudd, Chief Executive, Samaritans

Honours and awards

Chad Varah received numerous honours and awards in recognition of his humanitarian work and achievements. He was awarded the Albert Schweitzer Gold Medal in 1972; the Romanian Patriarchal Cross, and numerous honorary doctorates. He received the CBE in 1995; and was created Companion of Honour (CH) in 2000. He died on November 9, 2007.

> **OBITUARY**
> Chad Varah, founder of the Samaritans, has died in hospital, aged 95. The Prince of Wales led the tributes last night, describing Varah as an "utterly remarkable man" whose dedication has saved countless lives. "He was an outstanding humanitarian and a great Briton", the prince added... The Archbishop of Canterbury said he had made "a unique contribution to the life of our whole society, changing attitudes to suicide and bringing a distinctively pastoral and non-judgemental approach to people in need".
>
> The Guardian, 9 September 2007

Chad Varah quotes

> "(Listening) is a rare quality. (Samaritans) are in fact people who cannot bring themselves to pass by on the other side when somebody's needing them."

> "God intervened to supply the church with its memorable telephone number MAN 9000, ideal for an emergency helpline."

> "For people in distress there is nothing like a sympathetic ear."

> "Whenever I hear myself referred to as the Founder of the Samaritans I want to protest. The first of them found me, and without them the Samaritans would not exist."

Mother Teresa (1910–1997)

Few women in the world in the second half of the 20th century were better known than Mother Teresa of Calcutta. She had worked quietly for a number of years helping the poor and destitute of the city's slums. But in 1971 a programme featuring her work by the well-known television personality Malcolm Muggeridge (see above) brought her international fame. She was awarded the Nobel Peace Prize in 1987, and after her death ten years later she was declared by the Pope "Blessed Teresa" of Calcutta. In a remarkable tribute, Time magazine ranked her among the century's 100 most influential people.

Early years

Agnes Gonxcha Bojaxhiu was born in Skopie, Albania. When she was seven her father was murdered. At the age of 18 she travelled to Ireland to join the Sisters of Loreto, a teaching order of nuns with missions in India. After completing her training she was posted to Calcutta where she began teaching at St. Mary's High School. She remained there for seventeen years but became gradually disenchanted by the ivory tower nature of her life and work. The classroom seemed a long way from the grim realities of life around her. She said: "I wanted to leave the convent and help the poor while living among them . . . to fail would have been to break the faith".

Working in the slums

Calcutta had become well known for having the worst slums in India. People crowded into these desperately poor areas with few material resources, and often in poor health from malnutrition and disease. In Teresa's view, their biggest deprivation was spiritual as much as material: they were abandoned souls, ignored by society as wretched nobodies. Her mission then took shape: to offer some care and comfort to these people. From the first, Teresa found helpers to join her in her mission. They went among the poor, offering whatever care they could with limited resources. As time went by funds came in, and she was able to build emergency facilities: a clinic, a temporary shelter, an open-air school for slum children.

Missionaries of Charity

Realising the scale of the problem she decided, in 1950, to from a group of sisters who would dedicate themselves to the care of the poor, in the spirit of Christ. These became the Missionaries of Charity, a religious order of nuns officially sanctioned by the Pope, with Teresa as its Mother Superior. Today 4000 Sisters are operating some 610 mission centres in 130 countries, providing a range of services all directed to those whom Teresa called the "poorest of the poor".

Relief programmes

They provide help for victims of epidemics, natural disasters, and famine. They run hospices for the dying; homes for people with HIV/AIDS, drug addicts and alcoholics; tend victims of leprosy and tuberculosis; and other relief programmes. Its mission, in the words of its founder was to help: "the poorest of the poor ... those whom nobody was prepared to look after". Today the sisters have over one million Co-Workers in more than forty countries offering aid and support to people of all backgrounds, regardless of colour, class or creed.

Test of faith

But despite the strength of her Christian faith, Mother Teresa has admitted to feeling at times overpowered by the mammoth tasks she had undertaken, and being subject to moments of disappointment and frustration, if not despair. In a letter to her spiritual confidant she wrote, poignantly:

> "Jesus has a very special love of you. As for me the silence and the emptiness is so great, that I look and do not see—listen and do not hear—the tongue moves (in prayer) but does not speak ... I want you to pray for me ... that I let (God) have a free hand."

Faith and courage

To many people Mother Teresa remained an enigma during her life for her selfless dedication in working under conditions that most people would find impossible. To persevere for over 60 years in work that was physically strenuous, emotionally draining, and endlessly frustrating because of its no-quick-fix nature, was a sort of miracle. Denied the human satisfaction of seeing her patients ever escape the prison of poverty, or any chance that the problems she dealt with would ever be really solved, it took a super-human level of endurance to live and work as she did. As she put it: "Do not think that love, in order to be genuine, needs to be extraordinary. What is needed is to care without getting tired".

The enigma of inspiration

But this is to beg the question: what kept her going? To her fellow Christians the enigma of her life could partly, if not wholly, be explained in religious terms using the categories of vocation, grace, and divine inspiration. She could also be easily fitted within the tradition of heroic leaders whose lives were similarly faith-inspired. But to the ordinary observer, including the journalists and media figures that came to see her work, her ability to serve the poor without hope of earthly reward was simply another part of the enigma of human existence that defies explanation.

Honours and awards

In 1962 she received the Ramon Magsaysay Award (Philippines) for:

> "her merciful cognizance of the abject poor of a foreign land, in whose service she led a new congregation."

In 1972 she was awarded the Nehru Prize (India) for "her promotion of international peace and understanding". In 1985 she was awarded the Presidential Medal of Freedom (USA) by Ronald Reagan. But her biggest award was the Nobel Peace Prize in 1987. The Nobel citation recognised that her heroic efforts on behalf of the poor had been an inspiration to others, and in consequence was a significant contribution to the making of a better, more peaceful, world. As the citation put it, her award was:

> "For work undertaken in the struggle to overcome poverty and distress, which also constitutes a threat to peace."

In accepting the Nobel Prize, Mother Teresa said: "I am grateful to receive this Prize in the name of the hungry, the naked, the homeless . . . all those who feel unwanted, unloved, uncared for . . . people who have become a burden to the society and are shunned by everyone."

Death of Mother Teresa

Mother Teresa died of a heart attack on 5 September 1997 at the Sisters of Charity convent in Calcutta. Her body lay in state for a week, and she was given a state funeral by the Indian government in recognition of her life-long humanitarian work. Her remains were carried on the same gun carriage as Mahatma Gandhi and Jawaharial Nehru, while hymns were sung in Bengali, Hindi and English. In an extraordinary piece, Time magazine paid tribute to her moral example in catering for people in need, regardless of their background, race or origin, setting an example to a world all too ready to divide people into insiders and outsiders:

> "In fighting for the dignity of the destitute in a foreign land, she gave the world a moral example that bridged the divides of culture, class and religion. In this era of "ethnic cleansing", identity politics, and the dislocation of communities, it is heartening that one of the most marginalized people in recent history—a minority Albanian inside Slavic Macedonia, a minority Roman Catholic among Muslims and Orthodox Christians should find a home, citizenship and acceptance in an Indian city of countless non-Christians. She blurred the line between insider and outsider that many today are trying to deepen."
>
> Time Magazine 1999

Mother Teresa quotes

"I see God in every human being. When I wash the leper's wounds, I feel I am nursing the Lord himself."

"The other day I dreamt I was at the gates of heaven. St. Peter said 'Go back to Earth. There are no slums up here.'"

"Do not wait for leaders. Do it alone, person to person."

"Even the rich are hungry for love."

"Being unwanted, unloved, uncared for, forgotten by everybody. I think that is a greater poverty than the person who has nothing to eat."

"Every time you smile at some one, it is an action of love, a gift to that person, a beautiful thing."

"I know God will not give me anything I cannot handle. I just wish he didn't trust me so much!."

"I do not pray for success. I ask for faithfulness."

"It is a poverty to decide that a child must die so that you may live as you wish."

"One of the greatest diseases is to be nobody to anybody."

"The miracle is not that we do this work, but that we are happy to do it."

"There must be a reason why some people can afford to live well. They must have worked for it."

"I only feel angry when I see waste. When I see people throwing away things that we could use."

"Words which do not give the light of Christ increase the darkness."

Modern Activists

Trevor Huddleston (1913–1998)

> "I can remember a strange little incident when I was 12 or 13 years old. It was Christmas time and my father was at home. The night was quite cold and dark and I remember a knock at the door and I saw the face of an Indian at the window. My father, in a civilised way, told him "No there is nothing here for you." I thought this was a terrible thing, not only because he was black, but he was poor, and I couldn't believe that at Christmas you could turn anybody away."
>
> Trevor Huddleston

Trevor Huddleston was an Anglican parish priest who became internationally famous for his contribution to human inclusivity, seeing those of different colour and race as all too worthy to be invited in to the white man's table. Standing up for his black parishioners during the notorious years of apartheid in South Africa, he was attacked and villianised as an interfering outsider. So big a thorn did he become in the side of the apartheid regime, that he was expelled from the country for challenging the justice of its laws. He was praised and honoured by the anti-apartheid movement, the African National Congress, and was specially singled out for his work and courage by the later South African president, Nelson Mandela.

Early years

Born in Bedford, he studied at Lancing College, Sussex and Christ Church, Oxford. In 1939, he joined the Community of the Resurrection in Mirfield, Yorkshire, where he took the vows of poverty, chastity and obedience before being ordained for the Anglican ministry. In 1943, he was sent as priest-in-charge of the parish of Sophiatown, a black residential area of Johannesburg. There he came to appreciate the dignity of his black parishioners, and became devoted to ending the misery caused by apartheid. In his own words, he felt that fighting against the apartheid system was: "a moral battle against something profoundly evil, something that did not come to me through academic reading or study, but through its impact on the people I had responsibility for as a priest."

Apartheid

Apartheid, a system of segregation unique to South Africa, was a division of people on the basis of colour, one that was enforced by law. Under the system blacks had no equality with whites, and were *legally* made inferior. They were truly second-class citizens, with limited opportunities to gain employment; were denied equal wages with whites; and were denied access to the kinds of services and facilities (medical, educational, etc) that whites took for granted. Not only were they forbidden to live in areas designated "for whites only" (the best areas), they were often herded into so-called "townships." These were usually sited in remote and desolate areas distinctive for their overcrowding, poor housing and general material deprivation, conditions that, not surprisingly, often led to social unrest and violence.

Sophiatown

Sophiatown, a district of Johannesburg, was among many black areas that eventually came to be bulldozed and its people uprooted, transported away to the dreaded townships. Before that happened, Huddleston became a beacon of hope for the people, earning the nickname "Makhalipile" (the dauntless one). But he knew he was not alone. He was personal friends with other great opponents of apartheid such as Walter Sisulu, Oliver Tambo and Nelson Mandela of the Africa National Congress. In his own words: "I had to declare myself fully in supporting the resistance movement of the ANC. As a Christian priest that was what I had to do". He then wrote an article for the Observer attacking the Church in Britain for its failure to speak out against this evil and, by remaining silent, condoning it.

Honoured by ANC

Trevor Huddleston became so admired for his work that in 1955 the ANC did him the rare honour of bestowing on him the title "Isitwalandwe", meaning "the one who wears the plumes of the rare bird".

This was originally a tribal title reserved for the bravest warriors of the people, those who distinguished themselves for showing exceptional qualities of heroism and leadership. But it evolved in time into the *Medal of Honour* the highest award given by the South African people.

Expelled from South Africa

In 1956 he decided to go public with a book called *Nought for Your Comfort,* a devastating criticism of the apartheid system, and a stirring account of the struggle for freedom by black Africans. The book's title was derived from a poem of G. K. Chesterton (see above):

> *I tell you naught for your comfort,*
> *Yea, nought for your desire,*
> *Save the sky grows darker yet,*
> *And the sea rises higher.*

As a result of the impact of the book he was expelled from South Africa as an undesirable. He was recalled to England where he worked for awhile as Master of Novices for his order. In 1960, he was appointed Bishop of Masasi in Tanzania where he served from 1960 to 1968.

Later that year he was back in England again to take up an appointment as Bishop of Stepney, an area of London's east end full of racial tensions fanned by extremists.

International activist

In 1978, he was appointed bishop of Mauritius, retiring five years later to devote himself to travelling the world, lobbying governments to impose economic sanctions against South Africa and raising funds for the anti-apartheid movement. In 1981, he became President of the Anti-apartheid movement, a position he held until his death. But he never lived to see the end of the apartheid system.

Tributes and awards

In 1982 he was awarded the United Nations Gold Medal in recognition of his humanitarian work. In 1994 he was awarded the Torch of Kilimanjaro by Tanzania. In the year of his death he was made Knight Commander of the Order of St. Michael and St. George (KCMG). After his death he received a host of tributes from around the world, including the following from other anti-apartheid leaders in South Africa, by whom he was held in highest regard:

> "If you could say that anyone single-handedly made apartheid a world issue then that person was Trevor Huddleston."
>
> Archbishop Desmond Tutu
>
> "It is humbling for an ordinary mortal like myself to express the deep sense of loss at the death of so great and venerable figure... At a time when identifying with the cause of the equality of all South Africans was seen as the height of betrayal by the privileged, Huddleston embraced the downtrodden... He forsook all that apartheid South Africa offered the privileged minority. And did so at great risk to his personal safety and wellbeing... Father Huddleston was a pillar of wisdom, humility and sacrifice to the legions of freedom fighters in the darkest moments of the struggle against apartheid. His memory will live in the hearts of our people."
>
> President Nelson Mandela
>
> "We will always know him as a symbol of the justice of God, and a personification of the sacrificial love which gives life to all people."
>
> SA Anglican Bishops
>
> "He was a friend to all, a man of God, a committed churchman... he will be sadly missed for his profound liberation-theological insights."
>
> SA Catholic Bishops

Death

Trevor Huddleston died on April 20, 1998. One of his last wishes was that his ashes be spread near the church he served in Sophiatown. A commemorative window honours him in Lancing college chapel where he went to school. A memorial bust stands in the centre of Bedford where he was born, bearing the words of Nelson Mandela: "No white person has done more for South Africa than Trevor Huddleston".

> Whenever Trevor Huddleston spoke, however firmly, he sounded almost the caricature of the kindly, cultivated English vicar who might join you for tea on the lawn after croquet. Tall, pale and sweet-faced, he seemed an unlikely champion of poor, black South Africa against the bully boys of the South African police.
>
> Obituary, The Economist

Trevor Huddleston quotes

"God bless Africa. Guard her people, Guide her leaders. Give her peace."

"I wish to devote myself full-time to the South Africa I love."

"I always said I wanted to see apartheid dead before I am, so they got to get a move on!"

"My responsibility is always and everywhere the same: to see in my brother even more than the personality and manhood that is his . . . to see Christ himself."

> "Although he disparaged empty words, this man of action, who also lived a deeply contemplative life, inspired the world to action through his eloquent denunciation of our condition and the realities of forced removal and bantu education. His courage was not only of the kind which is needed to choose difficult and unpopular paths. He was also fearless where others might shrink from personal and physical danger . . . He did so not in any abstract and distant way. His sacrifices for our freedom . . . told of our capacity, on the basis of our common humanity, to touch one another's hearts across the social divides and across the oceans. In Father Huddleston we see exemplified in the most concrete way the contribution that religion has made to our liberation. Whenever the noble ideals and values of religion have been joined with practical action to realise them, it has strengthened us and at the same time nurtured those ideals within the political movement . . . He brought hope, sunshine and comfort to the poorest of the poor."
>
> Nelson Mandela (1998)

Desmond Tutu (1931–)

Long recognised internationally as a man of immense moral authority, he used his position as a prominent church leader to become a fearless critic of the apartheid system in South Africa. Outraged by the discrimination and injustice that apartheid represented, Desmond Tutu made it his job to call attention to the social and moral evils that it continued to perpetuate at the expense of black people. In 1988, as a voice of the oppressed, he declared his growing dissatisfaction with the South African authorities, saying: "we refuse to be treated as a doormat for the government to wipe its jackboots on." Since the ending of apartheid, he has continued his role as fearless moral critic of government behaviour, showing that the lines of morality do not run straight, as, say, between black and white, but follow a zig zag pattern engulfing humans regardless of colour, race or creed. At times, he saw the post-apartheid government as little better than their once ostracised predecessors. Tutu continues to be of the most recognisable faces on the international stage.

Early years

Desmond Tutu was born in 1931 in Klerksdorp, a small gold mining town in the Transvaal, but the family moved to Johannesburg when he was twelve. His father was a teacher, and his mother a cleaner and cook in a school for the blind. There he came into contact with the anti-apartheid priest Trevor Huddleston (see above) whom he would come to regard as his role-model. Beginning as a high school teacher he became frustrated by the apartheid system that permitted him to teach only in schools that were deprived of proper educational facilities, and therefore doomed to be second class. He decided he would make more use of his talents as a Christian minister.

Lecturer and church leader

After theological studies in London he was ordained to the Anglican priesthood. But after he returned to South Africa in 1970 he began to work as a lecturer in the University of Lesotho in Botswana. At this time he used his lectures to highlight the injustice of apartheid. Later, when he was appointed Dean of St. Mary's Cathedral in Johannesburg he continued to be an open critic of the system through talks, writings, sermons and lectures. In 1975, he became Bishop of Lesotho, a deprived black township, where he came into close contact with the inequalities and miseries of the apartheid system.

Peaceful advocate

After the Soweto anti- apartheid uprising in 1976, which led to major clashes between black youths and the police leading to the deaths of several hundreds, he went on to support an international boycott of South Africa that left it isolated and cut off from economic, social and sporting contacts with the outside world. But despite his avowed opposition to apartheid he always advocated peaceful methods of resistance. He believed that peace and reconciliation were possible and, given time, understanding and goodwill. He therefore lost no opportunity in his sermons to promote better relations between all conflicting parties. When apartheid finally ended in 1994, he became a widely acceptable figure in leading the task of healing and forgiveness that followed.

Peace and Reconciliation Commission

A close friend of President Nelson Mandela, he was chosen by him to chair the Peace and Reconciliation Commission that was set up to examine the evils committed on all sides during the apartheid regime. The Commission, which lasted from 1995 to 1998, held public hearings where victims and witnesses from both sides were able to recount their experiences and vent their anger. The aim was to create a climate where forgiveness and reconciliation could take place, enabling the new government to move forward with public support following the ending of apartheid. As chairman of the Commission, Desmond Tutu had to listen to hours of evidence which often involved harrowing accounts of brutality, torture and death. He later confessed that the experience left him traumatised. He said: "Listening to all the pain and anguish, you take it into yourself in many ways... maybe one day you will sit down when you think of all those things and you will cry".

> Forgiveness and reconciliation are not cheap, they are costly. Forgiveness is not to condone or minimise the awfulness of an atrocity or wrong. It is to recognise its ghastliness but choose to recognise the essential humanity of the perpetrator and to give that perpetrator the possibility of making a new beginning... Forgiveness is not opposed to justice, especially if it is not punitive justice, but restorative justice... justice that seeks to heal a breach, to restore a social equilibrium that the atrocity or misdeed has disturbed. There is no future without forgiveness.
>
> Desmond Tutu (2001)

Desmond Tutu Peace Centre

In 2000, he set up *The Desmond Tutu Peace Centre*, aimed at promoting international understanding and peace. He said: "I have given my name to an institution that will foster vision, understanding and the building of bridges. Its declared vision is the creation of a world committed to peace. Its mission is to nurture peace by promoting ethical, visionary and value-based human development. The centre will be the home of outreach programmes to promote peace. It will assimilate knowledge of the causes of conflict and the challenges facing leaders".

Continuing moral critic

As a former vigorous critic of apartheid Tutu maintained a consistent moral voice when the Africa National Congress, the new post-apartheid government, came to power. He spoke out against favouritism and elitism, questioning its slow progress in helping the poor. He was also alert to signs of corruption among the new leaders wittily pointing out that "they stopped the gravy train just long enough to get on themselves!" He was also scathing in his criticism of other failing black leaders, such as Robert Mugabe of Zimbabwe. He also spoke out on other international issues such as the Israel-Palestine conflict. It was a measure of his moral impact that he was frequently rebuked by international leaders for "interference". Today he continues to be a highly respected international voice in pursuit of justice, peace and reconciliation among peoples.

Honours and awards

In 1985, he became Bishop of Johannesburg, and the following year Archbishop of Cape Town, a position he held until his retirement. In recognition of his influence across religious boundaries, he was given the Catholic Pacem in Terris (peace on earth) award in 1987. He has gone on to receive numerous international awards, including the Gandhi Peace Prize in 2005, and the Lincoln Leadership Prize in 2008. He has also been awarded honorary degrees from many distinguished universities for his outstanding "humanitarian" work, for his contribution to international "peace and discourse", and "reconciliation and understanding".

Nobel Peace Prize

His biggest award was the Nobel Peace Prize in 1984 for his "role as a unifying leader figure in the campaign to resolve the problem of apartheid in South Africa".

> "I have great honour in receiving this prize. It is our prize . . . It is for you who down the ages have said that we seek to change this evil system peacefully . . . It is not Desmond Tutu's prize. The world recognises that, and thank God our God is God. Thank God that our God is in charge."
> (On receiving the Nobel Peace Prize 1984)

Desmond Tutu quotes

> "When the missionaries came to Africa they had the Bible and we had the land. They said "let us pray." We closed our eyes. When we opened them we had the Bible and they had the land."

> "I don't preach a social gospel. I preach the Gospel, period. The Gospel of Our Lord Jesus Christ is concerned for the whole person. When people were hungry Jesus didn't say "Now that's political or social." He said "I feed you." Because the good news to a hungry person is bread."

> "In the land of my birth I cannot vote whereas a young person of 18 can vote. That is because he or she possesses that wonderful biological attribute: a white skin."

> "We may be surprised at the people we find in heaven. God has a soft spot for sinners. His standards are quite low."

> "A person is a person when he recognises others as persons."

> "I am a leader by default because nature does not allow a vacuum."

> "Without forgiveness there is no future for a relationship between individuals or within or between nations."

> "Freedom and liberty lose out by default because good people are not vigilant."

> "Resentment and anger are bad for your blood pressure and digestion."

Chiara Lubich (1920–2008)

Deeply shocked by the capacity of human beings to kill each other during the Second World War which she experienced at first hand, Chiara Lubrich underwent a religious awakening as she sat in a bomb-shelter during an air-raid in her native town of Trento in northern Italy. The experience inspired her to form a movement devoted to overcoming conflict and violence, and through goodwill, to promote peace and brotherhood among men. Her profound spiritual vision of how to create a world at peace rather than at war, which she held throughout her life, was the driving force that made her brainchild, Focolare, a world movement.

Early years

Born Silvi Lubich, she later took the name Chiara (Claire) out of her admiration of St. Claire of Assisi who, with St. Francis, sought to live the gospel in a radically new way. She was brought up in a traditional Catholic home, but she was equally influenced by her father's socialist and anti-Fascist views. For holding such views he lost his job, leaving the family in poverty. Ever resourceful, to pay for her studies in philosophy at the University of Venice she began tutoring other students, as well as taking a series of part-time jobs. When her studies were interrupted because of the war, she worked as a teacher in an elementary school in Trento. It was during this time that she experienced the heavy bombing of the city and the destruction of her home. In a moment of enlightenment while cowering in a bomb shelter, she realised that only one thing could withstand the violence of bombs: the love of God. Her aim would be to spread this message through an organisation that came to be known as the *Focolare Movement*.

The Focolare Movement

The movement consists of small groups of lay (not clerical) volunteers who seek to create unity and understanding between people regardless of background. Its spirituality, designed to overcome centuries-old prejudices, beginning with the divisions between competing Christian churches, appeals to what is common in the Christian tradition: prayer, gospel values, and a passion for truth and justice. Focolare means hearth, or family fireside, which suggests an image of people at home with themselves in the company of friends. The keynote of the movement is, indeed, friendship.

International organisation

Today the movement has become an international organisation that promotes the ideals of unity and universal brotherhood, embracing people not only of every religion and creed (both east and west), but thousands who profess no beliefs whatever. It is present today in 182 countries, has over 140,000 members and over 2 million affiliates. By the end of the 1940's Focolare had spread throughout Italy; a decade later it had fanned out across Europe, and by the end of the 1960's it had reached every continent.

Social and political change

Although religious in its inspiration, Lubich always saw her movement as a vehicle for social and political change. She became actively involved in persuading politicians to adopt her ideals, and had famous collaborators in Inigo Giordani and Romano Prodi, both of whom became key figures in the development of the European Union. With the help of other volunteers she promoted the idea of trans-nationalism, an attitude to the social world transcending national political boundaries. She saw the narrowness of uncritical nationalism as one of the key causes of the world wars that ravaged Europe and beyond.

A vision of unity

With the idea of trans-nationalism she advocated "loving the nation of the other, as you love your own". In this way the old world of divisive nationalism would give way to a new world vision of people seeking common ground in the pursuit of unifying ideals. Gaining the support of the business sector, she was instrumental in the emergence of spin-off movements concentrating on the family and the youth culture. Today Focolare hold international congresses that seek to combat family breakdown and the social problems that both cause it and result from it, such as alcohol, drugs, domestic violence and prostitution. In this way unity is pursued at the roots of society as the promise of greater unity and brotherhood on a wider front. Later she helped to establish model towns intended to serve as laboratories for the reconstruction of society. Today there are 20 such towns in different continents around the globe, one of the more famous being Mariopolis in the USA.

> She was a messenger of unity and mercy among many brothers and sisters in every corner of the world.
>
> Pope John Paul II (2000)

Gospel inspiration

Lubrich's original vision was inspired by the gospel hope expressed in the words of Jesus "that they may all be one". Through its 18 branches and 6 mass movements its spirituality of unity is directed to all areas of religious and secular life. Its aim of bringing people together is inspired by the gospel's humanitarian call to unity addressed to all people. Since its foundation it has promoted dialogues among individuals, groups, movements and associations. Another focus of the movement is to foster unity among Christian Churches, a key stepping stone to greater social unity among believers. It also seeks to promote understanding between different religions in order to advance universal brotherhood; and encourages people of goodwill, whether believers or not, to work together to safeguard human values such as freedom, human rights, brotherhood and peace.

> Focolare is focused on a gospel base love which, when put into practice, revives individuals and communities bringing a new spirit to every expression of life.
>
> Chiara Lubich, on receiving honorary citizenship of Milan, 2004

Honours and awards

Chiara Lubich's widespread fame was such that she was the first Christian and the first woman to preach in the Malcolm X mosque in New York, where in May 1957 she addressed 3000 African-American Muslims. She was also the first woman invited to communicate her spiritual experience to 800 Buddhist monks and nuns in Thailand in 1997. Among the numerous awards she received was the Templeton Prize for Religion, presented by the Duke of Edinburgh in London in 1977; and the Order of St. Augustine, presented by Archbishops Runcie and Carey. In 1996 she was awarded the UNESCO Peace Education Prize in recognition of the fact that:

> "in an age when ethnic and religious differences too often lead to violent conflict, the spread of the Focolare Movement has also contributed to a constructive dialogue between persons, generations, social classes and peoples."

In addition to numerous honorary degrees from international universities she received a Doctorate of Divinity from Hope University in Liverpool in recognition of "Focolare's work in ecumenism and interreligious dialogue".

Death

Chiara Lubich died in Rocco di Papa, near Rome on March 14, 2008. Her funeral was held in the Basilica of St. Paul Outside-the-walls, attended by dignitaries from different faiths and political representatives from many countries. As a mark of recognition the chief celebrant was the Vatican Secretary of State.

> With death staring them in the face, Lubich and her disciples felt the urgency of penetrating to the heart of the Christian message by closely studying the gospels. By candle-light in a makeshift air-raid shelter, they discovered the phrase that was to be their inspiration for the next 60 years: "that all may be one" (John xvii, 21).
>
> Times Online Obituary 2008

Chiara Lubich quotes

"In life we do many things, say many things, but the voice of suffering offered out of love—which is perhaps unheard by and unknown to others—is the loudest cry that can penetrate heaven."

"We should not live in such a way that in our last hours we will not regret having loved too little."

"(Love) will be a radiant witness of the One who can bring this about on both a spiritual and social plane, through us His children, because he is Man as well as being God."

"I dream that the Holy Spirit may be present . . . for the world to be invaded by constant streams of new light, life and works . . ."

"I dream of gospel-based relationships not only among individuals but also among groups, movements, religious and lay associations . . . I dream of a world with unity in the diversity of its peoples under one single alternating authority."

Dorothy Day (1897–1980)

An American journalist turned social activist, Dorothy Day became known for her social justice campaigns for the poor, forsaken and homeless. But she paid the price for refusing to conform to public opinion in post-war America. Her simple and straightforward idealism brought her into conflict with both church and state, resulting in frequent arrests and terms of imprisonment. Suffering in this way for her beliefs she became the epitome of what happens to those who challenge the political status quo with their own deeply-held sense of equality and justice.

Early years

Dorothy Day was born in Brooklyn, but her family moved to San Francisco where they were lucky enough to survive the earthquake of 1906. Her father lost his job as a journalist, causing the family to fall on hard times. They eventually moved to the industrial midwest, finding a tenement flat in the poverty stricken south side of Chicago. After a promising start, she dropped out of university, disillusioned with the unreal, remote-from-reality nature of her academic studies. She later moved to the bohemian district of Greenwich Village, New York, then well known for its hippies and junkies. There she took a job as a reporter for a socialist newspaper, *New York Call,* a job that gave her new social awareness of the problems besetting the city and the country.

Spiritual awakening

In her semi-autobiographical novel, *The Eleventh Virgin (*1924)*,* she described a doomed affair with another journalist followed by an abortion and an attempted suicide. The title of the book was an allusion to the gospel parable of the foolish virgins. It reflected her new interest in the Catholic faith as she sought help in coping with the spiritual and psychological distress caused by her abortion. When her daughter, Tamar, was born she underwent a spiritual awakening which led her in 1927 to embrace Catholicism. Thereafter she became a devout believer with a profound sense that faith and worship were the key to happiness and fulfilment.

Catholic Worker Movement

Her new spiritual vision gave impetus to her social involvements. After meeting the French-Canadian philosopher Peter Maurin, who was also inspired by the social teachings of Christ, she began the *Catholic Worker Movement.* It began as a newspaper designed to promote the social teachings of the Church, but soon widened its scope to provide practical help to the unemployed and homeless. After people began calling to the paper's office looking for help and shelter she got the idea of setting up "houses of hospitality", inspired by Christ's words "I was a stranger and you took me in". By 1936 there were 33 *Catholic Worker* houses spread across the country offering hospitality to all in need regardless of religion, colour or class. Everyone was "a brother or sister in Christ". Many of those taken in were men who were poor and desperate, whom she grimly described as:

> "Grey men, the colour of lifeless trees and bushes and winter soil, who had in them as yet none of the green of hope, the rising sap of faith."

Work criticised

Critics of her work objected that her clients were not the "deserving poor" but drunks and layabouts. When she was asked how long they were permitted to stay in the Houses she responded fiercely:

> "We let them stay forever. They live with us. They die with us, and we give them a Christian burial. And when they are dead we pray for them. Once they are taken in they become members of the family. Or rather they always were members of the family. They are our brothers and sisters in Christ."

Anarchist and troublemaker

But in addition to her rescue work among the down-and-outs, she decided to seek more actively political ways to improve their lot. Joining demonstrations and protests, she actively sought ways to promote the interests of the outcasts and the povertystricken. She went so far as to oppose America's involvement in war which she saw as needless violence that only created further misery. But this was seen as both idealistic and unpatriotic. Branded an anarchist and a communist, she was arrested on a number of occasions for taking part in various human rights demonstrations and protest marches. She served a number of short prison terms, one as late as 1973 for joining a banned picket line in support of farm workers.

> When asked how she could reconcile her faith in the monolithic, authoritarian Church which seems so far from Jesus "who had nowhere to lay his head", and who said "sell what you have and give to the poor" with being an anarchist, she replied: "Because I have been behind bars in police stations, houses of detention, jails and prison farms, whatsoever they are called, eleven times, and have refused to pay federal income taxes and have never voted, they accept me as an anarchist. And I, in turn, can see Christ in them even though they deny Him, because they are giving themselves to working for a better social order for the wretched of the earth."

Honours and awards

Her fame as a social activist and humanitarian made her into something of an American heroine. A highly successful film was made of her life (Entertaining Angels); and a documentary (Don't Call me a Saint). But because of the controversial and often confrontational nature of her fight for social justice she was never an obvious candidate for political honours and awards. Still, in 1971 she received the Pacem in Terris Award for her humanitarian work and its "contribution to easing social unrest". Two years later, on her 75th birthday, the Jesuit magazine *America* devoted a special issue to her, describing her as the individual "who best exemplifies the aspiration and action of the American Catholic community during the past forty years". The same year she received the Laetare Medal award from Notre Dame University

> "for comforting the afflicted and for afflicting the comfortable."

In 2002, in posthumous recognition of her achievements, she was inducted into the National Women's Hall of Fame in New York. She is buried on Staten Island.

Dorothy Day quotes

"We do not have faith in God if we depend on the atom bomb."

"Don't call me a saint, I don't want to be dismissed so easily."

"Our rule is the works of mercy. It is the way of sacrifice, worship, a sense of reverence."

"Adoration, contrition, thanksgiving and supplication . . . were the noblest acts of which we are capable in this life."

"If I have achieved anything in my life it is not to be embarrassed to talk about God."

"Those who cannot see the face of Christ in the poor . . . are atheists indeed."

"I believe that we must reach our brother, never toning down our fundamental oppositions, but meeting him when he asks to be met, with a reason for the faith that is in us, as well as with a loving sympathy for them as brothers."

"Men are beginning to realise that they are not individuals but persons in society, that man alone is weak and adrift, that he must seek strength in common action."

"We have all known the long loneliness, and we have found that the answer is community."

"Women think with their whole bodies and see things as a whole more than men do."

"The church doesn't only belong to the officials and bureaucrats. It belongs to all people, especially its most humble men, women and children."

"As for ourselves, yes, we must be meek, bear injustice, malice, rash judgement. We must turn the other cheek, give up our cloak, go a second mile."

"It is easier to have faith that God will support each House of Hospitality and Farming Commune and supply our needs . . . than it is to keep a strong, hearty, living faith in each individual around us—to see Christ in him."

"I have long since come to believe that people never mean half of what they say, and that it is better to disregard their talk and judge only their actions."

"Didn't Jesus say that the poor will be always with us? Yes, but we are not content that there should be so many of them. The class structure is our making and by our consent, not God's, and we must do what we can to change it."

"Our faith is stronger than death, our philosophy is firmer than flesh, and the spread of the Kingdom of God upon the earth is more sublime and more compelling."

Simone Weil (1909–1943)

Whether the French philosopher and mystic should be listed as a thinker or mystic rather than an activist, is already a measure of how difficult it is to categorize one of the most provocative European voices of the early 20th century. Since much of her thought has centred on the human phenomenon of suffering, beginning with her own, it is not surprising that her writings have a melancholy tone. Yet this does not mean that she is negative about human life. On the contrary she believed that, with grace, all human misfortune can be for the good. But equally, she believed that evil can and must be challenged, a conviction that lay at the heart of her active involvement on behalf of the industrial workers of her day. Described as a philosopher, Christian mystic, resistance fighter, social activist and teacher, she received remarkable accolades after her death. Called by T S Eliot "a woman of genius", and by Albert Camus as "the only great spirit of our time", she was regarded by many as a "defining figure of the 20th century".

Early years

Simone Weil was born in Paris into an agnostic household, although both her parents were Jews. Her father being a doctor she grew up in comfortable circumstances. While at school, she showed signs of high intellectual ability, an early intimation of her later reputation as one of the most profound thinkers of her time. She was to become strongly influenced by Catholic teachings and examples, in particular the dynamism, spirituality and asceticism of St. Francis of Assisi. On a visit to Assisi in 1938 she experienced a spiritual ecstasy similar to the saint, an experience which, she said, led her to pray for the first time. She learned the *Lord's Prayer* in Greek, and recited it regularly for the rest of her life.

Search for spiritual help

After a short time she gave up teaching for good, and spent a cold winter in the famous Benedictine Abbey at Solemnes, near Le Mans. At the time she was troubled by severe headaches as well as plagued by an intense depression. During the Easter services she was enraptured by the singing of the monks, something she described as "an experience of mystical revelation." She said "It goes without saying that in the course of these services the Passion of Christ entered into my being once and for all". While at the monastery she was introduced by a priest to a poem by George Herbert which contained for her the moving words:

> "my miserable flesh
> shed in a heap on the porch -
> like in Solemnes at Easter."

Embracing Christian beliefs

After reading it she said "Christ came down and took possession of me." She converted to Christianity but, significantly, refused church membership, or baptism, because she wanted to avoid being identified with any one church, a view she expressed in *Waiting for God (1950)*. Her understanding of Christianity, however, was to prove controversial. She took to extremes its teaching on self-denial and penance, leading her to a life of extreme asceticism, one that, in the view of many of her friends, hastened her early death.

Social and political activist

She was not only a profound thinker and writer on philosophy, spirituality, mysticism and morality, but was prepared to participate actively in the social and economic struggles of her time. She had a special affection for downtrodden workers in the industrial towns. During her academic studies she took jobs in fields and factories in an attempt to understand the lives of the workers from inside. After graduating as a teacher of philosophy in 1931 she took up posts in Le Puy, Auxerre, Roanne and other French industrial centres. She had a strong sense that philosophical ideas were not just meant for study and discussion, but were meant to make a practical difference in life: to her own and the lives of others. This led her to became a political activist with radical ideas, always looking for opportunities to fight for just causes.

The worker movement

She became actively involved in the worker movement, wrote political tracts and took part in demonstrations for workers rights. While she was teaching in Le Puy she became involved in local political activity, supporting the cause of the unemployed, and joining striking workers on the streets. In 1934 she moved from the cosy surroundings of school teaching to work for a year in the factories of Renault, Alsthom and Carnaud. Not surprisingly, she was described as "hopelessly inept", a criticism that owed much to her poor physical and emotional health. During the first years of world war two Weil lived with her parents in Paris, Vichy and Marseilles but fled the Nazi occupation, first by going to America, then Britain.

In 1942, when she lived in London, she joined the French Resistance by working for De Gaulle.

Profound thinker

Weil never saw herself as either a philosopher or a theologian in any strict sense. Her thoughts on life, faith and God were never set forth systematically, but were later collected from her notebooks and published posthumously. One such book was *Gravity and Grace (1947)*. She sees the world as the direct creation of God and the expression of his love. In a thought-provoking passage she argues that every created thing is necessarily imperfect because it is "not God", and "only God is perfect." Therefore human beings are of necessity short in holiness, and always subject to evil. Evil is therefore part of the nature of created things, not something that "entered" the world. It is the task of humans to identify it and fight against it.

The problem of evil

She saw that evil, often in the form of injustice, leads to what she calls "affliction", something beyond mere suffering, something that can strike anyone regardless of their deserts. Showing an intense sympathy with those who are victims of it, she was driven by a desire to show how suffering could be redemptive. The alternative is an unacceptable despair, but with help, avoidable. She said, "the extreme affliction that overtakes human beings does not create human misery, it merely reveals it."

Suffering as redemptive

Weil believed that those things that lead to suffering have the potential to drive us out of ourselves and towards God, a truth revealed by the great mystics such as St. Francis, or St. John of the Cross, both of whom knew well about affliction. She saw both as examples of how to deal with the pain and suffering of concrete life while maintaining contact with the transcendent world of God. It was part of the reality of faith that "to stay with affliction is to find God in the silence that surrounds it." In a highly complex, typically deep, but thought provoking passage she writes:

> **AFFLICTION**
> The man who knows pure joy, if only for a moment... is the only man for whom affliction is truly devastating. At the same time he is the only man who has not deserved the punishment. But after all, for him it is no punishment; it is God holding his hand and pressing rather hard. For, if he remains constant, what he will discover buried deep under the sound of his own lamentations is the pearl of the silence of God... The absence of light, darkness, suggests light; the absence of goodness, evil, suggests goodness; the absence of beauty, horror, suggests beauty. Likewise the absence of God, distress, suggests the presence of God.
> Simone Weil, *Gravity and Grace*

Conscience and guilt

Weil had a profound sense of the sacredness of life and of other persons. She believed that one moral obligation takes precedence over all others: the obligation to respect and love the *Other*. The Other is ultimately God, but it is symbolised in, and means, other persons. Violating another person through exploitation or denial of their rights creates a profound sense that we have violated something holy or sacred, a vileness that eventually reveals itself to the conscience, and produces the torment of guilt.

Death

Simone Weil died, aged 34, of tuberculosis and self-neglect in Ashford, England. She refused food and medical treatment out of sympathy with the plight of the people in her native France.

Inevitably, both her motives and her ultimate sanity were questioned, but there were many whose estimate of her life was one of great respect and admiration. The following came from the poet T S Eliot on hearing of her death: "We must expose ourselves to the personality of a woman of genius, a kind of genius akin to that of a saint."

Simone Weil quotes

"Slowly, with suffering, I have rediscovered my feeling of the dignity of being human."

"The joy of learning is as indispensable in study as breathing is in running. Where it is lacking there are no real students, but only poor caricatures of apprentices who, at the end of their apprenticeship, will not even have a trade."

"The intelligent man who is proud of his intelligence is like the condemned man who is proud of his cell."

"A test of what is real is that it is hard and rough. Joys are found in it, not pleasure. What is pleasant belongs to dreams."

"An atheist may be simply one whose faith and love are concentrated on the impersonal aspects of God."

"As soon as men know that they can kill without fear of punishment or blame, they kill; or at least they encourage killers with approving smiles."

"Attachment is the great fabricator or illusions; reality can be attained only by someone who is detached."

"Beauty always promises, but never gives anything."

"Difficult as it is to listen to someone in affliction, it is just as difficult for him to know that compassion is listening to him."

"Evil being the root of mystery, pain is the root of knowledge."

"But the works of authentic genius from past ages remain, and are available to us. Their contemplation is the ever-growing source of an inspiration which may legitimately guide us. For this inspiration, if we know how to receive it tends—as Plato said—to make us grow wings to overcome gravity."

"Humanism was not wrong in thinking that truth, beauty, liberty and equality are of infinite value, but in thinking that man can get them for himself without grace."

"One cannot imagine St. Francis of Assisi talking about rights."

The danger is not lest the soul should doubt whether there is any bread, but lest, by a lie, it should persuade itself that it is not hungry."

The only way into truth is through one's own annihilation; through dwelling a long time in a state of extreme and total humiliation."

"Those who are unhappy have no need for anything in this world except people capable of giving them their attention."

"We can only know one thing about God—that he is what we are not. Our wretchedness alone is an image of this. The more we contemplate it, the more we contemplate him.."

"Those who are unhappy have need of nothing in this world but people capable of giving them their attention."

"The capacity to give one's attention to a sufferer is a very rare and difficult thing; it is almost a miracle; it is a miracle."

"Fictional good is boring and flat, while fictional evil is varied and intriguing, attractive, profound, and full of charm."

"The love of our neighbour in all its fullness simply means being able to say, "What are you going through?""

"All sins are attempts to fill voids."

"A science which does not bring us nearer to God is worthless."

"Science is voiceless; it is the scientists who talk."

"More genius is needed than was needed by Archimedes to invent mechanics and physics. A new saintliness is still a more marvelous invention."

"A hurtful act is the transference to others of the degradation we feel in ourselves."

Mary MacKillop (1842–1909)

A woman of rare energy, drive and commitment, Mary MacKillop used her religious faith as the driving force of a life dedicated to the service of the poor. Blessed with an ability to see the problems around her, and an equally clear vision of how to solve them, it was inevitably that her practical, down to earth approach would lead to conflict with her more politically correct clerical superiors. But the story of her life is one of surmounting obstacles, including this one. Described as reflecting the core values that Australians prize, "giving everyone a fair go, and standing up for the underdog", Mary MacKillop's recent rise to sainthood has called new attention to her life. The prime minister Julia Gillard, speaking of the need for government rules to prevent opportunists taking liberties with the saint's name for business purposes, said it was to recognise: "the significance that her life holds not only for Australian Catholics, but for all Australians".

Early years

Born in Melbourne of Scottish immigrants, MacKillop grew up in a large Catholic household that found it hard to make ends meet in the rural Australia of the early 1800's. At 16, she went out to work to support the family, later taking the job of governess of her uncle's farm. But inspired by the work of a local priest, Father Julian Woods, she became involved in what she believed was a major social issue at the time, the education of poor children. Together with Father Woods she opened a free Catholic school in the remote south Australian town of Penola, in 1866. It began in a converted stable, but later moved to improved premises thanks to help from two of her brothers.

Order of nuns

To consolidate her work, Mary decided to establish an order of nuns devoted to teaching the poor. In 1867, their first convent was opened at Grote Street, Adelaide. However, her intention was to break with the tradition of nuns living in convents rather than among the people they served. Within a short time the Sisters of St. Joseph had established themselves as the first Order of nuns in Australia, with a rapidly growing membership. From the beginning, the Order was committed to equality, concentrating on the education of children who were poor and deprived, including Aborigines.

Travelling Sisters

By the end of 1869, more than 70 Josephite nuns were educating poor children in Adelaide and its bleak surrounding territories. Soon they were called the "Sisters of the Outback" as they travelled to remote mining towns and farms to teach poor children, while living in temporary shacks like the people around them. Before long the Sisters widened their approach to include running orphanages, centres for the homeless, and homes for the aged. They set up a special mission to help young girls who had fallen into prostitution, and prevent others from doing so. Later in 1869, MacKillop and other sisters travelled to Brisbane to set up projects in Queensland. By 1871, 130 nuns were working in more than 40 schools and charitable institutions across southern Australia. Today 850 Josephite nuns live and work throughout Australia and New Zealand, operating through the well-known *Mary MacKillop Centres* in towns and surrounding areas.

Controversy

But alongside the Order's successes in its education and other relief work, Mary ran into organisational problems with local bishops. Keenly aware of the importance of on the spot decisions, she insisted in keeping the Order free from interference by church leaders. But this did not go down well. Smouldering resentment towards her came to a head when she accused a local Adelaide priest of involvement in sexual abuse. She was temporarily excommunicated for "insubordination" and forced to abandon her position in the Order. However this was later rescinded. Soon afterwards came a false accusation of alcoholism, which made her move from Adelaide to more sympathetic surroundings in Sydney where she spent the last 25 years of her life. After a visit to Rome in 1873 she received full papal approval for her Order, paving the way for the further expansion of their work.

Health problems

In 1883 MacKillop travelled to New Zealand where she remained for three years establishing the Order. By this time the sisters had begun receiving support from non-Catholic benefactors, enabling them to begin new projects. But the pressures of work, including intermittent friction with local bishops and other frustrations, eventually began to take their toll on MacKillop's health. As continually re-elected Mother Superior, she was constantly in the front line of the Order's work, always bearing the most responsibility. In 1902, she suffered a stroke which left her partly paralysed, but mentally unimpaired.

Death

Mary MacKillock died of a stroke on 8 August, 1909. She was laid to rest in the Gore Hill cemetery near the Pacific Highway in north Sydney. But following unusual interest in her grave, her remains were later removed to the newly built Mary MacKillop Chapel in Mount Street. As a measure of the admiration in which she was widely held, her vault was a gift from a Presbyterian friend. The chapel was for many years a pilgrims' shrine, containing, among its exhibits, a cross made from the floorboards of her first school.

Sainthood

After years of waiting for recognition of her enormous achievements and saintly character, she was declared a saint in Rome on October 17, 2010. As Saint Mary of the Cross, she is Australia's first canonised saint. At the canonisation, Pope Benedict XVI summed up her exceptional life in a few words:

> "She dedicated herself as a young woman to the education of the poor in the difficult and demanding terrain of rural Australia, inspiring other women to join her in the first women's community of religious sisters in that country."

Honours and awards

Although her rise to sainthood brought her life worldwide recognition, her life and achievements have long been recognised in her native Australia. Numerous, schools, colleges, institutions, reserves, and other landmarks have been named in recognition of her educational, cultural, and charitable contribution to Australian life. In 2008, she was the first to be honoured in a one dollar coin series of Inspirational Australians issued by the Royal Australian Mint.

It's been the better part of a week since Mary MacKillop was canonised as a saint of the Catholic Church. So many people seem to have partaken of the glow of the process that it's probably inevitable that there should have been scoffers and sneerers as well . . . You can argue, if you like, that there was something belated about Mary MacKillop's canonisation, that it would have meant more back in the 1950's—the last recent memory of an age of faith . . . But what's wrong with an old-fashioned saint? . . . A journalist friend, referring to Brunswick St. (the down and out area of Melbourne where Mother Mary worked) had been sanctified . . . We could do with a saint. It would be a sad thing if we lost even the ghost of a sense of what the ideal of sainthood could mean . . . The civilisation that we trail in the wake of has always exulted in the ideal of one blessed by God . . . Part of the strangeness of Mary MacKillop being a saint was that it happened in a world that was losing its grip on what the word meant . . . Well, in the land of "waltzing Matilda" we're still sinners enough to need our saints.

Peter Craven, Australian journalist and critic (Oct. 2010)

Modern Martyrs

Grand Duchess Elizabeth of Russia (1864–1918)

Of aristocratic birth and regarded as one of the most beautiful women in Europe, Grand Duchess Elisabeth married into the court life of Moscow under the Tsars. But despite her privileged live-style of balls, ballets, operas and concerts she became unsettled by the contrasting poverty of the ordinary people. Shocked by the poverty of the peasants both in the city and the countryside and, in particular, the high rate of child deaths, it was only a matter of time before she made her move. Events would intervene to shatter her privileged life, but she used them as a springboard to what she considered a higher form of existence: serving God and the poor. It was an existence that would end prematurely with her violent death at the hands of the Bolsheviks.

Early years

Elizabeth Fyodorovna was a German princess born into a Lutheran family of the house of Hesse, one of the oldest of the noble houses in the German aristocracy. So highly connected was she that her maternal grandmother was Queen Victoria. In 1884 she married the Russian grand duke Sergei Alexandrovich and converted to the Orthodox Church. Eight years later her husband became Governor General of Moscow.

Growing unrest

Before long she became unhappy with her privileged existence in the midst of grinding poverty. But her efforts on behalf of the poor paled against the injustice blamed on the regime. Bitterness towards the Czar was increasing among the people, leading to protest marches, strikes and sporadic acts of terrorism. The response of the government was increased police and military repression which inevitably made matters worse. On the outside things seemed to be going well. It was a time when Russian opera, ballet and theatre were gaining international fame, with names like Chaliapin, Pavlova and Diaghilev. But reality struck home in 1905 when her husband was assassinated by political rivals after a bomb was thrown into his carriage.

Religious Community

Afterwards she underwent a dramatic change, giving up her privileged position and her social life in order to dedicate herself to the poor whose plight had so long concerned her. In 1909 she gave away most of her jewellery, including her wedding ring, to found a religious community of women, named the convent of Martha and Mary in Moscow. Her inspiration was the words of Jesus: "I was hungry and you fed me . . . sick and you cared for me". When she accepted the position of Abbess of the community she spoke to the sisters with words of great poignancy:

> *"I am leaving the brilliant world where I occupied a high position, and now, together with all of you, I am about to ascend to a much greater world, the world of the poor and afflicted."*

But the idea of women working in poverty relief was new in Russia, and many did not agree with her work. She pressed on regardless, opening a hospital, a pharmacy, a chapel, a school and an orphanage in the grounds of the convent.

The Russian Revolution

At the outbreak of the First World War (1914) poverty got worse, and Russian troops suffered staggering losses. Then the economy collapsed and food became short, leading to social and political chaos. Rebellion, strikes, killings, terrorism and repression increased. In 1917 the Revolution happened, with the Bolsheviks seizing power. The new regime was openly atheistic, seeing the Church as belonging to the oppressive past. Persecution began with the closing of churches and the expulsion of priests and nuns to labour camps. Inevitably her convent came under attack, but she refused the opportunity to flee and faced certain arrest. Her convent would, like others, become a state-run institution.

> "Bless the Lord and may the holy Christ's resurrection strengthen and console you . . . I keep recalling the past day, all your faces so dear to me. O, Lord, how much suffering there was on those faces, how my heart ached. You are dearer to me with every passing minute. How shall I leave you, how can I comfort and strengthen you?"
>
> Letter written by Elizabeth to the convent sisters after her arrest.

Arrest, death and martyrdom

In 1918 she was arrested by the state security police on the orders of Lenin, along with her colleague Sister Barbara, who choose to be with her. They were imprisoned along with other members of the Czar's family, and the imperial household. The day after the Czar and his family were shot, they were to suffer the same fate. Forcibly thrown down a deep mine-shaft, they both died from injuries from two grenades which were thrown down after them to ensure their deaths. Their bodies were recovered and later transferred to the Russian Church of St. Mary Magdalen in Jerusalem. Today it is a revered shrine and a place of pilgrimage. In 1991, both were canonised as martyrs by the Russian Orthodox Church.

> Mother Elizabeth's statue stands with other 20th century martyrs over the west door of Westminster Abbey.

Grand duchess Elizabeth quotes

"We work, pray, and hope every day to experience God's mercy. Others begin to feel this and come to our church to give their souls a rest."

"I long to bring the Lord my insignificant gratitude, serving Him and his suffering children."

"It seems that from my childhood I had a great desire to help the suffering, especially those whose souls are in pain."

"We must rise from the mournful earth to heaven and rejoice with the angels over a single saved soul, over a single cup of cold water given in the name of the Lord."

Dietrich Bonhoeffer (1906–1945)

German pastor, and renowned religious thinker who was martyred by the Nazis for his alleged involvement in the plot to assassinate Hitler, his relatively short life left many wondering what great things he could have accomplished, especially in the theological field, had he lived. He is remembered for his uncompromising attachment to Christian beliefs and values, and for his challenging conviction that religion is about serving God in the neighbour in whatever capacity it is possible to do so. This meant that his brand of Christianity was serious and demanding, reminiscent of Kierkegaard, but born from the difficult times in which he lived. He is also remembered for his unique insights into the relationship between official Christianity and the secular or, in his term, "godless" world, which led to his paradoxical proposal for a "religionless Christianity". Such a form of Christianity would be costly, unlike its genteel counterpart that cost little, such as churchgoing, prayer and sacramental worship (although he did not discount the value of these in their proper place).

Early years

Dietrich Bonhoeffer was born in Breslau in Silesia of devout Christian parents. From an early age he decided he wanted to become a pastor. He travelled widely abroad including America, Spain and Britain. After his ordination as pastor he spent time in a temporary teaching post in New York. Here he became acquainted with the lively spirituality of the black community. Their ability to use their faith to cope with injustice and oppression, despite the ineptness of the church to fight for their integration, impressed him greatly. He recalled: "Here one can truly speak and hear about sin and grace and the love of God... the Black Christ is preached with passion and vision." He returned from America in 1931 to take up full time lecturing post at the University of Berlin.

The Third Reich

But he had already set his mind on the fateful path of social and political involvement at what he knew was an ominous time in his country's history. Two years after his return Hitler had come to power. Bonhoeffer immediately put himself in a dangerous position by making a radio broadcast about giving allegiance to the Furher, warning that he might be a *Verfurher* (a seducer, or false leader). The broadcast was cut off in mid air and Bonhoeffer became a marked man.

The Christian spirit

Concerned about the decline of the Christian spirit in Germany, he was convinced that the modern age tended to reject Christianity because it was seen to be too closely tied to church-going. He therefore laid new stress on the idea that true Christianity was essentially a way of life, a moral beacon that should not be hid under a bushel, but put into practice in the midst of the secular world. This he called "religionless Christianity", a term which meant that following Christ should not be confined to the pious practices of churchgoing, bible-reading and sacramental worship, all attempts, in his view, of trying to obtain "cheap grace". For it to mean something, the Christian spirit must show itself when all around it is being dominated by evil, tyranny and injustice. He wrote:

> "Cheap grace is the grace we bestow on ourselves... (like) baptism without church discipline... cheap grace is grace without discipleship, without the cross, without Jesus Christ... costly grace is costly because it costs a man his life; grace because it gives a man the only true life."

Serving God in the world

At the same time Bonhoeffer did not belittle the role of the Church in the world. For him it was a unique source of spirituality and leadership, one in which he himself had heavily invested. But he believed that the guiding model for the church and the Christian of today was moral and humanitarian witness, exemplified in the person of Jesus Christ whom, he noted, lived and served God in the midst of a godless world. He wrote:

> "Our relation to God is not a "religious" relationship... but our relation to God is a new life of "existence for others" through participation in the being of Jesus... The Church is the church only when it exists for others... In particular our own church will have to take the field against the vices of *hubris*, power-worship, envy and humbug, as the roots of all evil."

Need for action

Bonhoeffer went on to apply these principles to the darkening situation where he found himself. Observing the weak response of the German Church to the brutality and injustices of Nazism he became convinced that true Christianity called for defiance and resistance. Soon after Hitler came to power he helped to set up, and become a spokesman for, the "Confessing Church", a group of defiant Christians set up in opposition the so called "German Church" which sided with the Nazis. He wrote what was required: "The church had to share the sufferings of Christ at the hands of a godless world".

Travel and return

In 1936, disheartened by the feeble compliance of his fellow Christians, he was advised to take time out. He spent two years doing pastoral work in London, before later moving to America. Eventually he decided to return to Germany in what he described as "its darkest hour". He said:

> "I will have no right to participate in the reconstruction of Christian life in Germany after the war if I do not share the trials of this time with my people."

Back in Germany in 1939, he found himself, predictably, targeted by the Nazis. Denounced as a "pacifist and enemy of the state" he was forbidden to speak in public, his teaching licence had been withdrawn and he had to report to the Gestapo on all his activities. He knew that his time was running out.

Death in Flossenburg

After evidence emerged that he was involved in the plot to assassinate Hitler in March 1943, he was imprisoned, first in Berlin, but moved later to Buchenwald, and then finally to Flossenburg concentration camp near the border with Czechoslovakia. It was from here that he wrote his famous *Letters from Prison*. There in April 1945 he was tried without witnesses, court records or a defence. Condemned to death by hanging, his end had all the brutality reserved for the plot conspirators. He was stripped of this clothing and executed on the prison yard by strangulation with piano wire. It was the fate of history that in less than a week the camp would have been rescued by the Allies! The prison doctor left this moving account of his death:

> "Through the half-open door in one room of the huts I saw pastor Bonhoeffer before taking off his prison garb, and kneeling on the floor praying fervently to his God. I was deeply moved by the way this lovable man prayed, so devout and so certain that God heard his prayer. At the place of execution, he again said a short prayer and then climbed the steps to the gallows, brave and composed. His death ensued after a few seconds. In almost fifty years that I worked as a doctor, I have hardly ever seen a man die so entirely submissive to the will of God."

The ethical question

Many have questioned whether Bonhoeffer took ethical liberties in his decision to back the plan to assassinate Hitler. No doubt he did, judged from a traditional standpoint, but his decision was in line with his activist philosophy that evil has sometimes to be stopped by practical, sometimes violent, means. Nevertheless, he knew that he was caught in an ethical dilemma. He put it like this: "If a drunken driver drives into a crowd, what is the task of the Christian and the church? To run along behind to bury the dead and bind up the wounded? Or isn't it, if possible, to get the driver out of the driver's seat"? Elsewhere he restated the dilemma. If the state fails in its duty of providing justice for all, then it is the church's responsibility "not just to bandage the victims under the wheel, but to put a spoke in the wheel". It is obvious from these words that Bonhoeffer was acting from the highest ethical motives in wanting to remove an evil that seemed to defy all other means. The plot to remove Hitler did fail in the short term, but its longer term effect was to leave Hitler a badly shaken and eventually broken man, hastening the end of Nazism.

Legacy

Dietrich Bonhoeffer exercised exceptional influence after his death, both in the theological field, and the field of moral leadership. His provocative ideas spawned a huge literature among theologians and religious thinkers. His courage in standing up to Hitler was later to influence and inspire other champions of justice, like Martin Luther King and Desmond Tutu.

> And when this cup You give is filled to brimming
> With bitter suffering, hard to understand,
> We take it thankfully, and without trembling
> From so beloved and good a hand.
>
> Dietrich Bonhoeffer, hymn written shortly before his death

Dietrich Bonhoeffer quotes

"A God who would let us prove his existence would be an idol."

"In normal life we hardly realise how much more we receive than we give."

"To endure the cross is not tragedy; it is the suffering which is the fruit of an exclusive allegiance to Jesus Christ."

"We must learn to regard people less in the light of what they do or omit to do, and more in the light of what they suffer."

"It is very easy to overestimate the importance of our own achievements in comparison with what we owe others."

"Human love has little regard for the truth. It makes the truth relative, since nothing, not even the truth, must come between it and the beloved."

"The test of the morality of a society is what it does for its children."

"If you do a good job for others, you heal yourself at the same time, because a dose of joy is a spiritual cure."

"Cheap grace is the mortal enemy of our church. Our struggle today is for costly grace."

"Action springs not from thought but from a readiness for responsibility."

"Treason had become the true love of country and the new love of country (under Hitler) had become treason."

"The mark of solitude is silence, as speech is the mark of community . . . Right speech comes out of silence, and right silence comes out of speech."

"To be silent does not mean to be inactive; rather it means to breath in the will of God . . ."

"There is not a place to which a Christian can withdraw from the world, whether it be outwardly, or in the sphere of the inner life. Any attempt to escape from the world must sooner or later be paid for with a sinful surrender to the world."

"Earthly possessions dazzle our eyes and delude us into thinking that they can provide security and freedom from anxiety. Yet all the time they are the source of anxiety."

"Judging others makes us blind, whereas love is illuminating."

"In a world where success is the measure and justification of all things, the figure of him who was sentenced and crucified remains a stranger."

"For the working class world, Christ seems to be settled with the church and middle class society."

"If you board the wrong train, it is no good running along the corridor in the opposite direction."

> Dietrich Bonhoeffer is honoured among the nine 20th century martyrs on the west door of Westminster Abbey, and in the Martyr's Chapel, Canterbury Cathedral.

Edith Stein (1891–1942)

Well known philosopher, feminist, and a Jewish convert to Catholicism she had a promising, if interrupted, academic career before becoming a Carmelite nun, taking the name of Sister Teresa Benedicta of the Cross. Falling foul of the Nazis because of her Jewish heritage she was condemned to die in the death camp of Auschwitz–Birkenau. In 1998 she was canonised a saint by the Pope John Paul 11.

Early years

Edith Stein was born in Breslau, in the German province of Silesia, to a devout Jewish family. But following her father's death when she was only two, her mother was obliged to raise the family on her own, and carry on the father's timber business. Edith grew up with little interest in religion, but began to show serious promise as a high-flying student of philosophy and destined for the academic life.

Academic years

During her short academic career she met and worked with eminent philosophical thinkers such as Edmund Husserl, Martin Heidegger and Max Scheler. But her early studies were briefly interrupted with the outbreak of the Great War. She was posted as a nurse to an Austrian field hospital where she cared for victims of typhus and tended the wounded from the fighting. In 1917 she returned to her studies and received a doctorate in philosophy from the university of Gottingen.

Writer and lecturer

In 1920 she began writing, translating and lecturing on various issues, including women's rights, travelling across Germany, Switzerland and

Austria. In 1932 Edith became a lecturer in the Institute of Pedagogy (teaching) in Munster, but a year later Hitler came to power, and her Jewish identity meant that she was forbidden to teach, her first real taste of anti-semitism. At this time she began to work on ways to bridge the gap of understanding between Christians and Jews, resulting in a book called *Life in a Jewish Family (1933)*. Later, in 1936, she produced a work on the thoughts of Husserl and Thomas Aquinas. Both books were refused publication until after the war.

Contrasting fortunes

In 1929, her former colleague, Heidegger, achieved great fame as a philosopher of intelligence and originality. His deep philosophical analysis of what it means to be truly human, in which he highlighted the meaning of "authentic existence" brought him wide acclaim. He held that this meant a resolute facing up to death by each individual, rejecting the temptation to "follow the crowd" and live by other people's standards. When he was controversially rewarded with the post of Rector of Freiburg for his support of Nazism, the bottom seemed to fall out of his philosophy. As a Nazi sympathiser, there was little in his lofty philosophical message that could square with his new position. While Edith suffered persecution for being (thorough no fault of her own) a Jew, Heidegger went on to enjoy life as a privileged member of a tyrannical regime. But he would later pay with catastrophic loss of face for what many saw as his unacceptable double standards, promoting a philosophy that contained little more than unattainable ideals.

From Jew to Carmelite nun

A growing desire to embrace Catholicism emerged from her reading of the autobiography of the Spanish mystic, St. Teresa of Avila, resulting in her decision to convert. A visit to her mother in Breslau left her deeply upset: her mother strongly disagreed with her decision and both women departed weeping. Shortly afterwards she went a step further by deciding to become a Carmelite nun and joining the Carmelite Convent in Cologne. Here she stayed for five years, teaching and writing.

Fugitive

Edith, now aware of her liability as a Jew, began to identify herself openly with her fellow Jews who were suffering and dying under Nazi persecution. This impelled her to write a letter to Pope Pius IX asking him to denounce the Nazi regime "in Christ's name". By 1938 the persecution of the Jews took a new turn with the widespread burning of shops and synagogues in what became known as the "night of broken glass", *kristelnach*. Edith was quickly secreted to a convent in Echt in Holland for her supposed safety, but this was to be short-lived.

Arrest by Gestapo

Following the denunciation of Nazism by the Dutch bishops, she was caught up in the reprisals that ensued. The anti-Jewish net was now to extend to all Christian converts from Judaism. Witnesses testify that when Edith was summoned to the office of the Gestapo in Maastricht in 1942 she dared to open with the greeting "Praised be Jesus Christ". The following is a brief description of her arrest soon afterwards in her convent, and the grim journey that awaited her:

> It was at five in the afternoon of that bitter and bright 2 August that Edith Stein was taken prisoner. The community was assembled in choir... when two SS men rang the bell. "In ten minutes Sister Stein has to leave the house," was their command. While the prioress protested to no avail... several Sisters helped her pack her few belongings—a blanket, cup, spoon, and food for three days, were all the SS men thought she needed... At Westerbork a Jewish prisoner who escaped, remembered, "The distress of the camp and the confusion among the newcomers cannot be described. But Sister Benedicta stood out by her calm and composure, going among the women, comforting, helping, bringing peace, like an angel"... Three times on their way across Germany she was able to send a short message, through a former pupil, through a station master, through a stranger. "Greetings, I am on the journey to Poland. Sister Teresia Benedicta."
>
> Extract *The Walls are Crumbling*, J M Oesterreicher

Death camp Auschwitz

Edith and her fellow-sister Rosa, also a Christian convert, were transported to the death camp at Auschwitz–Birkenau. On arrival they were selected for instant death under the usual pretext that they were to be "de-loused and showered". Instead, they were herded and packed into tiled quarters that were mocked up to look like showers. Unknown to them, they had arrived at gas chambers where deadly zyklon-B crystals would soon be secretly released through air ducts. After half an hour of slow asphyxiation their remains were consigned to nearby industrial ovens and cremated. Her anonymous ashes were scattered, like countless others, in unknown places around the camp.

Saint and martyr

But her memory was to live on. In 1987 she was beatified in Cologne, and on 11 October 1998 she was canonised a saint and martyr by Pope John Paul II in Rome, in the presence of thousands of pilgrims, including her surviving relatives and members of the Carmelite Order.

Controversy

Controversy surrounded her canonisation. Jewish groups objected that she was murdered for her Jewish identity, not for her Christianity. Others insisted that, though this was indeed the case, she was no less entitled to the highest honours that her adopted Church can bestow, in recognition of the Christian spirituality (see box below) that became a major inspiration in her tortured and tragic life.

> Carmelites can repay God's love by their everyday lives in no other way than by carrying out their daily duties faithfully... with a loving smile, letting no opportunity go by for serving others in love. Finally, crowning this is the personal sacrifice that the Lord may impose on the individual soul. This is the "little way", a bouquet of insignificant little blossoms which are daily placed before the Almighty, perhaps a silent, life-long martyrdom that no one suspects, and is at the same time a source of deep peace and hearty joyousness and a fountain of grace that bubbles over everything we do, not knowing where it goes, and the people whom it reaches do not know from where it comes.
>
> Edith Stein

Edith Stein quotes

"As for what concerns our relations with our fellowman, the anguish in our neighbour's soul must break all precept. All that we do is a means to an end, but love is an end in itself, because God is love."

"In order to be an image of God, the spirit must turn to what is eternal, hold it in spirit, keep it in memory, and by loving it, embrace it in the will."

"Henceforth my only vocation is to love."

"One could say that in the case of need, every normal and healthy woman is able to hold a position. And there is no profession that cannot be practised by a woman."

"The nation . . . doesn't simply need what we have, it needs what we are."

"Things were in God's plan which I had not planned at all."

"Man no longer lives in the beginning—he has lost the beginning. Now he finds he is in the middle, knowing neither the end nor the beginning . . . He sees that his life is determined by these two facets, of which he knows that he does not know them."

"I believe that the deeper one is drawn into God, the more one must go out of oneself; that is, one must go to the world to carry the divine life into it."

"I had heard of severe measures against Jews before (1933). It now dawned on me that God had laid his hand heavily on His people, and that the destiny of these people would also be mine."

"I told Our Lord that I knew that it was his cross that was being placed on the Jewish people . . . What this carrying of the cross was to consist in, that I did not yet know."

"The ultimate test of a moral society is the kind of world it leaves to its children."

"The best informed man is not necessarily the wisest . . . To recognise the significant in the factual is wisdom."

"Worldly wisdom knows what distress and weakness and failure are, but it does not know the godlessness of man."

"In the presence of a psychiatrist I can only be a sick man; in the presence of a Christian brother I can dare to be a sinner who wants to confess, and yearns for God's forgiveness."

"One bears what was lovely in the past not as a thorn, but as a precious gift deep within, a hidden treasure of which we can always be certain."

"I accept the death that God has prepared for me in complete submission and with joy as being his holy will for me . . . I ask the Lord to accept my life and my death . . . so that the Lord will be accepted by His people and that His kingdom may come in glory, for the salvation of Germany and the peace of the world."

Titus Brandsma (1881–1942)

A Dutch Carmelite priest, professor of philosophy, journalist and writer, he laid his life on the line when he helped to expose the brutal tactics of the Nazis during their occupation of Holland. These included the sudden rounding up and deportation of Jewish families, as well as the imposition of serious restrictions on the freedom of the press either to report or comment on it. He was eventually arrested by the Nazis and taken to Dachau concentration camp where he died a martyr's death. The *Titus Brandsma Institute* of Nijmegen University honours the courage of its former Rector.

Early years

Titus Brandsma was born in the Frisian city of Bolsward, Netherlands, in 1881, the son of a dairy farmer. In 1898 he joined the Carmelite Order to become a priest. In 1909 he gained his doctorate in philosophy, and taught in various Dutch schools. Instrumental in founding the Catholic University of Nijmegen, he became its professor of philosophy in 1923. Later as its Rector Magnificus he was renowned for his care for the students well beyond their academic needs, regularly making himself available for counsel and advice outside the normal hours of duty. With his light usually on late, he was certain to be making coffee for students while chomping away on his favourite Dutch cigar. In the 1930's, during his work as a journalist, he began to fall foul of the occupying regime. He openly opposed the Nazi ideology which typically included silencing the truth about what was going on. This meant clamping down on press freedom, something he was very passionate about.

Spokesman for Dutch Bishops

Described as a "towering intellect as well as a man of humour, wit and sanctity", he was no pushover when it came to the fight for truth and justice. This was an issue he became dangerously involved in during his role as spokesman for the Dutch Catholic bishops. Since the Nazi invasion in 1940 they had shown courageous moral leadership in condemning the deportation and persecution of Dutch Jews. But the SS found out that it was Titus Brandsma who drafted the pastoral letter for the bishops in 1941, which included a scathing condemnation of Nazi policies:

> The Nazi movement is regarded by the Dutch people as not only an insult to God in relation to his creatures, but a violation of the glorious traditions of the Dutch nation.
>
> Dutch Bishops (1941)

Arrest and imprisonment

In January 1942, Brandsma was arrested for daring to persuade Dutch Catholic newspapers not to print Nazi propaganda as required by law. The urbane professor was taken, first, to the prison camp at Scheveningen, but in March he was transferred to a penal depot in Amersfoort. His introduction there was to find himself kept with 100 other prisoners for several hours in freezing rain. Disease, dysentery and despair was the predictable lot of the inmates, many dying from exhaustion from the penal labour chores that were coupled with meagre food rations. But the worst was to come. He wrote to his parents, showing a wry humour: "Keep up your courage and continue to be happy. Everything will right itself. Do believe this. I could be in Dachau for a very long time. It doesn't have such a very good name that you really long for it!".

Dachau concentration camp

After further interrogation he was duly transferred to Dachau, a concentration-slave labour camp near Munich. Symbolic of its cruelty was the confining of 1600 clergymen (of different denominations) to three small huts in the so-called "priestblok". Draconian prison rules were enforced by cruelty and brutality, and prisoners were worked to exhaustion, often being forced to draw wagons, ploughs and harrows in the camp farm. It was only a matter of time for Brandsma's health, never good at the best of times, to deteriorate as he came in for beatings and other punishments casually meted out for "slackness" or "laziness". Eventually a kidney infection made him so weak that he was no longer able to work.

> Dachau was the first slave labour camp opened by the Nazi in 1933. It was mainly for political prisoners and enemies of the regime. It held thousands of priests, the majority of whom were Polish. It was notorious for its brutality: photographs show prisoners suspended on poles, or trees, by means of their hands, which were tied behind the back. Discovered by the Americans, it joined Belsen and Auschwitz as bywords for the horrors of Nazism, later exposed through film and newsreels.

Experiments and lethal injection

There was a fatal progression in the scheme of things at Dachau, primarily a work camp. When you were fit enough you worked, and then you were worked to exhaustion. When you could no longer work you were declared ill, fit for the next stage: to be handed over to the medics in the camp "hospital" for experiments described as "excruciating and degrading". The final stage was death, either by intervention or neglect. After the experiments, and no longer of any use, Titus Brandsma was put to death by lethal injection on 26 July 1942.

Testimony and memorial

Titus Brandsma became well-known throughout his time in various prisons and camps as a saintly figure who made himself an outstanding friend to other prisoners and at risk to himself. He is known to have often shared his meagre rations with starving inmates. According to Carmelite records: "he brought comfort and peace to his fellow inmates and did good even to his tormentors". His experiences in Dachau became the basis for the prayer written on his memorial card under a sketch done by another inmate when he was still held at Amersfoort. It shows him dressed in the rough garb of prisoner "58".

> God our Father, source of life and freedom ... through your Holy Spirit you gave Titus Brandsma the courage to affirm human dignity even in the midst of suffering and degrading persecution, grant us that same Spirit so that, refusing all compromise with error, ... We may give coherent witness to your presence among us. Amen.
>
> Carmelite prayer

Declared blessed

On November 3rd 1985 he was declared Blessed by Pope John Paul II, the step prior to sainthood. In 2005, he was chosen by the inhabitants of Nijmegen as the greatest citizen to have lived there.

> **THE TITUS BRANDSMA AWARD**
> Given each year by the International Catholic Union of the Press to anyone who contributes to press freedom in the cause of human rights. It recognises initiatives for promoting dialogue and human dignity through the media. The Award recalls Brandsma's courage in defence of press freedom against Nazi repression.

Titus Brandsma quotes

> "He who wants to win the world for Christ must have the courage to come into conflict with it."

> "Blessed solitude. I already feel completely at home in this little cell . . . I am here alone, but never was our Lord so close to me."

> "Although neo-paganism (Nazism) no longer wants love, history teaches us that in spite of everything we will conquer this neo-paganism with love. Love will gain back for us the hearts of these pagans."

> "First of all we have to see God as the fundamental basis for our being. This basis is hidden in the inner depths of our nature. There we have to see him and meditate on him . . . We then not only adore him in our own being but also in everything that exists."

> "I have my own time, independent of Greenwich, Amsterdam or Berlin."

> "God bless the Netherlands. God bless Germany. May God grant that both nations will soon be standing side by side in peace and harmony."

Maximillian Kolbe (1894–1941)

Concentration camp victim who famously gave his life to save another inmate, he became a key figure in exposing the random cruelty and brutality that was the hallmark of Holocaust labour camps. His legendary act of self-sacrifice for reasons of absurd triviality has earned him a place among the 20th century martyrs honoured in the martyrs chapel, Canterbury Cathedral.

Early years

One of four brothers, Raymond Kolbe was born to an ethnic German father and a Polish mother near Lotz in the Russian occupied part of Poland His father joined the Polish resistance but was captured by the Russians and hanged. After a religious experience of the Virgin Mary in which he was shown two crowns, one white and one red he said: "The white one meant that I should persevere in purity, the red that I should become a martyr. I said that I would accept them both".

Priest, writer and founder

In 1919, after Poland gained independence, he became a Catholic priest of the Franciscan Order, a religious group dedicated to human welfare and works of charity. He took the name Maximilian. He began by establishing devout groups of Christians all over Poland, and in 1922 he began to publish a monthly magazine called *Faith and Life*. In 1927 he founded one of the largest Franciscan houses in the world near Warsaw.

Traveller abroad

Noted for his dedication and drive, he was sent with four fellow brothers to work in Japan, where he founded a monastery in the hills outside Nagasaki. When the atomic bomb was dropped in 1945 the monastery survived because of its fortunate position. Moved by the atmosphere of war and persecution under which he lived, he wrote, perceptively:

> "The real conflict is an inner conflict. There are two irreconcilable enemies in the depths of every soul: good and evil, sin and love. And what use are victories on the battlefield if we ourselves are defeated in our innermost selves?"

Nazi invasion

Six years later he was recalled to Poland where he became Prior of the original friary near Warsaw. When Germany invaded Poland in 1939, he used the friary to provide shelter for over 3000 Polish refugees, among whom were 2000 Jews. Inevitably, the friary came to the notice of the Gestapo and Kolbe and four companions were arrested.

Auschwitz labour camp

At first he was sent to the infamous Pawiak prison in Warsaw. There he was beaten and abused by the SS guards, and suffered the humiliation of having to surrender his Franciscan habit for a prison uniform. Soon afterwards he was deported to the original, and admirably brick-built, labour camp of Auschwitz, noted for the *Arbeit Macht Frei* greeting over its front gates. (This is not to be confused with the later, purpose built, wooden-hutted death camp of nearby Birkenau where millions were gassed). Here, as prisoner 16670 he was subjected to beatings, lashings, and other abuses, including having to run with heavy planks placed on his back for the amusement of the guards. At some point Kolbe managed to get this poignant letter to his mother which concealed more than it revealed:

> "Dear Mama, At the end of the month of May I was transferred to the camp at Auschwitz. Everything is well in my regard. Be tranquil about me and about my health... Do not write to me... I do not know how long I will stay here. Cordial greetings and kisses. Affectionately, Raymond."

Missing prisoner

His legendary moment came during the dreaded roll-call, when prisoners were counted. The guards believed that a prisoner was missing (he was found later dead in one of the latrines). The standard punishment meted out was the selection of 20 prisoners to be assigned to the starvation cells. The severity of the punishment was deliberate, designed to deter other prisoners from attempting to escape. Although he was not selected, he came forward to offer his life in place of another inmate who was a family man. After making an emotional scene about never seeing his wife and children again, Kolbe spoke up, telling the commanding officer: "I am a Catholic priest with no dependents. He is young with a wife and children. I wish to be taken in his place." The man later recalled:

> "I could only thank him with my eyes. I was stunned and could hardly grasp what was going on. The immensity of it; I, the condemned am to live and someone else willingly and voluntarily offers his life for me... I was put back in my place without having had time to say anything to Maximilian Kolbe. I was saved, and I owe to him the fact that I could tell you all this. The news quickly spread all around the camp... For a long time I felt remorse... But now, on reflection, I know that a man like him could not have done otherwise. Perhaps he thought that as a priest his place was beside the condemned men to help them keep hope. In fact he was with them to the last."
>
> Francis Gajowniczek

Lethal injection

His grim request was granted, and after a thee-week gruelling confinement in the death cells where the prisoners were forced to stand, and endure intense dehydration and starvation, he and four others were found to be still alive. His end finally came on 14 August 1941 when he was given a lethal injection of carbolic acid. His death certificate, made out with German precision, indicated the hour of death: 12:30 p.m. His remains were cremated at nearby Birkenau, like the anonymous millions who perished there. But Maximilian Kolbe was not forgotten. His fellow inmates remembered him for his courage, endurance and his time for other prisoners.

Memorable figure

Some recall how he made himself available to anyone who came for encouragement and consolation, with many coming to his bedside at night for help. He is said to have pleaded constantly with his fellow prisoners to forgive their persecutors and to overcome evil with good. When he himself was beaten, he refused to cry out, but heroically prayed for his tormentors. The camp doctor recalled:

> "I can say with certainty that during my four years at Auschwitz, I never saw such a sublime example of the love of God and of one's neighbour."

Another survivor, Jerzy Bielecki, said: "His death was a shock filled with hope, bringing new life and strength. It was like a powerful shaft of light in the darkness of the camp".

Martyr and saint

Maximilian Kolbe was declared a "martyr of charity" by the Church, and canonised a saint in 1981. Among the large crowd at his canonisation in Rome was the man he saved, who lived to be 95, and died in 1995 at Brzeg in Poland. Maximilian Kolbe's cell in death bloc 13 at Auschwitz is now a shrine.

Oscar Romero (1917–1980)

Shot dead in his cathedral by a military death squad for speaking out against the continuing repression of the country's poor, he has since been recognised as one of the true martyrs of the 20th century. In 1977, he was appointed Archbishop of San Salvador, the capital city of a country suffering mass poverty, but ruled over and dominated by a wealthy few. After a fellow priest had been assassinated for criticising the regime he was inspired to break his silence and speak out against the brutally repressive system that kept the poor in their place. It eventually cost him his life. He is remembered not only for his courage, but for the deep spirituality that inspired it. His image stands on the west door of Westminster Abbey among other 20th century martyrs.

> The murder of Archbishop Oscar Romero ... was not just a personal attack on a man who was a thorn in the side of El Salvador's corrupt ruling elite. It was the murder of an icon: a man who was prepared to "speak truth to power"; a bishop who stood side by side with the poor and oppressed.
> Christine Allen, The Guardian, 20 March 2010

Early years

One of a family of eight brother and two sisters, Oscar Romero was born in Cuidad Barrios, a small town in El Salvador. His father wanted him to follow in his footsteps and become a carpenter, to ensure for himself a career in a country of high unemployment and widespread poverty. But Oscar decided he wanted to join the priesthood and serve the poor as a pastor. Ordained in Rome in 1942 he took up pastoral work in various parishes when he returned. He was known as a conservative and loyal priest who saw little reason to become involved in anything beyond his normal pastoral duties. This separated him from many of his fellow priests who were becoming increasingly involved in challenging what they saw as the corrupt regime that kept bearing down on the poor. When he was rewarded for his loyalty by being made Archbishop of El Salvador, many of his fellow priests and local laity were shocked and disappointed. They expected someone who would support the growing movement of social and political criticism among priests called Liberation Theology.

> **LIBERATION THEOLOGY**
> Liberation theology is the name given to a movement among religious leaders which started in Latin America in support of the poor and oppressed. Supporters of the movement believed that staying within the confines of their traditional work as pastors was no longer enough. They believed that the example of Christ in the gospel meant that they should speak out in defence of their poor brethren, even at the risk of their own lives. This, unfortunately, brought them into conflict not only with the secular powers but also with the official Church which believed such involvement was not work for priests but politicians. Besides, it came too close to supporting elements in the country that had identified themselves with atheistic communism.

Change of attitude

Destined as he thought for a quiet life, Romero was shocked when a fellow priest, a Jesuit called Rutilio Grande, was gunned down by government forces for his liberation views. He decided then that he had no option but to align himself with the liberation movement and become involved in the struggle for social justice. As he put it:

> "When I looked at Rutilio lying there dead I thought if they have killed him for doing what he did, then I too must walk the same path."

The episode opened his eyes to what was going on. People who spoke out against government corruption and repression were attacked or imprisoned. It was common for many to "disappear," a recognised code for being killed. He could see that the church itself was becoming a victim, with many of his colleagues suffering and dying for their support of the peasants. He wrote:

> "In less than three years more than fifty priests have been attacked, threatened and slandered. Six of them are martyrs, having been assassinated. Various others have been tortured. Religious women have also been subjected to persecution... Christian institutions have been constantly attacked."

In speaking out he also knew what his own fate might be. As he told a reporter:

> "You can tell the people that if they succeed in killing me, that I forgive and bless those who do it. Hopefully, they will realise they are wasting their time. A bishop will die, but the Church of God, which is the people, will never perish. The church would betray its own love for God and its fidelity to the gospel if it stopped being a... defender of the rights of the poor... a humaniser of every legitimate struggle to achieve a more just society... that prepares the way for the true reign of God in history."

Murder in the cathedral

The way he was silenced caused international outrage. Shortly after finishing a homily during Mass he was shot to death in front of the congregation by military intruders. His funeral took place before a crowd of a quarter of a million mourners, including many who had come from abroad. As a grim symbol of the chaos and unrest that characterised his country, a bomb exploded in the cathedral square, killing many and causing further outrage. As the gunfire continued, his remains were interred in the cathedral crypt. Today it is a martyr's shrine in memory not only of the archbishop, but of all those in El Salvador who gave their lives during the days of the repression.

> During and after his time some twelve priests were assassinated in El Salvador by government death squads. The most notorious episode was when six Jesuits were gunned down together in San Salvador's Central American University on November 16, 1989.

Oscar Romero quotes

"I have been thinking of how far a soul can ascend if it lets itself be entirely possessed by God."

"Peace is not the product of terror or fear. Peace is not the silence of cemeteries.
Peace is the generous, tranquil contribution of all to the good of all."

"We suffer with those who have disappeared, those who have had to flee their homes, and those who have been tortured."

"A preaching that makes sinners feel good so that they are secured in their sinful state, betrays the gospel's call."

"We believe that placing ourselves on the side of the poor and attempting to give them life we will know what the eternal truth of the gospel consists of."

"Do you know if your Christianity is genuine? Here is the touchstone: Whom do you get along with? Who are those who criticise you? Who are those who do not accept you? Who are those who flatter you?"

"We are never embarrassed of saying: "The Church of the Poor.""

"If God accepts the sacrifice of my life, may my death be for the freedom of my people . . . a bishop will die, but the Church of God, which is the people, will never perish."

"If they kill me I shall rise in the Salvadoran people."

"I am bound as a pastor by divine command to give my life for those I love, that is all Salvadorans, even those who are going to kill me."

"When the Church hears the cry of the oppressed it cannot but denounce the social structures that give rise to and perpetuate the misery from which the cry arises."

"In the name of God, in the name of these suffering people whose laments rise to heaven, I beg you! I order you! In the name of God stop the repression!"

"May God have mercy on the assassins (last words)."

Oscar Romero joins the gallery of 20th century martyrs in Westminister Abbey, with Mother Elizabeth of Russia, Martin Luther King, and Dietrich Bonhoeffer.

Martin Luther King (1929–1968)

Charismatic and courageous leader of the civil rights movement in America, King became a world famous moral and religious leader whose efforts to end black oppression bore fruit with the passing of the 1964 Civil Rights Act, and 1965 Voting Rights Act which he never lived to see. The passing of such historic laws opened the way for new levels of justice and equality among the black community in America. For his efforts on their behalf which cost him his life he is honoured in the 20th century martyrs gallery on the west door of Westminster Abbey.

Early years

Born in Atlanta, Georgia the son of a pastor, he was educated at local black (segregated) schools before going on to theological college and, later, university. In 1955 he received a Doctorate in Philosophy from the University of Boston. At first he was co-pastor with his father in the Ebenezer Baptist Church in Atlanta, but moved later to become pastor at the Dexter Avenue Baptist Church in Montgomery, Alabama.

Anti-racist involvement

While pastor in Montgomery he became involved in local issues of racial segregation whereby black citizens were mostly excluded from health, education, transport and leisure facilities to which white citizens had full access. In effect blacks were second class citizens with little access either to the facilities or work opportunities normally available to whites. Following his efforts, he was asked to be leader of the first great negro non-violent demonstration in the United States: a bus boycott over a long-standing but petty source of injustice: the segregation of blacks to specified seating areas on Montgomery city buses.

Civil Rights Leader

The boycott lasted 382 days but in the end was successful. Blacks could now sit where they wanted. It was only a beginning, but King began to pay a heavy price. He became a target of local police, his home was bombed, and he was subject to regular abuse and harassment by racist groups, and eventually the Ku Klux Klan. Once, the trademark burning cross was lit on his front garden. But it was as much his ill-treatment as his anti-racist involvement that brought valuable publicity to the civil rights movement. In 1957 his election as leader of the Southern Christian Leadership Conference, an organisation formed to spearhead the civil rights movement, threw him further into the limelight. Soon he became an internationally known civil rights leader on behalf of black people in America, and his every action was news.

> "He led a mass struggle for racial equality that doomed segregation and changed America forever."
> Jack E. White, Washington Post

Non-violence

His spiritual inspiration was the Sermon on the Mount, but he admitted learning the tactics of non-violence from Leo Tolstoy and Mahatma Gandhi. During his leadership he travelled all over America organising peaceful, non-violent demonstrations, giving speeches and holding rallies publicising the injustices of discrimination suffered by blacks. A frequently used tactic was the sit-in, where demonstrators sat down outside buildings or institutions that upheld, or stood for, segregation. Sit-ins usually provoked violence and arrests, with local jails unable to cope. The resultant mayhem was part of his strategy to gain publicity and expose injustice. But his movements were constantly watched by both local police and the FBI. He was arrested at least 20 times, and was often subjected to physical abuse either by violent mobs or police brutality, or both.

Assassination

King's life was ended by a sniper's bullet on a humid evening of April 4, 1968, as he stood on the balcony of the Lorraine Motel in Atlanta. The place is now the national Civil Rights Museum. News of his death provoked riots in black neighbourhoods throughout the cities of America. His funeral was a national event covered by television stations worldwide, and attended by political leaders and representatives. But his assassination was not regarded as a surprise. Many felt that he had long been a target, surely destined for a violent end. The absence of police protection at the hotel confirmed for many his vulnerability. He himself was not unaware of the possibility of assassination, revealed with prophetic poignancy in a speech the evening before his death:

> We've got some difficult days ahead. But it doesn't matter with me now... And I don't mind. Like anybody, I would like to live a long life... But I'm not concerned about that now. I just want to do God's will. And he's allowed me to go up to the mountain... And I've seen the promised land. I may not get there with you... But we, as a people, will get to the promised land... And I'm happy tonight. I'm not worried about anything. I'm not fearing any man.
>
> King's last speech, the day before his death

Honours and awards

His greatest award was the Nobel Peace Prize in 1964, the money from which he donated to the Civil Rights Movement. His posthumous awards included the Presidential Medal of Freedom, 1977, and the Congressional Gold Medal, 2004. He was especially honoured by the establishment of the Martin Luther King Day in 1986. It is observed on the third Monday in January. He was the recipient of five honorary degrees, including Yale University, Amsterdam Free University and the University of Newcastle, England. He was named Man of the Year in 1963 by Time magazine, and voted third among Great Americans by the Discovery Channel and AOL.

Martin Luther King quotes

"Faith is taking the first step even if you don't see the whole staircase."

"A man who won't die for something is not fit to live."

"A nation or civilisation that continues to produce soft-minded men purchases its own spiritual death on the instalment plan."

"A riot is the language of the unheard."

"At the centre of non-violence stands the principle of love."

"Darkness cannot drive out darkness; only light can do that. Hate cannot drive out hate; only love can do that."

"Every man must decide if he will walk in the light of creative altruism, or in the darkness of destructive selfishness."

"We must learn to live together as brothers, or perish together as fools."

"I am not interested in power for power's sake, but I am interested in power that is moral, that is right, and that is good."

"I believe that unarmed truth and unconditional love will have the final word in reality. This is why right, temporarily defeated, is stronger than evil triumphant."

"I have decided to stick with love. Hate is too great a burden to bear."

"Our scientific power has outrun our spiritual power. We have guided missiles but misguided men."

"Science investigates, religion interprets. Science gives man knowledge which is power, religion gives a man wisdom which is control."

Index

Acts of the Apostles, 13–15
Adelaide, 229
Anna Karenina, 97
Anglican Church, 19, 60, 93
Antioch, 17
Apartheid, 208
Art and education, 56
Athens, 14
Atlanta, 258
Augustine, *Confessions,* 60-62
Auschwitz, 250
Auschwitz-Birkenau, 241, 243
Barnardo Homes, 181
Benedictine Rule, 23
Berlin, 236, 238
Bible, 50, 51, 70
Bishop Ambrose, 60
Brisbane, 230
Brothers Karamazov, 104f.
Calcutta, 139, 202
Campion, Edmund, 46
Canterbury Cathedral martyrs chapel, 241, 249
Carmelite Order, 242, 244, 246
Carthage, 60
Carthusian monks, 28, 41
Cathedrals, 58f.
Catholic Church, 32, 41, 44, 70-72, 152f., 193, 221
Catholic, 109, 114, 127, 133, 135, 139, 242
Catholic Worker Movement, 220
Chaucer, Geoffrey, 25
Cheshire Homes, 193
Chronicles of Narnia, 121
Church of England, 41, 50, 147, 149
Civil Rights Act, 256
Civil Rights Movement, 257
Copenhagen, 87

Dachau, 247
Descartes, Rene, 74
Dissolution of monasteries, 26
Druids, 21
Dublin, 179
Education, 169
El Salvador, 253
Emmaus Community, 186, 188
Erasmus, 41
Ethical dilemma, 235
Existentialism, 84
Faith, 86
Faith and freedom, 87
Faith and life, 75, 105
Faith and reason, 67
Faith and unbelief, 104
Franciscan Order, 24, 32, 33, 250
Freewill, 105
Geneva, 170, 195
Gestapo, 187, 238, 243, 250
Ghandi, Mahatma, 101, 185, 205, 267
God, existence of, 66, 82, 103
Gospel, 23, 25, 33, 45
Gothic architecture, 55
Grand Inquisitor, 105
Gulag Archipelago, 141
Gulliver's Travels, 92
Hawaii, 182
Hegel, G. F. W., 85
Heidegger, Martin, 242
Henry VIII, 26, 31
Holocaust, 249
Human spirit, 141-142
Industrial Revolution, 148
Josephite Sisters, 230
Joyce, James, 48
Kells, book of, 53f.
Lambarene, 172
Lotz, 249
L'Arche Community, 196
Latin America, 253
Leprosy (Hansen's disease), 173, 182
Liberation theology, 47, 253
Lindisfarne Gospels, 54
London, 43, 176, 179

Lord of the Rings, 124
Louvain (Leuven), 183, 185
Man, 75-76, 86, 106
Mandela, Nelson, 210, 211, 213
Madrid, 156
Martha and Mary Convent, 234
Martyrdom, 3
Melbourne, 229
Methodist movement, 150
Milan, 60, 218
Missionaries of Charity, 203
Monasticism, 24f.
Monte Cassino, 26
Moral education, 4
Morality and duty, 81
Moscow, 233, 234
Nagasaki, 250
Natural law, 67
New Testament, 15
New York, 220
Nijmegen, 246, 248
Nobel Peace Prize, 114, 140, 170, 174, 202, 214, 258
Noncorformists, 93
Nottingham, 176
Novelists, 93
Opus Dei, 156f.
Orleans, 38
Orthodox Christianity, 19, 59, 96, 98, 144, 235
Paris, 45, 67, 73, 173
Pascal's wager, 77
Philosophy and theology, 66
Protestantism, 26, 69f.
Protestant martyrs, 44
Puritans, 50, 57, 58
Quakers, 51
Red Cross, 171
Reformation, 26, 69f.
Religious education, 3, 56
Religious experience, 56, 61
Rome, 15, 19, 23, 244, 252, 253
Rouen, 39, 73
Salesian Order, 169
Salvation Army, 177
Samaritans, 200
San Salvador, 251, 255

Shaw, George Bernard, 40, 109
Slave Trade, 20, 164
Society of Jesus (Jesuits), 45f., 74
Sorbonne, 45, 67, 173
Stained glass, 57-58
Stevenson, Robert Louis, 182, 185
St. Petersburg, 102, 106
Sophiatown, 208
Sydney, 230
Taize, 158f.
Third Reich, 236
Time magazine, 27, 36, 184, 205
Toronto, 195
Trento, 215
Turin, 168
Voltaire, 74
Westminster Abbey martyrs memorial, 235, 256
Westminster Cathedral, 111
Warsaw, 250

Lightning Source UK Ltd.
Milton Keynes UK
175767UK00003B/193/P